BIG RIDES

BIG RIDES

GREAT BRITAIN & IRELAND

Vertebrate Publishing, Sheffield
www.v-publishing.co.uk

First published in 2021 by Vertebrate Publishing.

Vertebrate Publishing
Omega Court, 352 Cemetery Road, Sheffield S11 8FT, United Kingdom.
www.v-publishing.co.uk

A CIP catalogue record for this book is available from the British Library.

ISBN 978-1-83981-072-5 (Paperback)

Front cover: Road running north from Vatersay Community Hall. © Felicity Martin – *www.felicitymartin.co.uk*
Back cover (left): Riding alongside Loch Eriboll on the North Coast 500. © Stephen Ross
Back cover (right): Coverdale, Yorkshire Dales Cycleway. © Cycle England
Individual photography as credited.

Mapping contains OS data © Crown copyright and database right (2021) and Openstreetmap.org data © OpenStreetMap contributors.
Relief shading produced from data derived from U.S. Geological Survey, National Geospatial Program.
Cartography by Richard Ross, Active Maps Ltd. – *www.activemaps.co.uk*

Cover design by Jane Beagley, Vertebrate Publishing.
Interior book design by Ryder Design – *www.ryderdesign.studio*
Production by Cameron Bonser, Vertebrate Publishing.

Printed and bound in Europe by Latitude Press.

Vertebrate Publishing is committed to printing on paper from sustainable sources.

CRAGG QUARRY ON THE GREAT NORTH TRAIL. ▶
© JOOLZE DYMOND

Orkney Islands
Cape Wrath
Durness
John o' Groats
Wick
Isle of Lewis
Stornoway
Outer Hebrides
Ullapool
Moray Firth
Harris
North Uist
Skye
Inverness
South Uist
Barra
Vatersay
North Sea
Aberdeen
Cairngorms
SCOTLAND
Fort William
Atlantic Ocean
Perth
Dundee
Tyndrum
Firth of Forth
Helensburgh
Edinburgh
Dunbar
Glasgow
Alnwick
Moffat
Londonderry
Coleraine
NORTHERN IRELAND
Larne
Belfast
Ballyshannon
Sligo
Dumfries
Carlisle
Newcastle upon Tyne
Sunderland
Penrith
Whitehaven
Yorkshire Dales
North York Moors
Isle of Man
Lake District
Morecambe
Bridlington
Skipton
Hornsea
Hull
Shannon
Inny
Southport
Galway
IRELAND
Dublin
Manchester
Sheffield
Liverpool
Anglesey
Conwy
Lahinch
Snowdonia
Trent
Wirksworth
Irish Sea
Limerick
Peak District
King's Lynn
Norwich
Shrewsbury
ENGLAND
Great Yarmouth
Tralee
Waterford
Aberystwyth
Birmingham
Severn
Dingle
Blackwater
Cambrian Mountains
Cambridge
Cork
Wye
Bantry
Kinsale
WALES
Oxford
Cotswolds
Thames
Swansea
Swindon
London
Cardiff
Bristol
Bath
Exmoor
Dover
Calais
Winchester
South Downs
Bude
Exeter
Bournemouth
Brighton
Eastbourne
Dartmoor
Plymouth
Isle of Wight
Channel
Land's End
Falmouth
Penzance
English
Dieppe
Cherbourg-en-Cotentin
Le Havre
FRANCE
La Seine
Roscoff
Paris
01
02
03
04
05
06
07
08
09
10
11
12
13
14
15
16
17
18
19
20
21
22
23
24
25

CONTENTS

THE RIDES

WHAT IS A BIG RIDE?

A Big Ride is an opportunity to explore, an invitation to ride beyond the horizon. In the nineteenth century, bicycles opened up new vistas and rolling roads to ordinary people. Today, bikes offer escape from the city, adventures on the mountains and ascents and descents to steal your breath away. On a Big Ride, you will enjoy stunning seaside views, cycle historic tracks and reach deserted places discovered by few others. Sometimes, repairing a puncture in mizzling rain, or pushing an overladen bike up a boggy hillside, you will feel that you've embarked on an impossible odyssey. But a Big Ride is an experience of a lifetime, a maker of memories.

A Big Ride is an adventure to be had in the saddle. It is a long-distance route, suitable for cyclists on tourer, gravel or hybrid or mountain bikes, that usually takes several days or weeks to complete. This book presents the very best Big Rides in Great Britain and Ireland. The routes we have chosen for the Big Rides series are generally between 100 and 1,000 kilometres in length – although there are some longer iconic routes that are too good not to mention. Some of these routes are only rideable by experienced cyclists, but most are suitable for any rider with sufficient preparation, training and planning.

We believe that there is a Big Ride for everyone, whether you like fast roads, muddy singletracks, bouldered trails or quiet, well-surfaced cycleways. There are the iconic routes that we have all heard of, the routes that are mentioned in hallowed tones at every Sunday club or social ride. There are also the routes that you've never heard of, the routes that are just as beautiful, just as challenging, just as diverting as the famous ones. This book describes the rides that you've always wanted to know more about and the ones that you've never heard of before.

Every Big Ride is a unique challenge. Some climb over mountain ranges and some follow the country's coastline. Some offer sandy beaches and some chalky ridges. You might enjoy Britain's freshest seafood, or discover stone circles and abandoned villages. A Big Ride might reveal the countryside that inspired explorers, offer evenings of traditional music and camaraderie or follow routes that other riders have raced along for a fastest time. Scotland's bothies offer shelter to open-country bikepackers. On other rides, Britain and Ireland's traditional pubs wait for you at the end of each day to offer a hearty meal and comfy bed. Some of these rides won't appeal to you. They will be too hilly, too flat, too muddy, too urban or just the wrong length. But whether you're a speedy road racer, a mountain goat, a hill climber or a long luncher, this book has Big Rides to delight you.

ACKNOWLEDGEMENTS

We are indebted to David Belcher, and to Sam Jones and Sophie Gordon of Cycling UK, who generously shared their expert knowledge and offered advice on the introductory text and route descriptions. We are grateful to the following photographers who have generously allowed us to reproduce their stunning images: Graham Bland, John Coefield, Chris Coles, Penny Coombe, Toby Cummins, Chiz Dakin, Rachel Dickinson, Joolze Dymond, Richard Fairhurst, Richard Gower, David Harper, Jonathan Houseago, Nick Hubble, Calum James, Amy Jurries, John Kerr, Simon Long, Felicity Martin, Andy McCandlish, Sean McFarlane, Tom McNally, Gavin Morton, Matthew Price, Paul Rainbow, Kathy Rogers, Stephen Ross, Phil Stasiw, Markus Stitz, Barney Vaughan-Knight and Lizzie Vaughan-Knight. Thanks go to the following organisations who have helped us source the photography and provided information – many are tireless advocates for, and caretakers of, these Big Rides; Cycle England (*www.cycle-england.co.uk/en*), LakesMTB (*www.lakesmtb.co.uk*), North Coast 500 (*www.northcoast500.com*), Outer Hebrides Tourism (*www.visitouterhebrides.co.uk*), Outdoor Recreation Northern Ireland (*www.outdoorrecreationni.com*), Visit South Devon (*www.visitsouthdevon.co.uk*) and Yorkshire Velo Tours (*www.yorkshirevelotours.com*).

◀ LOCH ERIBOLL ON THE NORTH COAST 500. © STEPHEN ROSS

ABOUT THE ROUTES

Big Rides: Great Britain and Ireland provides descriptions of Big Rides in England, Scotland, Wales, Northern Ireland, Ireland and two English–French routes. The most westerly route is the **Wild Atlantic Way**, an epic route along the whole of Ireland's western coast, exploring quiet peninsulas, sandy beaches and towering cliffs. The most easterly is the **North Norfolk Cycleway**, a gentle road route that rolls through royal estates and past traditional seaside resorts. The **Land's End to John o' Groats (LEJOG)** stretches the length of mainland Britain from south-west Cornwall to Scotland's John o' Groats. The **Avenue Verte** is an Olympian route that connects London with Paris, via quiet roads and well-surfaced cycleways.

The volume offers picturesque road routes, such as the **Yorkshire Dales Cycleway** that takes you past Malham, Settle and over Askrigg Common; mixed-terrain adventures such as **King Alfred's Way** that winds a sometimes muddy, sometimes tarmacked loop between southern England's most interesting prehistoric sites; and challenging off-road routes, such as the **Highland Trail 550**, which takes you past bothies, beaches, breathtaking rugged mountains, deserted moors and lochside castles in Scotland's most remote countryside. Rides such as the **West Country Way**, which offers views across Dartmoor and pleasant railway tracks by Tarka the Otter's pretty river, are perfect for the first-time Big Rider; **Sarn Helen**, a Welsh coast-to-coast that traverses Snowdonia, the Cambrian Mountains and Brecon Beacons, has something to challenge even the most gnarled and saddle-worn of cyclists.

The routes in this book pass through some of Europe's most beautiful national parks and stunning coastlines. The **Tour de Peak District** encircles Britain's first national park, exploring its gritstone edges, green limestone dales, Roman roads across heathered moors and wide, blue reservoirs. The **Hebridean Way** reveals sandy beaches on ten islands of the Outer Hebrides, while **Coast and Castles South** follows Northumberland's golden coast past towering castles. **Lon Cambria** traces a gentle up-and-down route from England through the green heartlands of Wales.

THE RIDES AT A GLANCE

- Eighteen routes are linear (including **Ballyshannon to Larne** and the **Great Western Way**), six are circular or near circular while the **Highland Trail 550** consists of three interconnected loops.

- Seven are road routes; four are off-road routes, best suited only to mountain bikes; fourteen are mixed terrain, which may be rideable on a hybrid or gravel bike – some (such as the **Tour de Peak District)** offer road alternatives.

- The **South Downs Way** is a National Trail and the **John Muir Way** is one of Scotland's Great Trails. The **Great North Trail** follows the Pennine Bridleway and **King Alfred's Way** and the **Great Western Way** use sections of National Trails. Two routes (the **Wild Atlantic Way** and **North Coast 500**) follow popular driving routes.

- Two routes (**Ballyshannon to Larne** and the **Wild Atlantic Way**) cross the Irish border; two routes (**Avenue Verte** and **Tour de Manche**) cross the French border.

- Four English coast-to-coast routes are included (**Sea to Sea/C2C, Hadrian's Cycleway, Way of the Roses** and the **Trans Pennine Trail).** There are also two Scottish coast-to-coasts, two routes that traverse the whole of Wales and one north–south Irish coast-to-coast in addition to the iconic LEJOG.

OUR FAVOURITES

We think that every single Big Ride in this book is special, and there is something unique about every one of them that has earned them a place in *Big Rides: Great Britain and Ireland*. But if you're not sure what to look at first, here are six of our favourites.

- With Britain's longest road climb, Scotland's most northerly town and castles and lochs galore as you spin past kilometre after kilometre of Scottish coast, the **North Coast 500** is Britain's ***Most Epic Adventure***.

- The **Great North Trail,** which traverses the Peak District and the Yorkshire Dales and climbs through Scotland's remote Highlands on its journey to John o' Groats, is our ***Wildest Adventure.*** It offers experienced cyclists the opportunity to enjoy rugged off-road tracks and technical forestry trails, and on a fine day it presents stunning views across uninhabited moorlands.

- The **Yorkshire Dales Cycleway** offers a bumpy ride through the green Dales and Yorkshire's most charming towns, and supplies iconic hill climbs and panoramic views. If you love teashops, high pastures, Swaledale sheep, sparkling waterfalls and leg-testing hill climbs, the Way is ***Great for Road Riding.***

- The **Tour de Manche** will take you along the Jurassic Coast, through historic Dorchester and to the white sands of Studland Bay. You cross to France to enjoy Normandy's bocage and alabaster cliffs, with fresh seafood and wartime memorials to divert you from your ride. The **Tour de Manche** is an ***Undiscovered Gem*** that lets you explore both sides of the channel.

- The **Lakeland 200** is a little Big Ride with a lot of attitude. With climbs over Loughrigg and Harter Fells as well as Honister Pass, and trails in the shadows of Skiddaw, Scafell Pike, the Old Man of Coniston and Cat Bells, this is a route that gets you off the well-ridden track and into the heart of the Lakes. This is a great (long) ***Weekend Challenge***, but be prepared to fail on your first attempt.

- The **John Muir Way** crosses Scotland from west to east but is never too remote, too steep or too technical. There are often choices to be made so challenging climbs or urban roads can be avoided. With Scotland's capital city to explore and a sandy seaside finish, this route is ***Perfect for All the Family.***

LEE QUARRY ON THE GREAT NORTH TRAIL. © JOOLZE DYMOND

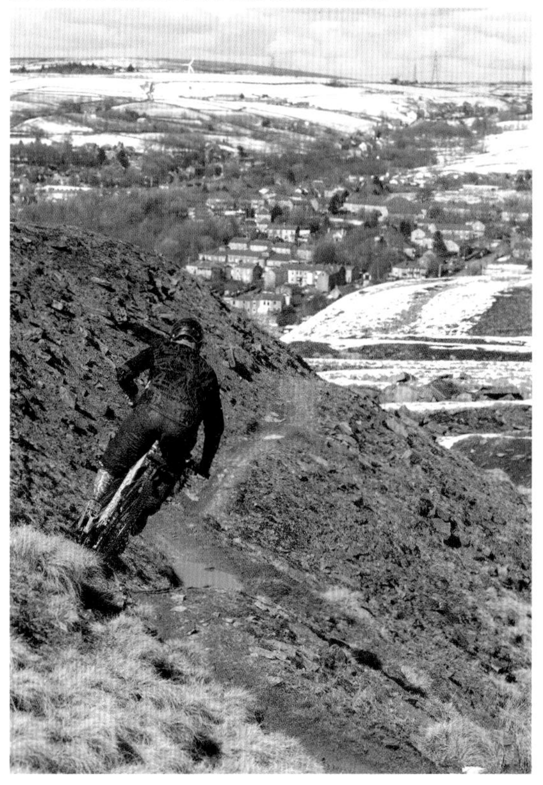

HOW TO USE THIS BOOK

This book provides descriptions of twenty-five of the very best European long-distance cycle rides in England, Scotland, Wales, Northern Ireland and Ireland, and two routes also cross into France. Each route description provides you with the following information.

- An overview of the route from start to finish.
- Useful information on how to get there, when to go and what to expect.
- Essential information on accommodation, weather and terrain.
- Highlights along the way – historical sites en route, wildlife to look out for, the best views.
- Interesting facts about the places you'll pass.
- A summary of route variations and detours.

This book is not intended to let you plan your next Big Ride adventure, but rather to inspire you. Whether you want a moorland challenge or a seaside amble, quiet roads or muddy singletracks, historic castles or hill climbs, this book has the ride for you. It includes iconic rides, such as **LEJOG**, the **Trans Pennine Trail** and the **South Downs Way**, but also undiscovered gems such as the **Tour de Manche**, which takes you – via two ferries – on a loop route along the English and French coast, and the **Lakeland 200**, a rugged, off-road route over the Lake District's high fells. Each route description is accompanied by beautiful photography to give you a sense of what to expect on the trail.

The rides are presented in alphabetical order so that you can easily find the one you're interested in. But if you're not sure where to start, why not turn to the back of the book where you'll find our unique ride index that quickly allows you to find a route based on bike type, where it is, how long is it (kilometres or days) or when to go?

In addition to detailed descriptions and inspiring photography, at the end of each route a handy double page of the following essential information is provided.

- An overview map of the ride, which shows the route (and major variations), terrain, nearby towns and cities and other local features.
- Route length and cumulative ascent and descent.
- An elevation profile of the route.
- Details of the start and finish and how to get there, including information on the closest international air, rail or ferry connections.
- Days to complete the ride.
- Pros and cons to offer a quick insight into the route.
- Information about the most common accommodation options available on or close to the route.
- Details about track characteristics that you will encounter on the ride.
- An indication of waymarking on the route.
- A calendar showing months when the ride can be safely completed.
- How to find further information – details of Vertebrate Publishing's guidebooks and guidemaps, route websites and other guidebooks or maps.

ICONS USED IN THIS BOOK

ACCOMMODATION

The accommodation icons highlight the different accommodation options available along the length of the route. If there are a number of hostels along the route, but you may have to spend one night in a bed and breakfast, the hostel icon will be shown. If there are hotels at the start of a route, but none on, or close to, the rest of the ride, the hotel icon will not be shown.

Camping – there are campsites on or close to the route, or properties, such as hostels, that will permit camping nearby. This icon is generally not used to indicate wild camping, unless wild camping is legally permitted (or at least well-tolerated) and applicable to the route.

Bothies – these small, basic shelters are generally in mountainous or remote locations. Often they offer little more than a roof over your head – there will likely be no lights, toilet facilities or water, although some have a basic fireplace (you will need to provide firewood).

Hostels – budget accommodation is offered in shared dormitory rooms (and sometimes private rooms); often reduced rates are available to members of hostel associations. Although hostels vary greatly in the facilities they offer, the European hostelling movement grew out of walkers' and cyclists' need for affordable accommodation, so they are often located close to the ride routes and cater specifically for cyclists.

Hotels – private rooms are offered, usually with en-suite facilities. In addition to breakfast, they will usually provide dining, and sometimes bar, facilities. They may offer additional services, such as laundry, a concierge and room service.

Bed and breakfasts or guest houses – similar to hotels but may be smaller with more limited facilities. They will generally offer private rooms, which may be en-suite, and prices will include breakfast. Check-in times may be limited and if there is provision for evening meals, you may have to pre-order.

ROUTE CHARACTERISTICS

The route characteristics icons provide information on the challenges that a ride presents.

Exposed – sections of these routes offer little protection from the weather. You may be exposed to torrential rain, hot sunshine or dangerous thunderstorms. Exposed routes are often in hills or mountains, on coastal tracks and sometimes on ridges or mountain edges, and exposed off-road routes may present the risk of steep drops or severely eroded trails.

Remote – these routes are distant from towns, villages and roads. If you need to abandon the ride in an emergency, it may be challenging and take some time to reach help.

Steep – these trails have sections of sharp ascent or descent. This icon is used to indicate where a ride has ascents or descents which may be challenging, rather than to identify rides with a lot of ups and downs.

Forest – these routes have (off-road) sections through forests. Forestry trails may be slippery, particularly during autumn leaf fall, are usually muddy and may be technically challenging because of tree roots.

TRACKS

The track icons indicate what type of roads and trails you will generally encounter en route; for example, a ride may have a short grassy section but the open countryside icon is only shown if grass-topped or mud trails make up a significant part of the route.

Roads – sections of the ride follow roads. There may be an on-road cycleway, but this is generally not segregated from the traffic, other than by paint. Many roads may be potholed and even on major roads the edge of the road may be guttered, strewn with debris or have surface water.

Hard tracks – the route follows well-defined stone or tarmac paths; these trails are often on shared pathways, converted railway tracks or surfaced canal towpaths. These tracks are often shared with pedestrians or horse riders.

Loose-topped tracks – the route follows compacted tracks that are covered with a loose topping (gravel, cinder or hoggin, for example). These tracks are reasonably straightforward in good weather, although caution should be exercised on turning or braking, but may be slippery in wet weather. They are also prone to track deterioration, may be potholed and there may be untopped patches.

Untopped tracks – the trail follows well-defined tracks that are grass-topped or muddy. These tracks may be muddy singletracks (wide enough for a single rider), grassy bridleways or technical tracks through forestry. These tracks are often technical and, even on a mountain bike, may involve hike-a-bike sections.

Open countryside – the route crosses open country-side, with little or no indication of a trail. You may need a map and compass to ride the route, and it may be boggy, bouldered or covered with vegetation. Open countryside is best tackled on a mountain bike and may involve hike-a-bike sections.

WAYMARKING

The waymarking icons indicate how easy or difficult the navigation is on the route.

The route is clearly waymarked along its entire length. You may need to pay careful attention to the waymarking where paths cross, or where there are route variations. In good weather conditions, you should be able to follow the waymarked route with minimal reliance on a map, guidebook or GPS route (although you should always have alternative means of navigation for emergencies).

The route has some waymarking but you will probably need to navigate using a map, guidebook or GPS route on some or all of the route. Some sections may be missing waymarks; waymarking may be out of date or poorly maintained; the route may only partially follow a waymarked route.

There is no waymarking or very little waymarking on the route. Some non-waymarked routes may also be remote and/or exposed, and you should be cautious about attempting these without significant route experience. You will need to rely on good navigational skills to safely follow these routes, or you might consider hiring a guide or joining an organised holiday.

BIKES

The bike icons indicate the best bikes for each Big Ride. Green icons indicate that a bike is the best choice for a route. Big Rides may be completed on bikes highlighted in orange by the experienced cyclist. Bike Types are described on page XVIII.

 **Road**

 **Tourer**

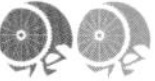 **Gravel**

 **Mountain**

WHEN TO GO

Each route has a calendar indicating the best time to tackle the ride. Months (or half months) may be highlighted in the following colours.

Green – these are the best months to hit the route. The entire route will be open; accommodation, food and public transport services will be operating at peak levels; normal weather conditions should not disrupt your trip.

Orange – it is generally possible to attempt the ride but it may require greater flexibility or better planning. Some accommodation may be closed; other tourist services may also operate over reduced hours, if at all. Parts of the route may be closed or diverted, and weather may mean that you are forced to abandon your ride.

Red – you should not tackle the ride unless you have significant skills and experience; you may have to be completely self-sufficient on the route in challenging weather conditions; you may require winter mountain skills and all accommodation may be closed. Some permissive trails may be closed at certain times of year; if significant sections of the route are closed, the calendar may be highlighted in red.

TIMINGS

Everyone tackles a Big Ride at their own pace, but in order to give you an indication of how long the ride might take, we have provided suggested minimum and maximum hours for each route. The timings have been calculated by bikepacker and route designer Markus Stitz, based on the route distance, ascent and descent and whether it is a road, bike touring, gravel or mountain bike route. The minimum represents the time in which an experienced cyclist might reasonably expect to complete the route, unless exceptional circumstances are encountered. Most cyclists, regardless of experience, could complete the route in the maximum number of hours, given reasonable riding conditions and no major technical difficulties. Minimum suggested days have been calculated, with regard to distance and climbing, on days of ten hours in the saddle. Many riders will prefer shorter days and distances, and the maximum days assumes an average of six hours a day riding, at an easier pace, based on the maximum hours. These timings are estimates; bad weather, favourable wind direction, your bike choice and how laden your bike is may all impact how long it takes you to cycle a Big Ride. As you tackle a Big Ride, you will quickly learn to adjust the timings to fit your preferred cycling style.

PLANNING FOR A BIG RIDE

PREPARATION

PICK YOUR ROUTE

Choose the ride that's right for you. Do you want a gravel bike adventure, a smooth road ride or a remote mountain bikepacking experience? Do you prefer coastal views, high moorlands or castles and churches? How many days and how far do you want to go? A circular route may be a good first Big Ride as you don't have to worry about how to get back to the start from the end. Most buses in the UK and Ireland will not transport bicycles. Some coach companies do, but it is space dependent and often requires a bike bag or similar. Most trains will carry bicycles, but space is often very limited (sometimes only two bikes per train), arrangements are different on different trains, even on the same route, and prebooking is often essential.

TAKE IT EASY

Don't overestimate the distance that you want to tackle in a day. This is meant to be fun, and not an endurance event. You are likely to enjoy your holiday much more if you have time to enjoy an ice cream on the beach, a hearty pub lunch or coffee in a cosy cafe while you wait for the rain to pass. Baggage transfer is available on popular routes, from as little as £10 a bag – you don't have to push an overladen bike up hill after hill. You may choose to book an all-inclusive cycling holiday – in addition to offering accommodation and route maps and guides, these may offer baggage transfer, emergency support, transfers from railway stations and bike and kit hire.

PREPARE YOUR BIKE

If you're not a confident bike mechanic, book a complete service for your bike before your trip. Even a fully serviced bike is no guarantee – it is worth taking a spare kit for repairs and learning the basics of bike maintenance before you set off; there are good guides and tutorials available online and local councils and charities often offer free introductory courses. You will need to check your chain (and oil it), tyres (particularly tread and pressure), gears (including cables), brakes (and cables), your frame, headset (handlebars), pedals, saddle and other fixtures. Look for signs of corrosion, cracks, loose bolts or fittings and excess wear or tear.

A few simple additions to your bike will make your trail more comfortable. Mudguards will protect you from the worst of the rain and mud. A kickstand (not advised on carbon frames) means you don't have to find somewhere to lean a heavy bike. Consider how you will carry your luggage – there are panniers (which require racks) and bags that attach to the main frame, handlebars, over the front or back wheels or under the saddle. You may find it uncomfortable to cycle for hours with a heavy weight on your back, although a lightweight water bladder rucksack can be convenient. Think about navigation – you will want your GPS device or map clearly visible on or by your handlebars.

If you are being accompanied by children who are too young to cycle on their own, a tagalong bike (a bike that attaches to the back of another bike) may be a good alternative to a child seat or bike trailer, particularly for older children – some can be detached and cycled independently.

TRAIN

Try and get out on your bike at least a couple of times a week and build up the distance. Ride in different weather conditions and after dark, and with a fully loaded bicycle. Running can increase your cardiovascular fitness and improve aerobic performance; circuit training and high-intensity interval training can help develop core strength on the days when you're saddle sore. Spin sessions in a dry, air-conditioned gym are no replacement for rides done in driving rain or against a strong headwind. Hard-worn kilometres on the road or trail will make your trip easier and more enjoyable.

TEST YOUR KIT

Small changes can make a big difference to your comfort on a long-distance cycle adventure. Find the saddle that suits you best, discover the food that gives you the boost you need to conquer the hills, check that your waterproofs DO keep you dry and work out what is missing from your toolkit.

RECOMMENDED KIT LIST

Kit can be highly subjective and vary depending upon the person, the season, ride type and the level of experience or comfort. These recommended kit lists may be slightly different for tourers, bikepackers and road, gravel or mountain rides, and are endorsed by our equipment partner **Alpkit** – the ideal resource for sourcing equipment for your adventure. ***www.alpkit.com***

Safety

- Helmet
- Hi-vis vest/Sam Browne belt/reflective arm and ankle strips
- Cable lock and/or D-lock
- First aid kit
- Survival bag
- Whistle
- Phone & charger
- GPS navigation device and/or maps, and case

Essentials

- Toiletries & wet wipes
- Travel towel & travel wash
- Sunscreen
- Insect repellent
- Chamois cream/nappy cream
- Rucksack
- Camera
- Earplugs

Clothing

- Cycling jersey (long back & rear pockets)
- Long- & short-sleeve technical T-shirts
- Arm warmers
- Cycling gilet
- Cycling skorts, shorts or bib shorts
- Cycling leggings or bib tights
- Underwear & socks
- Buff
- Gloves (full-length waterproof for cold/wet weather, fingerless for warm weather)
- Sunglasses
- Shoes & waterproof covers
- Waterproof & windproof cycling jacket, or cape
- Waterproof trousers
- Helmet rain cover (or hat)
- Evening clothes & shoes

Paperwork

- Passport and visas/Photographic ID
- Bank card
- Cash
- Proof of travel/activities/cycling insurance

Bike

- Bike – consider fitting a kickstand, mudguards, mirror, luggage fittings, bottle holders
- Bike lights
- Panniers – waterproof
- Bags (handlebar, topbar, saddle, frame)
- Bike pump
- Multi-tool (including screwdriver and Allen keys)
- Chain tool, quick-link, spare chain links
- Chain lube
- Spoke nipple tool
- Bungee cords
- Spare tube & puncture repair kit
- Sealant (tubeless or mountain bike riders)
- Tyre levers (three)

- Cable ties
- Gaffer tape (wrap short strips around water bottle, for emergency repairs)

Bikepacking and camping

- Tent/bivouac/tarpaulin
- Sleeping bag & mat
- Stove & fuel
- Cooking gear & utensils
- Trowel
- Head torch – with spare batteries
- Water purification system/tablets

Food and drink

- Snacks & gels
- Water bottles and/or bladder
- Rehydration tablets
- Knife

Useful extras

- Spare brake and gear cable
- Pliers
- Spare spokes
- Adjustable wrench spanner
- Tyre 'boot' patches or toothpaste wrapper
- Helmet or bike-mounted camera
- Power bank/battery pack

BIKE TYPES

ROAD

Road bikes have a lightweight frame, dropped handlebars and slick, or smooth, tyres and are designed to be ridden at speed over tarmacked or paved surfaces. Road cyclists often cycle in a crouch position on the bottom of the drop handlebars.

TOURER

Touring bikes are similar to road bikes, but are designed to cover long distances on the road. They have a frame strong enough to withstand luggage carrying, and adaptations such as luggage mounts and mudguards. They have a longer wheelbase (the horizontal distance between front and back wheels) than road bikes.

HYBRID

Hybrid bikes are a blend of road and mountain bike and are designed to tolerate riding over a wide range of terrains and in different weather conditions. They tend to have the mountain bike's straight handlebars and upright cycling position but the narrower wheels of a road bike, as well as the luggage mounts of a tourer bike.

GRAVEL

Gravel bikes are a road–mountain bike hybrid, designed to facilitate long-distance riding over varied terrains, both on- and off-road. They usually have drop handlebars and a road-style frame but wider, knobblier tyres and a longer wheelbase, and the front wheel is further forward to provide better stability. They have much wider tyre clearance than road or hybrid bikes.

MOUNTAIN

Mountain bikes are designed to ride over rough terrain, and generally have wider, stronger wheels with knobbly tyres, straight handlebars and up to twenty-seven gears. They may have suspension/shock absorbers on both the front and back wheels (full suspension), front suspension (a 'hardtail'), or no suspension (rigid). Fat tyres are all-terrain bikes with extremely wide, often low-inflated, tyres (in excess of 3.8 inches/97 millimetres). You generally cycle in an upright position on a mountain bike.

EBIKES

Any type of bike can be an e- or electric bike. An ebike has a battery and a motor; ebikes are either pedal assist (they provide power when the pedals are turned) or power on demand (controlled by a throttle). Ebikes can be ridden without a licence or registration but both the UK and Ireland places restrictions on the maximum speed and motor power on ebikes. An ebike can be a good choice for a long-distance cycle trail as they 'flatten' the hills, compensate for riding with heavy loads and can enable longer daily distances. However, particularly with off-road routes, it may be hard to find recharging points. Ebikes are heavier than their conventional equivalents, limit your luggage carrying options and are more difficult to pedal with a dead battery.

OTHER

Tandem bikes are built for two or more people and recumbent bicycles are ridden in a laid-back, rather than seated, position. Tricycles have a pair of wheels (usually at the back) and a single wheel and unicycles have a saddle above a single wheel. Handcycles are cycles, usually tricycles, powered by movement of the arms and hands rather than legs and feet.

TYRES

One simple adaptation you can make to your bike to improve your Big Ride experience is to choose the right tyres for your trip.

Width – tyre widths range from 23 millimetres (road tyres) to 127 millimetres (fat tyres). Although the width of your wheel and tyre will be constrained by your bike choice, even a few millimetres on a road tyre can make your tourer more stable on the roads and better at handling the additional load, while a slightly narrower mountain bike tyre will help you make faster progress on road sections.

Tread – switching slick road tyres for those with slightly more grip will give you more stability on a tourer bicycle. Consider the best tread for mountain bike tyres based on what types of surface you will encounter on the trail, what time of year and weather conditions you will face, and how far you will travel on roads.

Tubeless – most wheels use a thin rubber inner tube filled with air, and a thicker outer tyre. Tubeless tyres seal under the wheel rim to provide an air cushion with no need for an inner tube. Tubeless tyres are less susceptible to flat tyres, as this is generally a result of punctures to the inner tube, and small holes in tubeless tyres can be sealed with liquid sealant. Tubeless tyres can also be ridden at lower pressures than conventional tyres, which offers better traction over rough terrain. Tubeless tyres are difficult to repair when they do acquire a large puncture, so it is worth carrying a spare tube for a repair of tubeless tyres.

SAFETY AND RESCUE

Always carry a **mobile phone** in order to alert emergency services in the event of an accident. Phone signal may be intermittent, particularly in remote or mountain areas. An SMS message may connect when voice calling is unavailable, and some local rescue services provide the option to contact them by text.

If cycling off-road, do not rely on a single form of navigation. Mobile signals may be intermittent; electronic devices may be broken or lose charge; waymarking may be vandalised. It is advisable to always carry a map, and consider downloading GPX files to your navigation device or storing routes offline in your route-planning app.

Emergency services: 112 is the single EU emergency number and will connect you to emergency services in every European Union country, including Ireland and France (it also works in Great Britain). **999** is the British and Irish emergency number.

In Great Britain, the emergency services can also be contacted by SMS text – useful if you have low battery or intermittent signal. Although primarily aimed at deaf and speech impaired people, EmergencySMS is available to anyone, if your service provider supports it, but it requires registration; you can register by sending an SMS message, 'register' to 999 (the UK) or 112 (Ireland). It is particularly useful in areas of the countryside where mobile signal is too weak to sustain phone contact but a text message might be sent. **EmergencySMS should only be used when voice call contact with emergency services is not possible.**

Mountain and other countryside rescue services in Great Britain and Ireland are provided as part of national emergency services and by voluntary organisations. Organisations such as Mountain Rescue are charitable organisations, financed by public donation and reliant entirely on volunteers.

In event of needing to call for rescue, prepare the following information.

- **Your name** – normally you are asked your full name, and sometimes your address, to identify you. Your mobile number will show on the emergency operator's screen, but you may be asked to confirm it.

- **Where you are** – make sure you know how to locate your UTM coordinates using your mobile phone or smartwatch.

- **Phone number** – if you are low on battery, tell the operator and provide an alternative phone number of another group member.

- **What occurred** – detail the event that occurred in terms of numbers involved, their ages and injuries and how they were sustained. Provide any detail you feel pertinent, such as fractures, medication, or the time elapsed since the accident.

- **Rescuer details** – you may be asked various details that the rescue teams might require, such as local weather conditions.

Try and remain calm when providing this information, as your clarity and quality of the information is of vital importance to the rescue team.

INSURANCE AND EMERGENCIES

It is essential that anyone planning a Big Ride considers whether insurance is advisable for their trip, particularly if not riding in their home country. Standard travel insurance policies often provide cover for cycle touring, but you may be required to pay an extra premium for bikepacking, particularly on mountainous or remote trails. You should always check the terms and conditions to ensure that you have adequate cover both for the duration of your time on the ride and for the type of ride.

CYCLING: THE LEGALITIES

KIT

In both Great Britain and Ireland, the law places a legal responsibility on cyclists to ensure that their bike is maintained in good working order. On public roads, bikes must have a rear reflector, working front and rear lights (between sunset and sunrise) and front and rear braking systems. In addition, in Ireland, Northern Ireland and the Isle of Man, bikes must have a working bell and in Great Britain, pedal reflectors. Cyclists are not required by law to wear helmets or high-visibility clothing although both the Highway Code (Great Britain) and Rules of the Road (Ireland) strongly advise that cyclists do.

OFFENCES

Cyclists are obliged, in Britain, to adhere to the Highway Code and can be charged with cycling under the influence of drink or drugs, and although no speed limits are applicable to cyclists, they may be charged with cycling carelessly or furiously.

Although cycling on the pavement is technically illegal, unless it is also a cycle path, government ministers have encouraged a lenient application of the law.

In Ireland, cyclists must adhere to the Rules of the Road and may be charged with dangerous, inconsiderate or careless cycling, or cycling under the influence of drink or drugs. Cycling on a pavement is technically not allowed in Ireland, although it is not one of the seven fixed charged offences introduced in 2015. In both Great Britain and Ireland, cyclists can be disqualified from driving for cycling offences (although this is rare).

RIDING

In both Britain and Ireland, cyclists are permitted to ride two abreast, and may ride in the middle of the lane ('primary position'). In Ireland, cyclists must not ride two abreast in heavy traffic. In the UK, cyclists are generally not required to use a cycle lane (exceptions being in pedestrianised areas and contra-flow lanes). In Ireland, cyclists must use the cycletrack where one is provided. You must not carry passengers on your bike, unless it is designed to do so.

OFF-ROAD

The Highway Code and Rules of the Road apply to public roads, but different rules apply off the road network. It is trespass (currently a civil offence, although this is under review) to cycle on footpaths in England, Wales and Northern Ireland unless the landowner gives permission; Cycling UK's Trails for Wales campaign is making progress in extending the public rights of way for cyclists in Wales. Cyclists may use bridleways and byways in England and Wales, but technically not in Northern Ireland. Scotland's freedom to roam gives cyclists the right to ride on paths and across open country. Ireland has few off-road public rights of ways although attempts have been made to improve permissive routes; the Irish government invested €13.6 million in 2019 to develop new mountain bike trails.

CYCLING ORGANISATIONS

SUSTRANS (*www.sustrans.org.uk*) is a charity formed in 1977, whose aim is to create and promote better walking and cycling routes. It is the custodian of the National Cycle Network.

Cycling UK (*cyclinguk.org*) is a charitable membership organisation, founded in 1878 and formerly known as the Cyclists' Touring Club. It promotes and enables cycling for everybody – by promoting flagship routes, organising local events and rides, offering practical support to cyclists and lobbying for safer cycling environments

British Cycling (*www.britishcycling.org.uk*) is the sports governing body for most competitive cycling in the UK. It also promotes leisure cycling, through initiatives such as Breeze and Let's Ride.

Cycling Ireland (*www.cyclingireland.ie*) is the sports governing body for competitive cycling in Ireland, but also promotes tour and leisure cycling.

The National Cycle Network (NCN) is a signposted network of national cycle trails, developed by Sustrans, since the 1980s. The network consisted of waymarked routes on well-maintained, well-surfaced paths and trails, and roads. However, Sustrans reviewed the network in 2018 and removed or reclassified approximately quarter of its 25,000 kilometre network. It is in the process of removing all signage from 1,200 kilometres of road that once formed part of the network but are now deemed too busy or dangerous to form part of the network.

THE CLIMB UP ON TO HIGH STREET ON THE LAKELAND 200. © CALLUM JAMES – *WWW.EXPLOREEVERYTHING.CO.UK*

THE
RIDES
SRAM

01

01 AVENUE VERTE – 394km

The Avenue Verte is an iconic 394-kilometre route that links the capitals of Britain and France, from the London Eye to Notre-Dame cathedral. Created in celebration of the 2012 Olympics, this family-friendly route is largely on hard-surfaced, off-road tracks but occasionally uses quiet country lanes or rougher bridleways. It offers you the opportunity not only to see the sights of the cities, but also to enjoy the rolling South Downs, the towering Seven Sisters, Normandy's Alabaster Coast and green farmland as well as Gothic cathedrals and chateaux.

The Avenue begins on the banks of the Thames by the London Eye, with views across the river to the Houses of Parliament at Westminster. This start is on one of the poorer pieces of London's cycling infrastructure, on a narrow, unsegregated lane on the busy Lambeth Road. You might prefer to push your bike along the riverside Queen's Walk to Lambeth Bridge and continue along the river on the Cycleway 8 rather than the original road-based route. From Battersea Park you face a pleasanter, segregated route and soon cut across Clapham and Wandsworth Common to join the Wandle Trail at Earlsfield, which takes a green riverside path alongside the River Wandle.

At Carshalton you rejoin residential, double-parked roads. The narrow Ditches Lane offers spectacular green views over Farthing Downs. You are climbing across the high ridge of the North Downs and take hard tracks past the lakes in Mercers Country Park. South of Redhill, you enjoy well-surfaced tracks parallel to the railway with short, quiet road sections. The peace is soon shattered as you ride around the perimeter of Gatwick Airport and through Crawley. The Worth Way follows the disused railway, east not south, to East Grinstead. You continue on the line of an old railway along the Forest Way, crossing the High Weald Area of Natural Beauty, where you may encounter dragonflies, deer and foxes.

The trail takes a hilly road route over the South Downs on tree-shaded country lanes. You will find some of the prettiest trail on the English section of the Avenue on the Cuckoo Trail, with its wild garlic and orchid verges. The trail is decorated by sculptures and benches carved from oaks felled during the Great Storm of 1987. There is a challenging section on rough, unsurfaced forestry trails through Abbot's Wood which may be difficult on a tourer or for inexperienced riders. It is difficult to circumvent, and you may prefer to push your bike through the trees instead.

The Avenue follows quiet roads by the River Cuckmere as it cuts through the South Downs, and you get good views of the Litlington White Horse. There is an off-road path along the coast from Seaford to Newhaven, with the white cliffs of the Seven Sisters behind you, first along the top of a shingle beach and then on a gritty track that runs parallel to the road through wetlands. You take the ferry from Newhaven, although there are link routes on to Eastbourne and Brighton. There are two or three crossings a day, which take four hours – there is a time difference of an hour.

You arrive in Dieppe on Normandy's Alabaster Coast, with its fresh seafood and fish markets. The route leaves town on roads, but quickly joins a cycleway along the Dieppe–

◀ TYPICAL NORTHERN FRENCH ROAD – QUIET AND BEAUTIFUL.
© SIMON LONG

Paris railway line. The tarmacked track offers a quick, easy route through green farmland, orchards and past village churches. You are heading towards the Pays de Bray, where the clay soil supports verdant pastures beloved by dairy cows, so this is a region famed for its cheese.

You pass the sixteenth-century chateau at Mesnières-en-Bray, which was restored after it was badly damaged in a fire in 2004. At Neufchâtel, you can visit the cheese market; the town is famous for producing one of France's oldest cheeses – a soft, crumbly, white-rinded cheese that has allegedly been produced in the area since the tenth century. The trail passes Forges-les-Eaux, the spa town made popular by the visits of Louis XIII and Anne of Austria in the 1630s. On quiet roads fringed by hedges and trees, you pass Gournay-en-Bray, where you have a choice of routes towards Paris.

The longer eastern route takes you through the beautiful region of Oise, with its historic chateaux, cathedrals and churches. You ride a railway track through green and golden farmland. On the outskirts of Beauvais, you pass the pretty, landscaped gardens – with waterlily lakes, tumbling cascades and pastel flowers – of the painter André Van Beek. Beauvais was badly damaged during the world wars, but you can still enjoy the Gothic cathedral and other historic buildings in a city that dates back to the Romans. This is a landscape shaped by kings and bishops, and you pass the isolated sixteenth-century Saint-Ouen Church on the road out of Beauvais. You follow well-maintained cycle paths on what was once a royal road linking Beauvais to Bresles. After Clermont, there are some sections on quiet, tree-lined roads, but also sometimes rough forestry tracks.

As you follow the banks of the Oise through the Natural Park, you pass Philip the Fair's Royal Moncel Abbey. You can enjoy the cloisters of the thirteenth-century Royaumont Abbey, once Cistercian, now a cultural centre. The skyline of the pretty town of Senlis is dominated by the spire of its gothic cathedral, and you cycle through ancient forests to reach the horse-racing town of Chantilly, with its stately chateau. After passing through Auvers-sur-Oise, resting place of Vincent and Theo van Gogh, you rejoin with the western alternative at Neuville-sur-Oise.

The western option climbs gently through the verdant Normandy countryside, passing the abbey at Saint-Germer-de-Fly, one of France's earliest Gothic buildings. After Gisors, with its octagonal eleventh-century castle, you take the greenway along an old railway line through the Epte Valley. You are cycling through the wooded Vexin Français Regional Natural Park, a rural and rolling landscape interrupted by the occasional chateau (at Villarceaux and Vigny), continuing on quiet roads and cycle paths to reach Neuville-sur-Oise.

With the routes reunited, you reach France's waterway capital of Conflans-Sainte-Honorine on the outskirts of Paris. The route takes cycle paths through the Saint-Germain-en-Laye forest and then follows the Seine on the Promenade Bleue through the capital's suburbs. Saint-Denis has been the burial place of almost every French king since Dagobert I, although the royal necropolis was vandalised during the French Revolution. From here you ride along the Villette Canal basin towards the Île de la Cité and the Avenue Verte's end in the shadow of Notre-Dame cathedral.

While both sides of the channel have their charming sections, the route through Normandy may make British cyclists jealous of their French counterparts. The route is waymarked, although different signs are used on different sides of the channel and the signs may be difficult to spot or missing altogether in towns and cities. You can tackle the Avenue Verte at any time of year, but there will be more ferry crossings in the summer. France and England have a long and complicated history as neighbours, but cycling through the green hills, golden farms and blue rivers that separate two of Europe's most magnificent capitals will remind you just how close they are. The Avenue Verte is a relaxed route, where you can have bacon and eggs in a British seaside cafe, feast on *la marmite Dieppoise* fish stew at lunch and set off for an easy afternoon's cycling with a saddlebag full of emergency Normandy cheese, on roads and tracks that have linked London and Paris for centuries.

BEAUBEC-LA-ROSIERE, NEAR THE END OF THE *VOIE VERTE* THROUGH THE PAYS DE BRAY. © *CYCLE.TRAVEL*

A GENTLE INCLINE IN THE VALLEY OF THE EPTE. © *CYCLE.TRAVEL*

01 AVENUE VERTE: ESSENTIAL INFORMATION

RIDE ESSENTIALS

Start: **London, England**
End: **Paris, France**
Distance: **394km**
Ascent/descent: **2,180m/2,150m**
England: 1,170m/1,170m
France: 1,010m/980m

HOW TO GET THERE

London's closest international airports are Heathrow and Gatwick (you pass the latter en route). You can take bikes on Eurostar services, although not to all destinations, and you should prebook.

Paris has Charles de Gaulle and Orly international airports, and international and national rail connections. You can take a Eurostar train back to London, but will need to book a space for your bike.

TIME TO COMPLETE

Minimum days: **England 1 days/12 hours**
France 2 days/16 hours
Maximum days: **England 3 days/16 hours**
France 4 days/22 hours

PROS

- **Cheese** – Normandy is famous for its cheeses. Calva d'Auge is camembert soaked in Calvados. Neufchâtel, one of France's oldest cheeses, is crumbly and white rinded. Livarot and camembert are famous for their pungency.

- **Chateaux and cathedrals** – the route starts opposite the Palace of Westminster and finishes by Notre-Dame Cathedral, passing chateaux, cathedrals and historic churches on the way. Highlights include the fort at Gisors, Saint-Germer-de-Fly's abbey and the Chateau de Monte-Cristo.

- **Capitals** – the route links two of Europe's most fascinating capital cities. In London, you can visit the Tower of London and Hyde Park. In Paris, you can enjoy a stroll by the Seine, climb the Eiffel Tower and visit the Louvre art gallery to view the *Mona Lisa*.

CONS

- **Provisional** – this is a trail quickly devised for the 2012 Olympics. The route is not set in stone, and some improvements are being made as new cycling infrastructure is created. The French eastern variation involved hilly roads before the railway cycle path was opened.

- **Railway tracks** – in both England and France, the route makes frequent use of old railways. These trails tend to be straight and flat, and don't offer the best views of the countryside – they are often lined with trees or hedges. Surface quality varies, although in France they tend to be wide tarmac trails.

VARIATIONS

In France, you have the choice between a western ride through Normandy's bucolic countryside or a longer eastern route that threads through historic cities. There are many link routes that take you from the trail to overnight accommodation.

GOOD TO KNOW

Thomas Stevens, the first person to circumnavigate the globe on bicycle, rode from London to Paris on his round-the-world trip between 9 and 13 May 1885. He took advantage of the Newhaven to Dieppe steamer and rode into Paris along the Champs-Élysées. His trip – on a penny farthing – began in April 1884 and concluded on 17 December 1886.

FURTHER INFORMATION

www.avenuevertelondonparis.co.uk

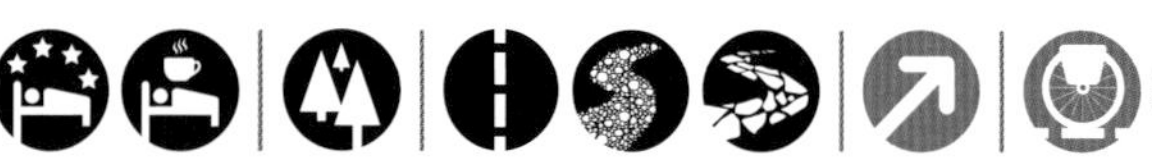

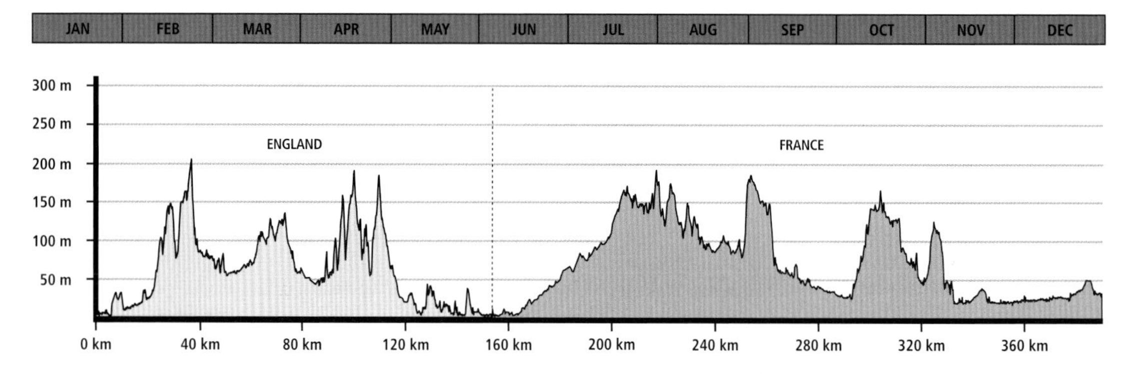

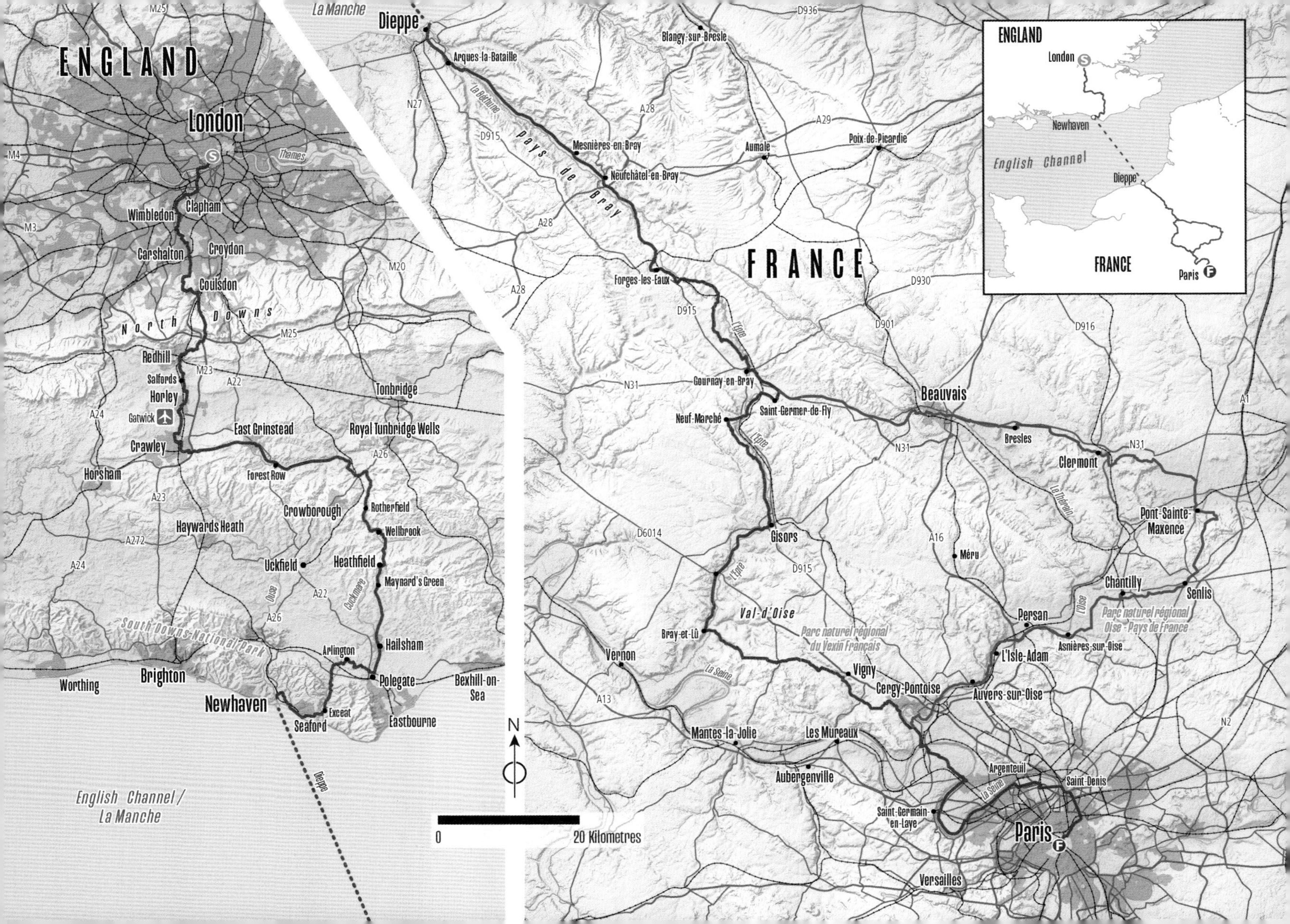
ENGLAND
London
Thames
Wimbledon
Clapham
Carshalton
Croydon
Coulsdon
North Downs
Redhill
Salfords
Horley
Gatwick
Crawley
Horsham
East Grinstead
Forest Row
Tonbridge
Royal Tunbridge Wells
Crowborough
Rotherfield
Wellbrook
Haywards Heath
Uckfield
Heathfield
Maynard's Green
Cuckmere
Ouse
South Downs National Park
Hailsham
Arlington
Polegate
Worthing
Brighton
Newhaven
Seaford
Exceat
Eastbourne
Bexhill-on-Sea
English Channel / La Manche
Dieppe
La Manche
M25
M4
M3
M20
M23
A22
A24
A23
A272
A26
N
0
20 Kilometres
Dieppe
Arques-la-Bataille
La Béthune
Pays de Bray
Mesnières-en-Bray
Neufchâtel-en-Bray
Blangy-sur-Bresle
Aumale
Poix-de-Picardie
FRANCE
Forges-les-Eaux
L'Epte
Gournay-en-Bray
Saint-Germer-de-Fly
Neuf-Marché
Beauvais
Bresles
Clermont
Le Thérain
Pont-Sainte-Maxence
Gisors
Val-d'Oise
Parc naturel régional du Vexin Français
Bray-et-Lû
Vernon
La Seine
Vigny
Cergy-Pontoise
Mantes-la-Jolie
Les Mureaux
Aubergenville
Méru
Persan
L'Isle-Adam
Auvers-sur-Oise
Asnières-sur-Oise
Chantilly
Senlis
L'Oise
Parc naturel régional Oise - Pays de France
Argenteuil
Saint-Denis
Saint-Germain-en-Laye
Paris
Versailles
D936
A28
A29
N27
D915
D930
D901
D916
N31
A16
A1
D6014
A13
N2
ENGLAND
London
Newhaven
English Channel
Dieppe
FRANCE
Paris

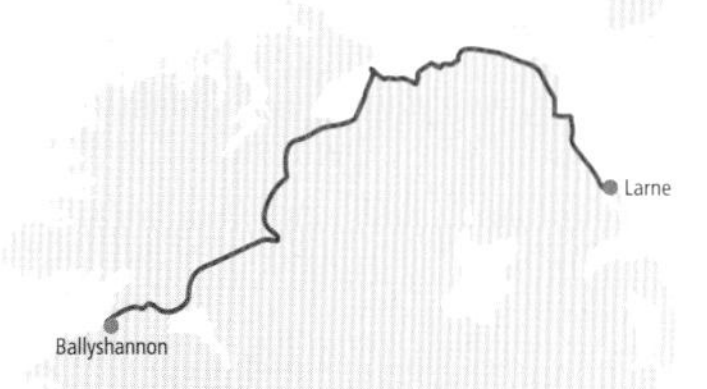

02 BALLYSHANNON TO LARNE – 357km

Ballyshannon to Larne is a 357-kilometre Irish coast-to-coast that takes you from Ballyshannon on Donegal's western coast in the Republic of Ireland to Northern Ireland's port town of Larne. It offers you the opportunity to enjoy the greenest of Ireland's moors and hills, beautiful sandy beaches, dramatic clifftop castles and charming villages. It is often on narrow country lanes, sometimes on shared pathways and very occasionally on busier roads or on-road cycletracks.

Sitting on Erme's estuary, Ballyshannon is one of the oldest towns in the Republic of Ireland, and excavations suggest it has been settled since the Neolithic period. The route leaves town on a poorly surfaced tarmac lane on the shores of the artificial Assaroe Lake. You continue into Ireland's green countryside on gorse-fringed, moss-topped lanes, crossing the border into Northern Ireland near Belleek – the route meanders along the border, traversing it several times on its way north. There is a brief section on the still-quiet A47 main road before turning into roads narrowed by hedgerow to ride above Lough Scolban, a popular fishing spot. The trail now enters the Fermanagh Lakelands area of reed-fringed lakes and rivers.

On gently climbing roads you head for the border again near Tullynasiddagh Lough, passing between it and Lough Vearty. You have left green farmers' fields behind you for heathered moorland, dotted with loughs, which occasionally gives way to evergreen plantations. Near the Cross Bar pub you join the R234 main road heading towards Pettigo, a village bisected by the border.

At Pettigo you can head north on a wooded route past Lough Derg and then follow the River Derg towards Castlederg. Alternatively, you can take a longer route east on a road that hugs the border before turning south past Drumskinny Stone Circle. The eastern route continues through the holiday village of Kesh, down the shores of Lough Erne and through the Castle Archdale Forest. You pass through Irvinestown, Ballinamallard and Trillick on narrow, undulating roads. On the quietest of back roads, some with a grassy ridge in the middle, you finally head north – you are very briefly on the busy A5 as you approach Omagh, but only to make a staggered crossing.

At Gortin you reach the Strule Valley Loop. This route connects Gortin, Newtownstewart and Sion Mills, and whether you have taken the northern or eastern variation you can proceed clockwise or anticlockwise around the Loop. Between Gortin and Newtownstewart, as you follow the River Owenkillew, you'll enjoy spectacular views of the Sperrin Mountains, an Area of Outstanding Natural Beauty. Newtownstewart is worth a visit for the circular towers of the fourteenth-century Harry Avery's Castle. You leave the Strule Valley Loop, whichever way you go, just south of Strabane. The route follows the River Mourne through Strabane, and then a short section of shared pathway by the A38 leads you to the Lifford Bridge, another border crossing from Northern Ireland into the Republic.

The fast-flowing River Foyle marks the border, and you follow the river, on the Irish side, towards Derry (or Londonderry). You do not enter the walled city of Derry,

◄ LOUGH DERG NEAR KILLALOE. © SHUTTERSTOCK/MARION HORAN

A CYCLIST ON TORR HEAD DURING THE GIANT'S CAUSEWAY COAST SPORTIVE. © OUTDOOR RECREATION NORTHERN IRELAND

but instead cross the river on cycletracks on the top deck of the double-decker Craigavon Bridge, which once also carried the railway. Now, on the opposite bank of the Foyle, you follow the river upstream again on a narrow shared pathway beside the A5 main road. You turn off to take a meandering route along hawthorned lanes that rise and fall through gorsey, green farmland, punctuated by occasional villages.

The route follows the River Roe into the Roe Valley Country Park, once the site of an old linen mill. You can visit the Dogleap Rock, where a faithful canine sprang across the river to warn the O'Cahan clan of advancing enemies – the town of Limavady gained its name from this tale. A section of shared pathway takes you through the town centre. Leaving town on the ominously named Windyhill Road, you climb towards through the Ballyhanna and Binevenagh forests. As the curve of coast appears before you, you can enjoy a hard-earned freewheeling descent towards Downhill. You pass the National Trust's Mussenden Temple, a library built by the Fourth Earl of Bristol – the cliff edge is moving perilously closer to the building.

You reach the northern shores at the sandy-beached village of Castlerock, although you skirt the village, following the busy A2 main road on high-quality shared pathway. The trail follows quiet country roads into Coleraine, the port town built during the seventeenth-century Plantation (or colonisation) of Ulster. You are again on the A2 main road, on cycleway that begins as an inadequate painted strip on the road but becomes good-quality shared pathway. The route arrives in Portstewart, with its long, golden strand, perfect for an ice cream. The next section of route is one of the finest, easiest stretches of cycling in Northern Ireland and makes an idyllic day trip if you don't want to tackle the whole route.

Occasionally on roads as you pass through seaside towns, you can make fast progress on good-quality shared pathways along the low, sandy coast. Portrush, home to the Royal Portrush Golf Club, is one of Northern Ireland's most popular seaside resorts. Quiet country roads, away from the popular coastal road, take you to the sixteenth-century Dunluce Castle, home to Clan MacDonnell, which stands on an outcrop surrounded by steep drops to the sea. You turn inland to the town of Bushmills, home to the

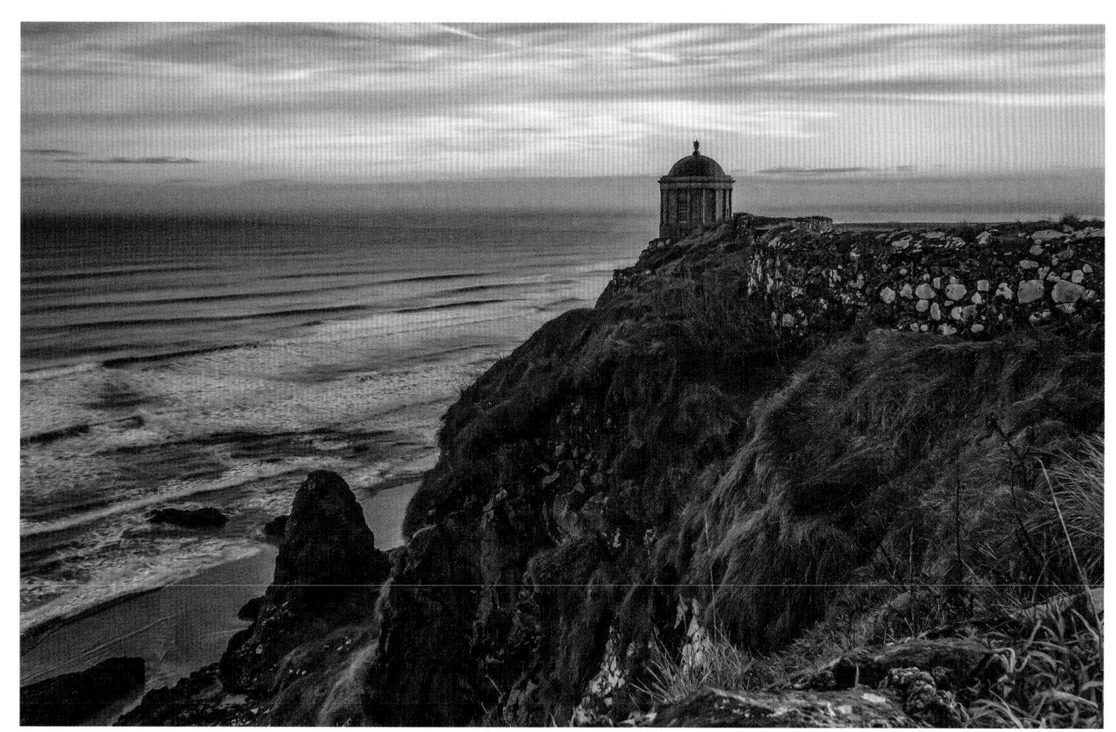

MUSSENDEN TEMPLE. © SHUTTERSTOCK/SHAUN TURNER

Old Bushmills Distillery, which has been licensed since 1608. Another good stretch of cycling infrastructure awaits you as you follow the line of the heritage railway to the Giant's Causeway, the basalt columns disappearing into the sea that are said to be the remains of a bridge built by the giant Finn MacCool. The route turns on to the busy A2 Causeway Road that may be thronged with coaches, before reaching quieter roads that take an inland route to Ballycastle on Ireland's north-eastern tip – you can catch ferries to Rathlin Island from the town.

After Ballycastle, you cut inland on the busy A2 road, passing the ruins of the sixteenth-century Bonamargy Friary. At Ballyvoy, you leave the main road behind you to climb across the green Glens of Antrim to reach Torr Head, where you are rewarded with views of the Mull of Kintyre on the Scottish coast on a fuchsia-fringed road. You undulate over quiet clifftop roads to reach the white houses at the sheltered harbour of Cushendun and then Cushendall. The trail joins the tourist-heavy A2 main road as it hugs the sand and shingle of the beaches, with the cliffs towering above you to reach the end of your journey at the ferry port town of Larne.

This is a route perhaps best tackled in spring or autumn, as the coastal roads are popular summer tourist routes. A spring ride will offer you flowered pastures, lambs in the meadows, sunshine on quiet beaches and fresh sea breezes. Ballyshannon to Larne is not the ride for an off-road adventurer, but it is the trip to make if you want to enjoy loughs and rivers, historical towns, dramatic cliffs and impossibly long, sandy beaches.

02 BALLYSHANNON TO LARNE: ESSENTIAL INFORMATION

RIDE ESSENTIALS

Start:	**Ballyshannon, County Donegal, Ireland**
End:	**Larne, County Antrim, Northern Ireland**
Distance:	**357km**
Ascent/descent:	**3,540m/3,560m**
AKA:	**NCN 93 (Derry to Larne)**

HOW TO GET THERE

Ballyshannon has no train station – the closest station is at Sligo, forty-four kilometres away. There is a Belfast to Ballyshannon route (389 kilometres) for those wishing to complete a loop. The closest international airports are at Belfast, although Donegal and Derry offer flights to the UK mainland.

Larne has ferry services to Cairnryan on the Scottish coast, and is served by two train stations (Town and Harbour) which have services to Belfast, with its ferries and international airports.

TIME TO COMPLETE

Minimum days:	**3 days/23 hours**
Maximum days:	**5 days/32 hours**

PROS

- **Glens of Antrim** – the route takes you right across the Glens of Antrim, an Area of Outstanding Natural Beauty.

- **Coast** – the sandy beaches of Portrush and Portstewart are the perfect place to relax after a day in the saddle, but you can also enjoy the natural wonder of the Giant's Causeway, clifftop castles and quaint harbours.

- **Castles** – in this fiercely fought-over land, you can see Dunluce Castle, the castle at Castlederg, as well as the Stewart Castle ruins and Harry Avery's Castle in Newtownstewart.

CONS

- **Villages** – you pass through very few towns and villages, particularly on the route before Derry. When you do pass a village, it is often a cluster of houses tucked into the hillside with no facilities.

- **Cycling infrastructure** – both Ireland and Northern Ireland have little in the way of cycling infrastructure. A legal oddity means that cyclists should not use bridleways in Northern Ireland. Where there is cycling infrastructure, much of it is so impressively haphazard that it makes England look progressive – a narrow strip painted in the gutter of a busy road or shared pathway that is barely wide enough for two walkers to pass.

- **A2 main road** – the route along the Causeway Coast often follows the A2 road. Even when you are cycling off the road on shared pathway, you may be inhaling heavy traffic fumes and there may be walkers or runners on narrow-ish pavements.

VARIATIONS

There are two loop variations on the Donegal/border section near the start of the route. The route often skirts towns, avoiding traffic in the centre, but you may want to detour for food, accommodation or sightseeing.

GOOD TO KNOW

In 2014, the Giro d'Italia set off from Belfast. On the second day, riders cycled from Belfast through Larne, Cushendun and Cushendall, past the Giant's Causeway to Bushmills, before taking an inland route back to Belfast. The stage was won by German Marcel Kittel who rode the 219-kilometre route in five hours thirteen minutes.

FURTHER INFORMATION

www.cycleni.com/106/ballyshannon-to-larne

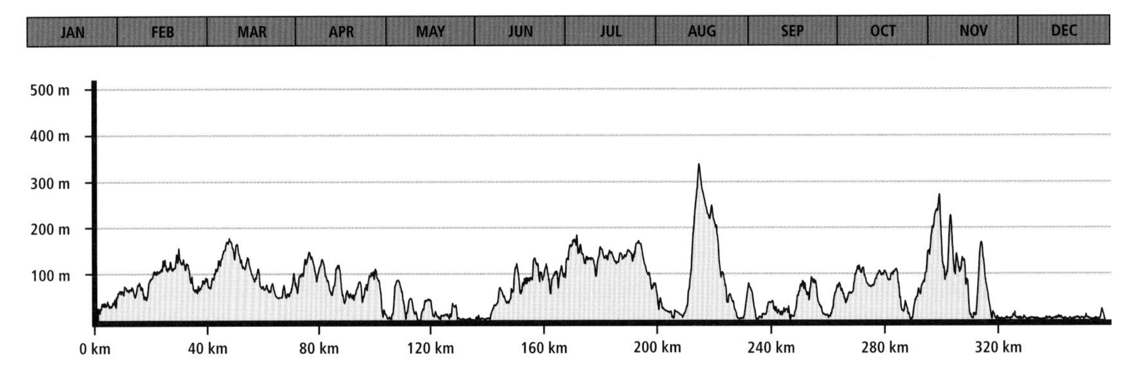

North Channel
Rathlin Island
Giant's Causeway
Torr Head
Red Bay
Portrush
Portstewart
Castlerock
Articlave
Coleraine
Bushmills
Bush
Ballycastle
Ballyvoy
Cushendun
Cushendall
Waterfoot
Antrim Mountains
Carnlough
Glenarm
Ballygally
Cairnryan
Larne
Lough Foyle
Londonderry/ Derry
Limavady
Ballymoney
Carrigans
Newbuildings
St Johnston
Foyle
Gortnahey
Foreglen
Dungiven
Straidarran
Letterkenny
IRELAND
Deele
Lifford
Strabane
Castlefinn
The Sperrins
Glenelly
Maghera
Ballymena
Magherafelt
Randalstown
Antrim
Carrickfergus
Newtownabbey
Liverpool / Douglas / Cairnryan
Bangor
Belfast
Lisburn
Derg
Castlederg
Newtownstewart
Gortin
Killeter
NORTHERN IRELAND
Lough Neagh
Donegal
Lough Derg
Omagh
Donegal Bay
Pettigo
Kesh
Ballyshannon
Lower Lough Erne
Irvinestown
Fintona
Belleek
Lisnarick
Trillick
Ballinamallard
Portadown
Enniskillen
Armagh
Newry
N
0
20 Kilometres
N56
N15
A2
A6
A5
A29
A54
A44
A26
A43
A42
A36
A8
M2
A505
A47
A46
A4
M1

03

03 COAST AND CASTLES SOUTH – 324km

The 324-kilometre Coast and Castles South route begins in the bustling city of Newcastle upon Tyne and follows the Northumberland coast past castles and golden beaches to the Scottish border, with a brief diversion to the Holy Island of Lindisfarne. At Berwick-upon-Tweed it turns inland to follow the Tweed Valley though the tranquil borders country, although you can choose to hug the coast on a variation that leads to Dunbar.

The Coast and Castles South route begins at the Millennium Bridge in Newcastle. There are routes on both banks of the Tyne, although there are longer road sections on the southern bank through Hebburn. The more popular northern version follows Hadrian's Cycleway (see page 33) on good tarmac tracks through Wallsend and on to North Shields, where it joins the National Cycle Network (NCN) 1 route – this is where the southern route rejoins, via the South Shields Ferry. You follow a wide, tarmac, traffic-free road to reach the coast at Tynemouth, with its headland castle jutting out into the sea.

The route hugs the coast on well-made tracks, with short road sections, through Whitley Bay, passing the white-fronted Edwardian pleasure dome of Spanish City and the decommissioned lighthouse on the tiny sandstone St Mary's Island. You are leaving Tyneside now and arriving on the castle-rich Northumberland coast. The medieval town of Blyth, its name meaning merry, built its fortune on salt, coal and fish.

The trail continues along the coast on roadside cycleways and gravel tracks, with occasional road sections. It skirts around Newbiggin-by-the-Sea, the town that lost its beach – a new beach was constructed in 2007 when 500,000 tons of sand were brought in from Skegness. A wide, tarmac track just above the bay leads you through the tranquil Druridge Bay Country Park; the quiet beaches are a popular naturist destination and an annual skinny dip takes place here at the autumn equinox to raise money for the mental health charity Mind.

You arrive at Amble, the 'kindliest port', via the coast path as it hugs the top of sandy beaches – the harbourside is a great place to stop for fresh fish. On the cycleway that runs between the River Coquet and the main road you reach Warkworth. The village's twelfth-century castle, the first of the Northumbrian castles you encounter, was once host to Edward I. The roadside cycle path continues to Alnmouth, where you have a choice of continuing on the road or taking rutted, sometimes muddy farm tracks along the coast.

Near Craster, you follow the road through the eighteenth-century Gothic arch over The Avenue. The road passes above the village, but you might want to descend to the harbour, which is famous for its smoked kippers. You may also want to detour to the crumbling, clifftop Dunstanburgh Castle, although the only access is by footpath. After a short section on concrete tracks, interrupted by cattle grids, you are on roads all the way up the Northumbrian coast until you approach the Holy Island of Lindisfarne. The route passes through the busy seaside resort of Seahouses, where you can take a boat trip to the Farne Islands and Bamburgh, with its castle built on the cliffs where an ancient Celtic fort once stood.

◀ APPROACHING BAMBURGH CASTLE ALONG THE B1340 LINKS ROAD.
© ANDY MCCANDLISH – *WWW.ANDYMCCANDLISH.COM*

You face a steep uphill before Belford and cross the A1 main road and mainline railway. If you want to visit Lindisfarne, there is a shared pathway that keeps you off the busy road through Beal, but you will have to take your place in the queue of cars on the causeway – be sure to check the safe crossing times. This section of loose-surfaced coast track, with some steep climbs and tracks through the dunes, is the toughest off-road section of the route, but it is short enough to get off and push. The trail returns to the roads at Tweedmouth and over the river to reach Berwick-upon-Tweed, the historic border town.

The main route meanders along the banks of the Tweed, crossing the border between Scotland and England several times. As you approach Norham you pass the red walls of the moated twelfth-century castle. Near Coldstream, you skirt around Hirsel Country Park, with its teashop, museum and craft workshops. On the outskirts of Kelso, near Floors Castle which is still the seat of the Duke of Roxburghe, you take a short ride along the A6089 main road. You can see the top of Smailholm Peel Tower, one of many built in the borders to protect from English raiders.

The route takes you past the ruins of Dryburgh Abbey on the banks of the Tweed. It was burned by the English in 1322, then again in 1385 and finally destroyed in 1544, although it is said still to be haunted by the spirit Fatlips, who has a penchant for tidying. In the historic town of Melrose, the abbey, burial place of Robert the Bruce's heart, was built on the instruction of David I in the twelfth century. You take a railway path on to Galashiels.

After Innerleithen, you leave the Tweed and face a challenging climb over the moorlands and bare hills of the Southern Uplands. The trail descends through farmland on hawthorn-lined lanes. From Dalkeith, you are largely on disused railway tracks and finish by riding up the Royal Mile to the castle.

ON THE BACK ROADS OF NORTHUMBERLAND, NEAR WOOLER. © ANDY MCCANDLISH – *WWW.ANDYMCCANDLISH.COM*

From Berwick, an alternative is to continue north up the Berwickshire coast in the direction of the East Coast Main Line. On quiet country roads you cycle past the red sandstone Ayton Castle and return to the coast at Eyemouth. This low, exposed coastal area is scattered with wind farms, but you also pass the imposing Torness nuclear power station before you join an old railway path to Dunbar. From Dunbar, you can take the John Muir Way (see page 51) back to Edinburgh or continue on quiet roads on NCN 76 to Haddington. From here you take a railway path towards Longniddry, Cockenzie and Port Seton and Prestonpans. You join the main route into Edinburgh near Musselburgh.

While much of the trail is on quiet roads or well-made tracks, sections are on farm tracks or across sandy dunes. The roads through Northumberland's seaside towns are often clogged with cars. A hybrid or gravel bike is a good choice for the Coast and Castles South route. If you attempt it on a touring bike you may have to take an alternative route to circumvent the sandy trails between Lindisfarne and Berwick, and mountain bikers may want to switch to slicker tyres. Scotland's open access laws mean that a gravel or hybrid bike allows you to take alternatives to some of the road sections.

The Scottish borders were fiercely contested territories, and the legacy of this remains in the imposing castles that stand on the coast and along the Tweed. Coast and Castles South is a ride that allows you to enjoy historical ruins, coastal views, sandy beaches and quiet country roads. You can stop for afternoon tea at a country estate or enjoy a fish supper on the seafront. The coastal route that takes you through North Berwick's beautiful seashores is a shorter and easier alternative for those who do not want to tackle the hillier inland route. Scotland's capital, Edinburgh, offers you the very best of Scottish cuisine at the end of your adventure.

OFF-ROAD SECTION NEAR SCREMERSTON. © STEPHEN ROSS

03 COAST AND CASTLES SOUTH: ESSENTIAL INFORMATION

RIDE ESSENTIALS

Start:	**Newcastle, North Tyneside, England**
End:	**Edinburgh, Scotland**
Distance:	**324km**
Ascent/descent:	**2,220m/2,130m**
Also known as:	**NCN 1**

HOW TO GET THERE

Newcastle is on the East Coast Main Line rail service, with fast, direct services to London and Edinburgh. It also has an international airport and ferry services to Amsterdam.

Edinburgh is on the East Coast Main Line and has direct services to Newcastle and on to London, as well as to Glasgow and other Scottish cities. Both Glasgow and Edinburgh are well-served by international airports.

TIME TO COMPLETE

Minimum days:	**3 days/21 hours**
Maximum days:	**5 days/29 hours**

PROS

- **Castles** – you will encounter imposing castles at Warkworth, Bamburgh and Tynemouth. The dramatic clifftop ruins of Dunstanburgh are worth a detour. The fifteenth-century Smailholm Peel Tower provided inspiration to Sir Walter Scott.

- **Coast** – you not only get to enjoy the sandy Northumbrian coast, but also Tyneside's vibrant seaside towns and the bird-rich red cliffs of north Berwick's coast.

- **Fine food** – you can enjoy the finest Scottish produce in Edinburgh, including oysters, salmon, beef and whisky. Edinburgh has four Michelin-star restaurants and also has rich Italian and Indian culinary traditions.

CONS

- **Seaside roads** – road sections through Northumberland may be busy with tourists, particularly in summer, and are also travelled by regular coastal bus services.

- **Cities** – it is easy to lose the routes as you travel through Newcastle and Edinburgh. Edinburgh's cobbled streets, thronged with sightseers and busy with buses, are not the most cycle-friendly.

- **Railways and roads** – the East Coast Main Line and A1 main road are arterial routes through Northumberland's coast towards Edinburgh. There are sections of the route that are close to the busy road or railway, and occasionally besides both.

VARIATIONS

The main route follows the Tweed inland and then climbs over the Southern Uplands, but you can stick to the coast on NCN 76 and make use of the John Muir Way to reach Edinburgh. Coast and Castles North continues from Edinburgh to Aberdeen.

GOOD TO KNOW

Robert the Bruce was the Scottish king who secured independence from the English, with his decisive victory at Bannockburn near Stirling. He instructed that after his death his heart should be taken on pilgrimage to Jerusalem, although it only made it as far as Spain before its courier, Sir James Douglas, died. In 1921, an embalmed heart was excavated under Melrose Abbey's Chapter House – it has since been reburied, with a commemorative plaque. The abbey is also Alexander II's burial place, as well as the resting place of several Earls of Douglas.

FURTHER INFORMATION

www.sustrans.org.uk/find-other-routes/coast-and-castles-south-newcastle-to-edinburgh

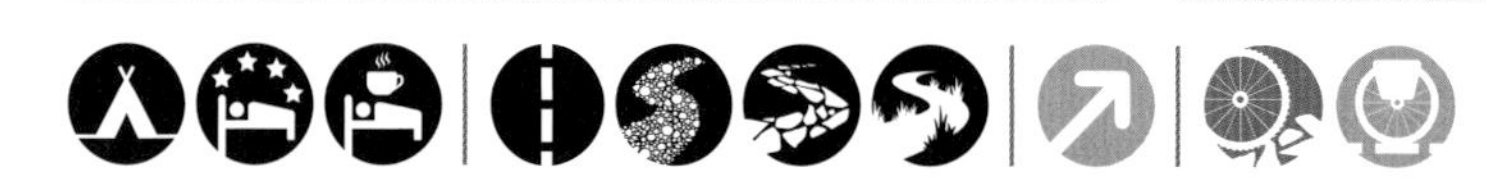

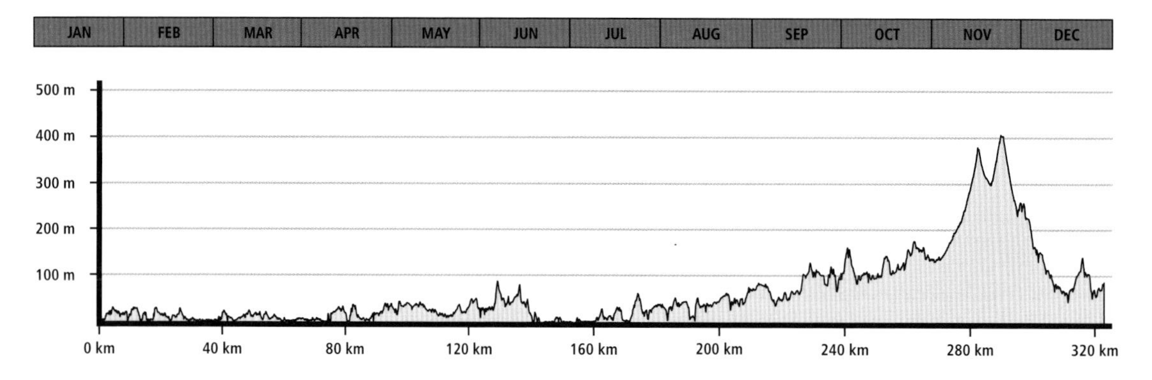

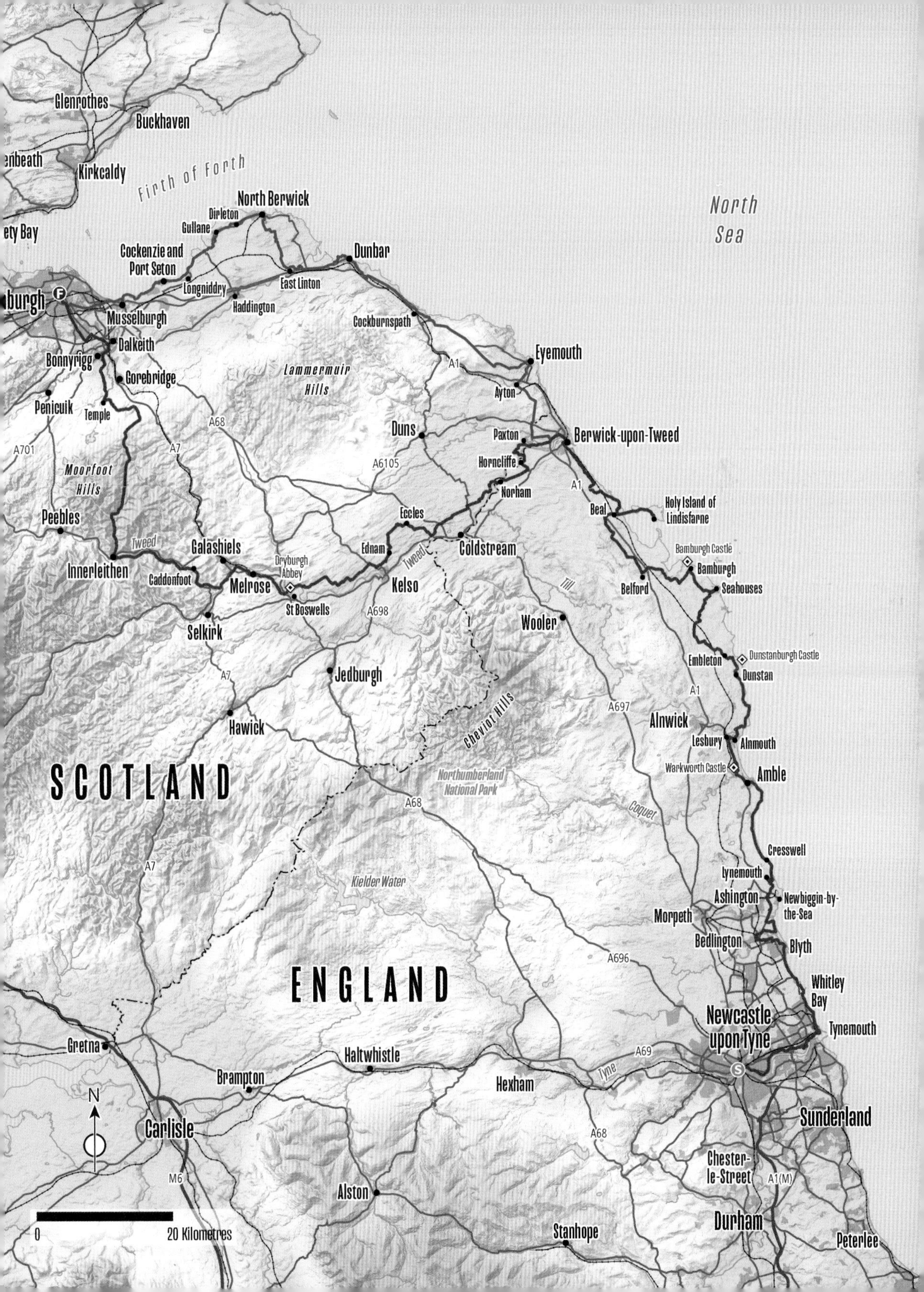
Glenrothes
Buckhaven
enbeath
Kirkcaldy
Firth of Forth
ety Bay
North Berwick
Dirleton
Gullane
North Sea
Cockenzie and Port Seton
Dunbar
Longniddry
East Linton
burgh
F
Musselburgh
Haddington
Cockburnspath
Dalkeith
Bonnyrigg
Eyemouth
Gorebridge
Lammermuir Hills
A1
Ayton
Penicuik
Temple
A68
Duns
Paxton
Berwick-upon-Tweed
A701
A7
A6105
Horncliffe
Moorfoot Hills
Norham
A1
Holy Island of Lindisfarne
Beal
Eccles
Peebles
Tweed
Galashiels
Ednam
Coldstream
Bamburgh Castle
Dryburgh Abbey
Tweed
Bamburgh
Innerleithen
Caddonfoot
Melrose
Kelso
Belford
Seahouses
Till
St Boswells
A698
Selkirk
Wooler
Embleton
Dunstanburgh Castle
Jedburgh
A7
Dunstan
A1
Cheviot Hills
A697
Hawick
Alnwick
Lesbury
Alnmouth
Warkworth Castle
Amble
SCOTLAND
Northumberland National Park
A68
Coquet
Cresswell
A7
Lynemouth
Kielder Water
Ashington
Newbiggin-by-the-Sea
Morpeth
Bedlington
Blyth
A696
ENGLAND
Whitley Bay
Newcastle upon Tyne
Tynemouth
Gretna
Haltwhistle
A69
Tyne
S
Brampton
Hexham
N
Sunderland
Carlisle
A68
Chester-le-Street
M6
A1(M)
Alston
Durham
0
20 Kilometres
Stanhope
Peterlee

Cape Wrath
John o' Groats
EDINBURGH
Middleton Top

04

04 GREAT NORTH TRAIL – 1,292km

The Great North Trail is an ambitious 1,292-kilometre route, developed by Cycling UK, that runs up the spine of the country from the centre of England to the very northern tips of Scotland. It is a challenging, rugged, off-road journey that traverses the Peak District, Yorkshire Dales, wild Cumbrian Hills and the Scottish Highlands, taking in Britain's most beautiful and remote scenery. This adventurous trail, often on rough, unsurfaced tracks, is not for the novice, although canal towpaths, quiet roads and disused railways offer occasional relief from hilly countryside.

The route begins in the White Peak at Middleton Top on the Pennine Bridleway, Britain's only National Trail specifically created as a bridleway. You take advantage of the Cromford and High Peak Railway. You join an old packhorse route across Wye Dale on to the hillier, grittier trails of the Dark Peak, contouring up and down around Mount Famine on technical trails. If you want an extra challenge, you can follow the alternative route over Mam Tor and up the steep Jacob's Ladder with the Pennine Way.

The trails rejoin at Hayfield in the shadow of Kinder Scout and follow the Sett Valley Trail. A steep, stony track leads you over Lantern Pike, and you skirt moorland and reservoirs near Manchester's urban sprawl, often on boggy packhorse trails. After crossing the M62 motorway, you can enjoy the deep, green Calder Valley, riding through Mankinholes beneath Stoodley Pike. You can ride the Mary Towneley Loop, named for the keen equestrian who was a riding force behind the Bridleway's creation, through Hebden Bridge, Todmorden and along the border between Yorkshire and Lancashire. You face a stern climb out of the valley on dirt track and sett (stone slab) trails heading for Brontë country and the Wycoller Country Park.

The route now reaches Craven Fault countryside, geological faultlines responsible for the dramatic limestone scenery that you cycle through on grassy, sometimes slippery trails. A tricky, stony descent leads you into the market town of Settle – you can divert on to the Settle Loop which takes you close to Malham Cove and Tarn. At mossy Catrigg Force, you can pause for a refreshing swim before a challenging climb over Long Scar in the shadow of Ingleborough. After passing under the iconic Settle–Carlisle Railway, you face a tough climb, past Dismal, Fair Bottom and Hard Turf Hills, to join the gravelly Pennine Way and reach the top of Cam Fell. You have good views of the Ribblehead Viaduct as you climb the grassy Bridleway around Dent Fell.

The Pennine Bridleway contours high on the hillside above the River Eden as it emerges in the Mallerstang Valley, on an old, high road which passes Mary Bourne's Watercut sculpture. You leave the Pennine Bridleway just before its end at Ravenstonedale and, passing the grey ruins of the twelfth-century Lammerside Castle, arrive at Kirkby Stephen. Quiet country roads lead you through the Eden Valley to Appleby-in-Westmorland, where you face a challenging climb over the ridge of the Pennines. The access road (to the golf ball radar station) leads high on to Great Dun Fell. A stony descent spins you down to Alston, England's highest market town.

◀ A STIFF CLIMB UP LOW GATE LANE HEADING TOWARDS HEBDEN BRIDGE, LEAVING CASTLESHAW RESERVOIRS AND ROMAN FORT IN THE VALLEY. © JOOLZE DYMOND

THE VIEW TOWARDS LOCH OSSIAN FROM THE GREAT NORTH TRAIL, WHICH FOLLOWS THE OLD ROAD TO THE ISLES FROM LOCH RANNOCH. © MARKUS STITZ

The South Tyne Trail is a well-surfaced, stony track that runs beside England's highest narrow-gauge railway to Haltwhistle, the centre of the UK. You ride across Hadrian's Wall, near Milecastle 42 and the Great Chesters fort, close to Walltown Crags. The route takes forestry tracks through Kielder Forest, a Dark Sky Park. You reach Scotland at the Bloody Bush on the Cross Border Trail and follow disused railway tracks through the Liddel Valley, and then roads to the textile town of Hawick. The Borders Abbeys Way offers grassy tracks through fields and muddy woodland sections. You can stay close to the River Tweed or follow a technical trail over Minch Moor.

The Trail climbs out of Peebles on the well-surfaced, gorse-lined Cross Borders Drove Road and passes North Esk Reservoir, built by nineteenth-century mill owners. You must climb over the Pentland Hills (on good tracks) but will be rewarded with views of Edinburgh and the snaking Firth of Forth. The Water of Leith takes you towards the city, but you turn west when you meet the Union Canal. You follow the canal to the Falkirk Wheel, the unique rotating boat lift that connects the canal to the lower Forth and Clyde Canal. You remain on the towpath to reach the outskirts of Glasgow.

From Glasgow you may choose to follow the John Muir Way north, or the An Turas Mor route, developed by Obscura Mondo Cycle Club.

The Great North Trail turns north through a forested river gorge, along dirt singletracks, to join the West Highland Way at Milngavie. You follow the popular Way to Drymen near Loch Lomond, where you turn on to the Rob Roy Way. The route follows forestry tracks through Loch Ard Forest, and then climbs through the Queen Elizabeth Forest before descending to Loch Venachar. You have been roughly following the line of the Highland Boundary Fault as it cuts north-east across the country, and on the old Callander and Oban Railway, you cross the fault into the Highlands at the Falls of Leny.

You continue to the follow the railway past waterfalls and lochs. At the tip of Loch Tay, near the beautiful Falls of Dochart, you can see Inchbuie, the ancient island burial ground of the MacNabs. You ascend gently up the green glen of Lochay, with the munros rising ahead of you. Glen Lyon, Scotland's longest enclosed glen, stretches before you; entering the wildest of Scotland's Highlands, you face

RIDING THROUGH THE PENTLAND HILLS REGIONAL PARK NEAR EDINBURGH.
© JOOLZE DYMOND

a steep climb up the old drovers' Kirk Road to the remote Rannoch Moor. The trail becomes more rutted as you pass Corrour, the UK's highest mainline rail station, heading for the isolated youth hostel on the shores of Loch Ossian.

Although you are now in remote countryside, the Trail takes advantage of access roads across moors and by lochs. You pass the highest point on route as you take General Wade's stony road over the Corrieyairack Pass, to be rewarded with panoramic wilderness views. You can rest weary legs on the twenty-kilometre descent to Fort Augustus, on Loch Ness's shores.

Another military road leads you through the sprawling Inchnacardoch Forest. Near Plodda Falls (a short diversion), you climb up and down on muddy tracks and rocky trails that follow a stream towards Marybank. You face a busy main road (the A835) for three kilometres, but you escape on to forestry tracks near Little Garve and then take the road to Black Bridge to access tracks and old drove roads past Loch Vaich. These deserted moors, with their abandoned croft, owe their quietness to the nineteenth-century Highland Clearances' eviction of tenants. You cycle through Amat Forest's pinewoods, in the Alladale Wilderness Reserve, famous for its plans to reintroduce wolves. You reach Oykel Bridge on good, yet remote, flat trails. Northwards, much of the route is A roads that, despite their designation, are quiet, singletrack tarmac lanes. At Rosehall, you follow the salmon-rich River Cassley northwards.

At Allnabad, you face the choice of heading west to Cape Wrath or east to John o' Groats. Though the western road is shorter, it is more demanding and involves a challenging river crossing at Cashel Dhu (not passable in bad weather). It does, however, offer you the opportunity to visit the Iron Age broch roundhouse, Dun Dornaigil, by the Strathmore. The ferry to Cape Wrath only operates from May to September. You may want to conclude your adventure with a night in the remote Kearvaig bothy. If you choose instead to go to John o' Groats, the route is largely on quiet roads through low, grassy peatlands, although you might choose a more challenging (and rutted) off-road track around Loch Choire.

The Great North Trail is perfect for the mountain bike adventurer, although it might also be completed on a gravel or hybrid bike with wide, grippy tyres. It is a route that lets you cycle deep into Britain's wildest and most remote country, and takes advantage of Scotland's right to roam to let you discover the best of Scotland's hills, moors and forests.

04 GREAT NORTH TRAIL: ESSENTIAL INFORMATION

RIDE ESSENTIALS

Start:	**Middleton Top, Derbyshire, England**
End:	**John o' Groats, Caithness, Scotland OR Cape Wrath, Sutherland, Scotland**
Distance:	**1,292km**
Ascent/descent:	**17,400m/17,670m**

HOW TO GET THERE

Middleton Top is four kilometres from Cromford train station. The closest airports are Manchester and East Midlands.

Cape Wrath can only be reached via the Kyle of Durness ferry. Summer bus services from Durness to Lairg, the closest railway station, carry bicycles but advance bookings have to be made. You might choose instead to follow the North Coast 500 (see page 81) to Thurso's train station. Inverness is the closest international airport.

John o' Groats is approximately thirty kilometres from Wick and thirty-five kilometres from Thurso, which both have local train stations that connect to Inverness. Bus services from John o' Groats to Wick and Thurso will not transport bikes – there are several local courier operators.

TIME TO COMPLETE

Minimum days:	**12 days/115 hours**
Maximum days:	**27 days/160 hours**

PROS

- **Highs** – this is a route with plenty of climbing. Plenty of climbs mean plenty of descents, the highlight being the twenty-kilometre roll down into Fort Augustus.

- **Countryside** – this trail takes you not only through the Loch Lomond and the Trossachs National Park, but also the Highlands and the Southern Uplands. You also get to enjoy the Peak District and Yorkshire Dales National Park.

- **Technical trails** – the Trail offers several variations and more technical trails for those seeking a mountain bike challenge. You can test your skills at Lonesome Pine, Bloody Bush, Glentress and Contin, and explore the trails at Aberfoyle and the Callander Estate.

CONS

- **River crossings** – there are several rivers to be forded in the northern Highlands, and this may be dangerous or impossible in spate, particularly in winter and spring. The ferry across the Kyle of Durness only runs between Easter and October.

- **Midges** – these biting pests are at their worst in Scotland between May and June. Take plenty of insect repellent (although some swear by Avon's Skin So Soft), mosquito nets and try to avoid being outside at dawn and dusk.

VARIATIONS

There are several loops on the Pennine Bridleway – the Settle Loop, Charlie's Loop and the Mary Towneley – which can be used either to extend, or as alternatives to, the main route. You have a choice of end destinations, but particularly in Scotland, there are many opportunities to pick a more challenging off-road route.

GOOD TO KNOW

If you choose Cape Wrath as your end destination, you become a member of the Cape Wrath Fellowship, devised by cycling journalist Rex Coley. To become a member now, you should take a photo of yourself by the lighthouse, and fill in the form at *www.cyclinguk.org/capewrath* (Cycling UK are now custodians of the Fellowship).

FURTHER INFORMATION

www.cyclinguk.org/offroadcampaigns/great-north-trail – Cycling UK also produce a print guidebook; *Pennine Bridleway* (Vertebrate Publishing, 2021).

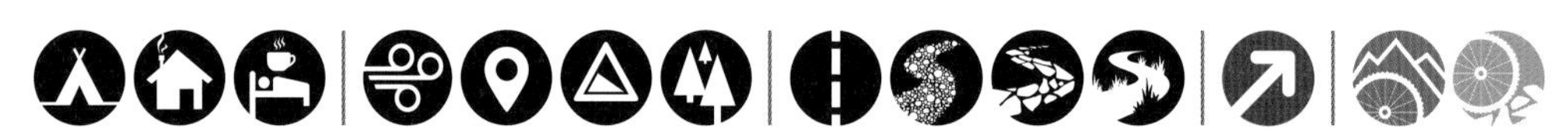

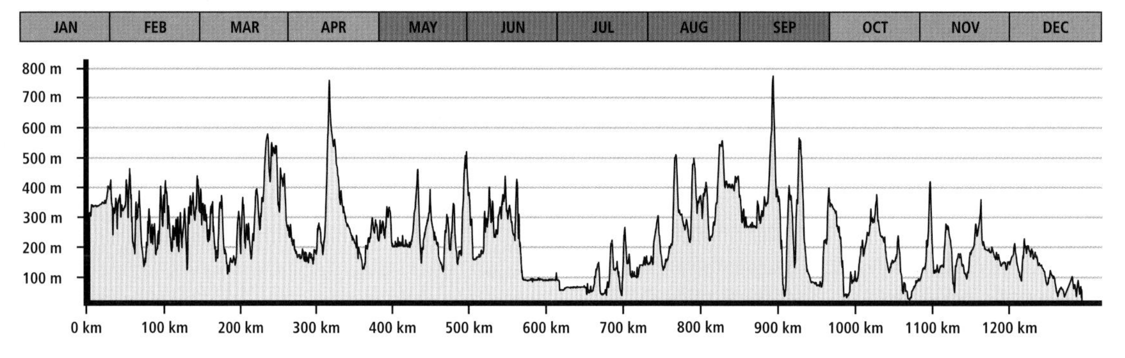

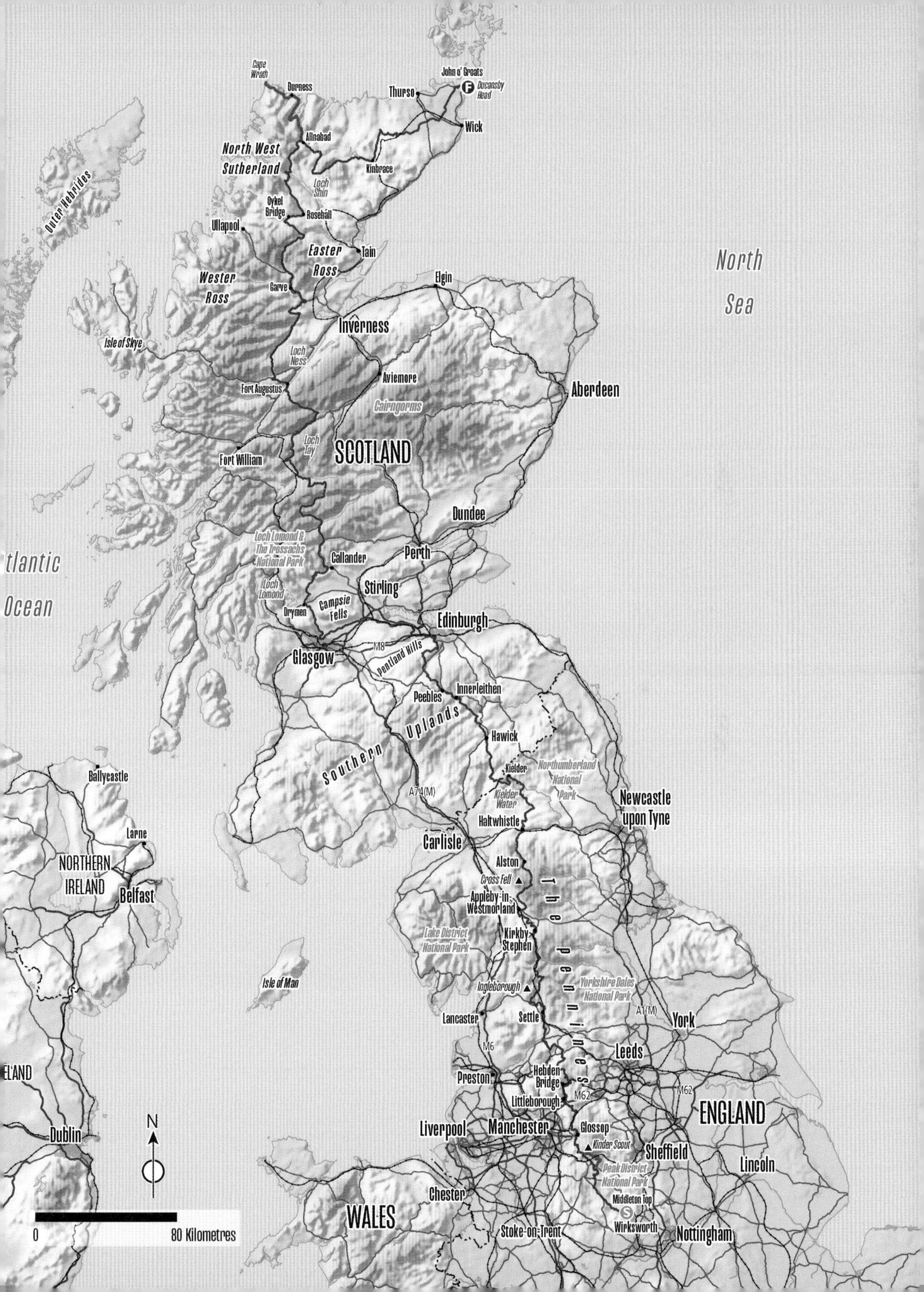

Cape Wrath
Durness
John o' Groats
Thurso
F
Duncansby Head
Wick
Allnabad
North West Sutherland
Kinbrace
Outer Hebrides
Loch Shin
Oykel Bridge
Rosehall
Ullapool
Easter Ross
Tain
North Sea
Wester Ross
Garve
Elgin
Inverness
Isle of Skye
Loch Ness
Aviemore
Fort Augustus
Aberdeen
Cairngorms
Loch Tay
SCOTLAND
Fort William
Dundee
Loch Lomond & The Trossachs National Park
Callander
Perth
tlantic
Ocean
Stirling
Loch Lomond
Drymen
Campsie Fells
Edinburgh
M8
Glasgow
Pentland Hills
Innerleithen
Peebles
Uplands
Southern
Hawick
Kielder
Northumberland National Park
Ballycastle
A74(M)
Kielder Water
Newcastle upon Tyne
Haltwhistle
Larne
Carlisle
NORTHERN IRELAND
Belfast
Alston
Cross Fell
Appleby-in-Westmorland
The Pennines
Lake District National Park
Kirkby Stephen
Isle of Man
Ingleborough
Yorkshire Dales National Park
A1(M)
York
Lancaster
Settle
M6
Leeds
ELAND
Preston
Hebden Bridge
M62
M62
Littleborough
ENGLAND
Liverpool
Manchester
Glossop
Dublin
N
Kinder Scout
Sheffield
Lincoln
Peak District National Park
Chester
Middleton Top
S
WALES
0
80 Kilometres
Stoke-on-Trent
Wirksworth
Nottingham

05

05 GREAT WESTERN WAY – 256km

Isambard Kingdom Brunel's Great Western Railway, nicknamed 'God's Wonderful Railway', linked the shipping powerhouse of Bristol with London, curving around the Marlborough Downs. The 256-kilometre Great Western Way provides a cycle link between the two cities, following canal towpaths, riverside tracks and quiet country lanes. En route you can enjoy views of the Cotswolds, the Roman city of Bath, waterfront pubs, royal castles and hunting grounds and London's tourist attractions.

You start your journey in London at Rotherhithe, on the banks of the Thames next to the Brunel Museum. It is here that Marc Isambard Brunel, a French engineer, and his son Isambard Kingdom bored the first Thames Tunnel, a feat previously believed impossible. The route follows the river westwards, often along the route of the Thames Path. Sustrans's route is largely on roads, but new segregated solutions are rapidly being created through London, and routes such as Cycleway 4 (which is being extended but currently runs from Rotherhithe to Tower Bridge) and Cycleway 8 (between Lambeth and Battersea) offer you traffic-free alternatives to the long-established NCN 4. Your waterfront route through London offers views of Westminster and the Tower of London, and passes the tourist attractions of the Globe theatre, World War II ship *HMS Belfast* and, if you want panoramic views of the city, the London Eye.

You cycle through the green space of Richmond Park, once a royal hunting ground and still home to red and fallow deer. The Way joins the largely traffic-free Thames Valley Path near Teddington Lock – the lock marks the limit of the legal powers of the Port of London Authority, meaning that you are now on the stretch of the Thames where wild swimming is permitted. The route passes Hampton Court Palace, the red-brick Tudor palace built by Cardinal Wolsey that became King Henry VIII's beloved residence.

At Weybridge, you either have to take the ferry across the Thames to Shepperton (the boat takes bikes and runs every quarter of an hour) or take a longer detour around the Roman Catholic St George's College. You can also make another route choice at Chertsey Bridge – the northern route follows the riverbanks, first on-road through Laleham (once home to Matthew Arnold) then on the tarmacked Thames Path. The southern route winds inland on quiet roads, riverside paths and segregated cycleways, close to the M3 and M25 motorways and past the Thorpe Park amusement resort, home to the UK's fastest rollercoaster (Stealth). The routes reunite near Staines-upon-Thames.

At Egham you skirt the edge of the green water meadows at Runnymede, where King John sealed the Magna Carta in 1215 – the site was chosen because it lay between the rebels' stronghold at Staines and Windsor Castle. There is a long road section to Windsor on tree-fringed residential roads, past large semi-detached houses and then on the roads that run through Windsor Great Park. There is a small route variation when you return to the Thames that takes you to Windsor Castle, the longest occupied palace and castle in Europe.

◀ BEYOND THE OUTSKIRTS OF BRISTOL THE PATH PASSES THROUGH BITTON STATION, HOME OF THE AVON VALLEY STEAM RAILWAY.
© DAVID HARPER – *WESTERNASPECT.COM*

BITTON STATION. © DAVID HARPER – *WESTERNASPECT.COM*

You enjoy a pleasant riverside section to Maidenhead, but then cut inland on quiet roads and traffic-free tracks to cut off the river's wide loops, skipping Marlow and Henley-on-Thames. The route rejoins the Thames near Wargrave for a short time. Just before Reading, you reach the Kennet and Avon Canal, that links navigable parts of the Kennet and Avon rivers to provide a waterway route between Bath and Reading. Significant restoration work has been carried out to create a navigable canal, but also to improve the towpaths.

A pleasant, flat route takes you through to Hungerford, and although there are grassy and bumpy sections of towpath that are perhaps best tackled on a gravel or hybrid, the route is generally passable on a tourer with caution. You are often cycling close to the canal edge, with nothing to protect you from the water. Near the pretty waterfront village of Aldermaston Wharf, you pass the Aldermaston Gravel Pits – these flooded workings are now a Site of Special Scientific Interest and a haven for waterfowl. You are occasionally diverted from the canal – at Thatcham, for example – although you could choose to remain on the towpath through the muddy Monkey Marsh Lock. Between Newbury and Hungerford, you skirt the edge of the bio-diverse conservation areas of Kennet Valley Alderwoods.

The Way leaves the canal near Marsh Benham to follow country lanes, through the pretty but hilly Vale of Pewsey. You can remain on the canal towpath, although narrow, stony and grassy tracks will be challenging even on a gravel or hybrid bike and you may have to push along some sections. The official route gently rolls along hawthorn-lined lanes and past chocolate box villages, thatched cottages and golden fields. You may encounter local traffic and occasionally tractors or other large farm vehicles as you cycle through the North Wessex Downs. As you pedal past Pewsey you should get a good view of the white horse, the smallest of the eight Wiltshire white horses, carved for the coronation of George VI.

Near Devizes, you return to the Kennet and Avon Canal and quickly encounter the Caen Hill Locks, a flight of twenty-nine locks that rise seventy-two metres in a little over three kilometres, reaching gradients of up to one in thirty. You descend past the locks, and should proceed with caution

RIVER AVON AT SALTFORD. © MATTHEW PRICE ARTIST

unless you want an impromptu swim. The route passes the pretty Cotswold town of Bradford-on-Avon – it is here that the first sods were turned for the canal in 1794. The stunning Dundas and Avoncliff aqueducts carry the canal across the Avon. This section of the canal beneath the backdrop of the Cotswold hills is particularly spectacular. You briefly return to the roads to enjoy a ride through Bath's historic centre, past the city walls, abbey and Pump Rooms. The Bristol and Bath Railway Path follows the route of an old Midland Railway branch line on pleasant tarmac trails; developed between 1979 and 1986, this flagship route was one of Sustrans's first projects. You have a short section on-road to reach the Way's end at Bristol Temple Meads, where you can still see parts of Brunel's original mock-Tudor station.

The Great Western Way may be ridden at any time of year although the low, flat route may be flooded during winter and spring. It is the ideal family route, with plenty of places to stop on the way, and good public transport connections – the route often runs parallel to the modern railway. There are direct, high-speed trains between Bristol and London making it a very straightforward linear route to return to the start, whichever way you choose to cycle it, and you can enjoy a journey from London all the way to Land's End if you combine it with the West Country and Cornish Ways.

The Great Western Way is the perfect choice if you want to keep your wheels spinning over easy trails, to travel hawthorn-scented lanes and to see England's green hills without climbing too many. You can enjoy thatched cottages, golden farm fields and quiet villages, and if you wonder at Brunel's incredible achievements you can visit the museum dedicated to him in London, stop at the *SS Great Britain*, the first steel ship in the world, in Bristol or could cycle further down the Avon to the Clifton Suspension Bridge. The Great Western Way will show you how easy it is to leave the city behind and find England's calm countryside.

05 GREAT WESTERN WAY: ESSENTIAL INFORMATION

RIDE ESSENTIALS

Start:	**London, England**
End:	**Bristol, England**
Distance:	**256km**
Ascent/descent:	**780m/770m**
AKA:	**NCN 4**

HOW TO GET THERE

London has international rail and air services. Bicycles – whether boxed or not – can be carried on the Eurostar for an additional fee, although prebooking is advised.

Bristol has an international airport and is on the mainline rail network, with direct, high-speed connections to London and other UK cities.

TIME TO COMPLETE

Minimum days:	**2 days/17 hours**
Maximum days:	**4 days/24 hours**

PROS

- **Villages** – the Great Western Way has more than its fair share of quirkily named villages. The route takes you through, or past, Ram Alley, Clench, Crazies Hill, Little Abbots, Cuckoo's Knob and Sheffield Bottom to name a few.

- **Waterfront pubs** – from the Barge Inn near Devizes, Staines's community-owned Wheatsheaf and Pigeon and the Boatman by Windsor Castle, to Woolhampton's traditional Rowbarge and the gastro Kingfisher at Chertsey, there are plenty of waterside pubs with good food and riverside terraces to choose from.

- **Flat** – this is a route with very few climbs. River, canal and railway tracks are flat. There is some climbing in the section through the Vale of Pewsey but nothing to exhaust even the novice cyclist.

CONS

- **Roads** – there are sections on-road in London on painted cycle lanes, and through Bath's busy city centre. The road section between Marsh Benham and Devizes is generally quiet, but may be busy with farm traffic during harvest, for example.

- **Accidental dips** – the towpath is often close to the canal edge, and there is little to prevent you from falling in. Care should be taken when the towpath surfaces is bumpy, or when descending past locks.

VARIATIONS

There are route choices to be made at Chertsey, and you can choose to remain on the canal towpath between Marsh Benham and Devizes (there are direct trains between Hungerford and Devizes if you want to avoid the roads but do not want to tackle the bumpy canal towpath).

GOOD TO KNOW

The Great Western Railway Company was founded in 1833, and Isambard Kingdom Brunel, aged twenty-seven, was appointed Chief Engineer. He devised the route, designed London's Paddington and Bristol's Temple Meads station and constructed viaducts, tunnels and bridges. The line – which was later to be nicknamed the 'Holiday Line' as it whisked Londoners to Devon and Cornwall – was the site of the world's first commercial telegraph line, installed to improve signalling on the railway.

FURTHER INFORMATION

www.sustrans.org.uk/find-other-routes/great-western-way

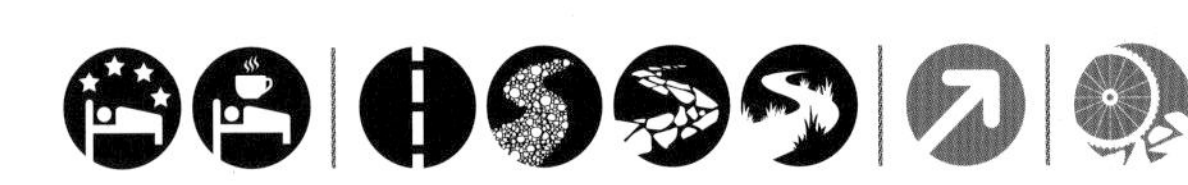

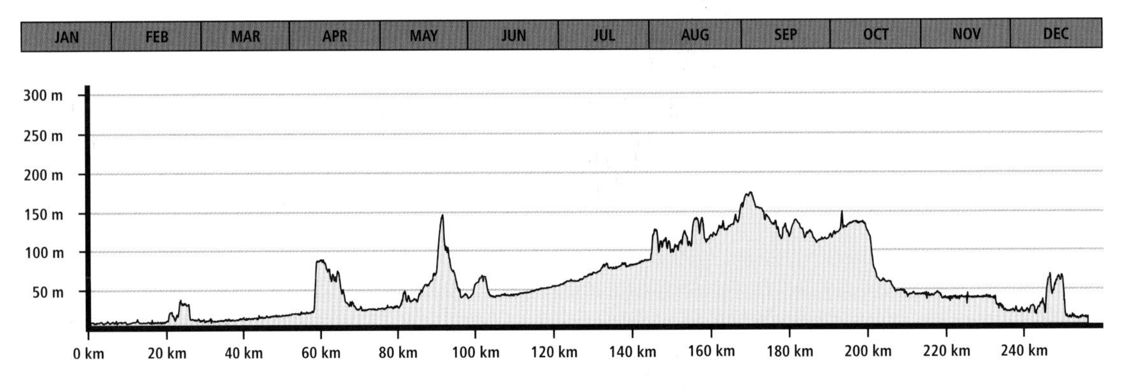

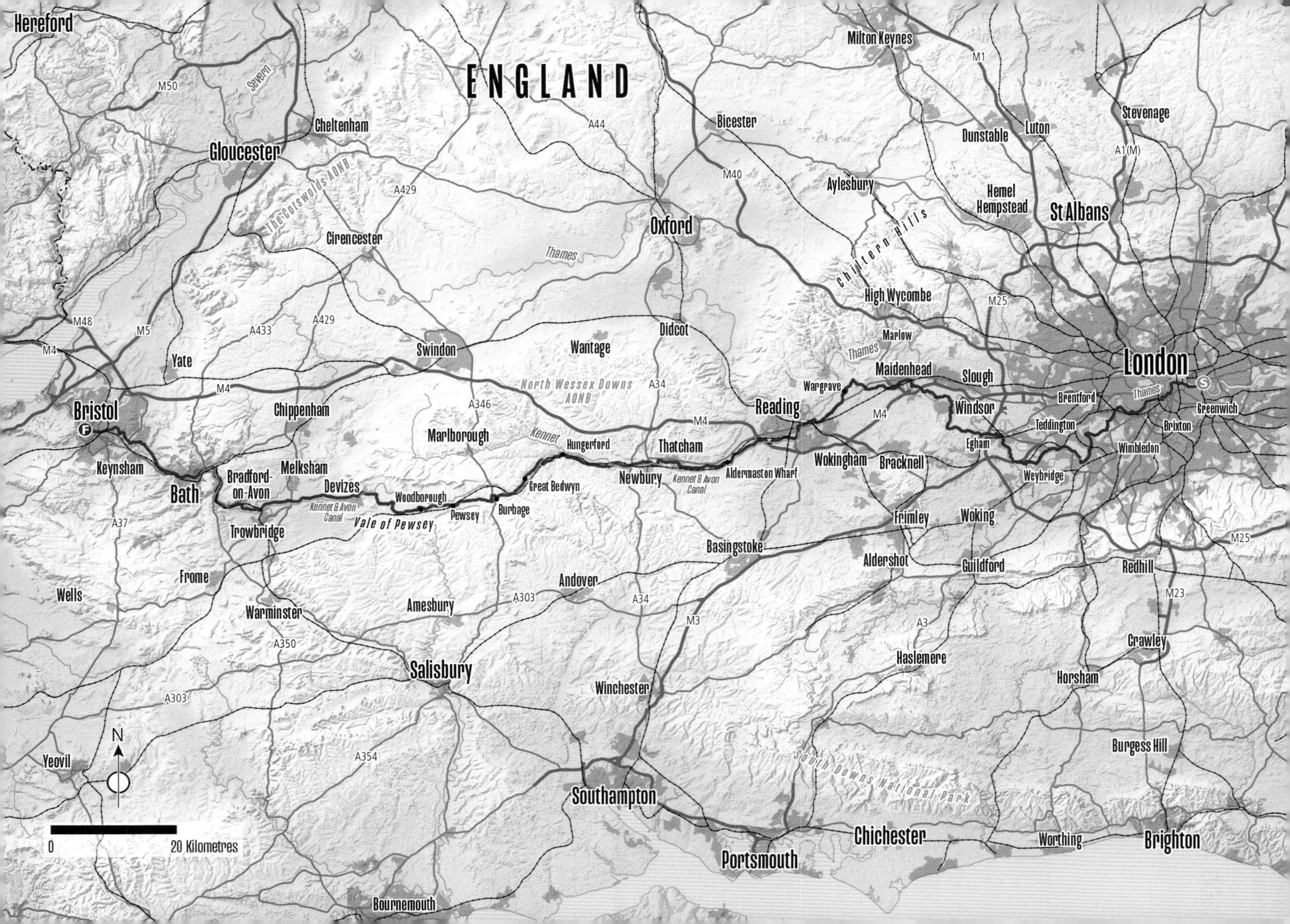
ENGLAND
Hereford
M50
Severn
Cheltenham
Gloucester
The Cotswolds AONB
A429
A44
Bicester
M40
Oxford
Cirencester
Thames
Milton Keynes
M1
Stevenage
Dunstable
Luton
A1(M)
Aylesbury
Hemel Hempstead
St Albans
Chiltern Hills
High Wycombe
M25
M48
M5
A433
A429
Didcot
Marlow
Thames
M4
Yate
Swindon
Wantage
Maidenhead
Slough
London
Wargrave
North Wessex Downs AONB
A34
Reading
Windsor
Brentford
Thames
Greenwich
Bristol
Chippenham
A346
M4
M4
Teddington
Brixton
Marlborough
Kennet
Hungerford
Thatcham
Egham
Wimbledon
Keynsham
Melksham
Wokingham
Bracknell
Bradford-on-Avon
Devizes
Great Bedwyn
Newbury
Kennet & Avon Canal
Aldermaston Wharf
Weybridge
Bath
Woodborough
Kennet & Avon Canal
Pewsey
Burbage
Frimley
Woking
A37
Vale of Pewsey
Trowbridge
Basingstoke
M25
Aldershot
Guildford
Redhill
Frome
Andover
Wells
A303
A34
M23
Amesbury
Warminster
M3
A3
A350
Crawley
Haslemere
Salisbury
Horsham
Winchester
A303
Burgess Hill
South Downs National Park
N
Yeovil
A354
Southampton
Chichester
Worthing
Brighton
0
20 Kilometres
Portsmouth
Bournemouth

06

06 HADRIAN'S CYCLEWAY – 265km

Hadrian's Cycleway is a coast-to-coast route with a lot of history thrown in. The 265-kilometre trail begins on the Cumbrian coast, in the Lake District National Park, and follows the line of Roman fortifications up the Solway Firth and along the course of Hadrian's Wall. You will enjoy riverside paths, old railway tracks and the occasional hedgerowed country lane on a route that never climbs mountains but offers plenty of ups and downs as it spins across Northern England towards the vibrant city of Newcastle upon Tyne.

Hadrian's Cycleway begins in Ravenglass, the only coastal village in the Lake District National Park, chosen as the start because it was once the site of the Glannaventa Roman fort, a continuation of the fortifications of Hadrian's Wall. You leave Ravenglass on the main A595 road, which can be busy and has little space to spare at the edges. At low tide, you might instead choose to ford the River Mite on the sandy track next to the railway line.

However you cross the river, you take quiet roads along the coast and past Seascale, site of the Sellafield nuclear plant. Taking advantage of a disused railway line, the route heads inland through the market town of Egremont. Although you are briefly on roads through towns and villages, you are largely on the railway tracks back to Whitehaven, the coastal town that was once a thriving port, its fortunes built on tobacco and rum.

You are now on the Sea to Sea/C2C route (see page 99), and you can enjoy good-quality tarmac tracks that follow the Cumbrian coast north towards Silloth, through the old steel and coal town of Workington. At Maryport, you can visit the clifftop Senhouse Roman Museum or the Lake District Coast Aquarium; hungry pedallers can also tuck into fish and chips or a prawn sandwich at the aquarium's Harbourside Cafe. On easy-going trails, you enjoy views along the Solway Firth and the Galloway Hills rising in Southern Scotland.

This countryside is rich not only in Roman remains but also reminders of Cumbria's industrial and agricultural past – near Crosscanonby, you pass the hollows of Elizabethan salt pans. The route returns to roads near the sandy seaside resort of Allonby. Silloth, the town whose sunsets over the sea were beloved by J.M.W. Turner, is still home to Carr's Flour Mill, established to mill flour for Carr's table biscuits.

The trail heads inland on quiet, green-fringed country lanes to ride through the South Solway Mosses Nature Reserve; the firth's bog and salt marshes are rich and unique wildlife habitats. You reach the coast again near Anthorn and meet the end of Hadrian's Wall Path National Trail at Bowness-on-Solway. Your route into Carlisle along flat, low roads by the water's edge is often shared with the walkers. At very high tides, sections of this road may be flooded – you should check the tide tables for any high tides above nine metres.

At Burgh by Sands you can loop out to visit the King Edward I monument, erected on the sands where Edward, Hammer of the Scots, died of dysentery. You are reaching the outskirts of the castled city of Carlisle. With the

◀ THE STEEP CLIMB OUT OF GREENHEAD TOWARDS HALTWHISTLE.
© *CYCLE.TRAVEL*

VINDOLANDA ROMAN FORT. © SHUTTERSTOCK/JAIME PHARR

Hadrian's Wall walkers, you take an often-muddy riverside path out of Carlisle but join the roads to follow an indirect route to Brampton – fortunately there is a shared, albeit narrow and tussocky, tarmac path beside the busy A689 main road.

Hadrian took advantage of the high Great Whin Sill to build his wall, and this section of the route, as it climbs towards the Wall, is bumpy. On the banks of the River Irthing, you reach the remains of the twelfth-century Lanercost Priory. At Banks, you get your first glimpse of the stone wall against breathtaking views over the Pennines. The Wall accompanies you as you follow the road to Birdoswald, one of the best-preserved forts on the Wall.

You enter Greenhead on a riverside trail that passes the twelfth-century Thirlwall Castle. On a tarmac trail next to the Military Road, you face the toughest climb of the route over Greenwhelt Bank before descending to Haltwhistle, the town that claims to be the centre of Britain. The route follows the course of the South Tyne river towards Bardon Mill, before climbing again towards the Wall. Just below the Youth Hostel Association's flagship The Sill and the Twice Brewed Inn in the village of Once Brewed, you turn on a singletrack road that leads past the Vindolanda fort.

Following a Roman road beneath the high ridge of the Wall, you reach the highest point of the Cycleway. It is a short detour if you want to visit the Roman fort of Chesters on the outskirts of Chollerford. The Cycleway takes you south, away from the Wall, towards the market town of Hexham. You remain on roads on your way towards Prudhoe; the grey-walled castle, once home to the Percys, is the only fortification in Northumberland never to have fallen to the Scots.

Although no longer enjoying views of the Wall, you now enjoy one of the best sections of the Cycleway – an off-road route that follows the Tyne towards Newcastle through low, green fields, and along the Wylam Waggonway.
The route passes the cottage where George Stephenson, railway pioneer, was born – he was perhaps inspired by William Hedley's steam locomotives, built to transport coal down the Tyne on the Waggonway. The route sometimes coincides again with the Hadrian's Wall Path, and you head for the busy, vibrant riverfront of Newcastle.

SUNRISE OVER THE FIELDS ABOVE HENSHAW, CLOSE TO VINDOLANDA.
© PENNY COOMBE

A SIGNPOST ON THE ROUTE NEAR THE ROMAN FORT OF MARYPORT ON THE CUMBRIAN COAST. © PENNY COOMBE

Your riverside route takes you to Wallsend, where the Hadrian's Wall Path begins, and you can visit Segedunum Fort and Museum, opposite a large supermarket. On wide, tarmac tracks you reach North Shields, once a busy fishing port but now the departure point for the South Shields Ferry. You could choose to continue on the off-road route to the seaside resort of Tynemouth, with its weekend markets, castle and priory ruins, although technically the Cycleway ends with a crossing of the Tyne to reach the Roman Arbeia Gatehouse in South Shields.

Hadrian's Cycleway is readily completed on a tourer, but it is the perfect first big adventure on a gravel or hybrid bike. It is a route best tackled slowly, and a gravel or hybrid bike will give you more options with respect to exploring off-route. You will want to make detours to the Wall, explore the coast and visit the many castles, abbeys and forts. The route from Ravenglass to Silloth is still subject to change but the rest of the Cycleway is clearly waymarked, although the distances on the signs sometimes seem contradictory. The middle Wall sections may feel remote but, despite the panoramic views over green hills, you are rarely far from the next country pub, farmyard ice cream parlour or cosy cafe. The route is never particularly high or steep, but the middle section is bumpy. Hadrian's Cycleway is a low, easy coastal route interrupted by a high, green middle section that undulates through moorland, in the shadow of the Wall. The Romans built the Wall here for its high vantage points and as you cycle through the heart of England, it will sometimes feel like you can see forever.

06 HADRIAN'S CYCLEWAY: ESSENTIAL INFORMATION

RIDE ESSENTIALS

Start:	**Ravenglass, Cumbria, England**
End:	**South Shields, Tyne and Wear, England**
Distance:	**265km**
Ascent/descent:	**1,510m/1,510m**

HOW TO GET THERE

Ravenglass is a station on the Cumbrian Coast Line; this regional line connects with the West Coast Main Line services at Carlisle. Manchester is the closest international airport.

South Shields is on Newcastle's metro line; bicycles are allowed on the metro during off-peak hours (but not through central Newcastle) and also on the South Shields Ferry. Newcastle is on the East Coast Main Line with high-speed connections to London and Scotland. Newcastle is the closest international airport, and Newcastle's ferry port offers services to Amsterdam.

TIME TO COMPLETE

Minimum days:	**2 days/17 hours**
Maximum days:	**4 days/24 hours**

PROS

- **Romans** – you are on the northern fringe of the Roman empire, and in addition to the Wall with its milecastles and forts, you can visit museums, temples and even Roman latrines.

- **Coast and country** – Hadrian's Cycleway is the route where you don't have to choose between sandy beaches or green moorland. With a long stretch along the Cumbria coast, Tyneside's seaside resorts and a mid-section through the wild Northumbrian countryside, Hadrian's Cycleway offers the best of both and is one of the easiest English coast-to-coast routes.

- **Market towns** – as it veers away from the Wall, the route takes you through Northumberland's charming traditional market towns. Haltwhistle has fine independent cafes; Hexham's centre is a beautiful park, surrounded by historical buildings; Prudhoe has castle ruins and fine stained-glass windows in Prudhoe Hall and the Catholic church.

CONS

- **Wall** – the Cycleway generally follows the route of the Wall, but is often one or two kilometres away from it. If you want to see the Sycamore Gap, Milecastle 39, Sewingshields Crags or any of the other iconic Wall views, you will have to schedule extra time to leave the route.

- **Walkers** – at times you share the trail with the extremely popular Hadrian's Wall Path National Trail, and at other times, the routes criss-cross. Particularly during the summer, you may have to give way to lots of hikers.

VARIATIONS

There are no variations to the main route, although some choose to start from Silloth so that the route is easier to complete in a weekend. Most riders will detour to visit the Wall.

GOOD TO KNOW

If you're looking for a return route, you could attempt the 278-kilometre Reivers Route, a challenging on- and off-road route that takes you from Tynemouth through the wild countryside of the Northumberland National Park, Kielder Forest and border country to return you to Carlisle and the Cumbrian coast.

FURTHER INFORMATION

www.sustrans.org.uk/find-other-routes/hadrians-cycleway; Hadrian's Cycleway (Cicerone, 2020).

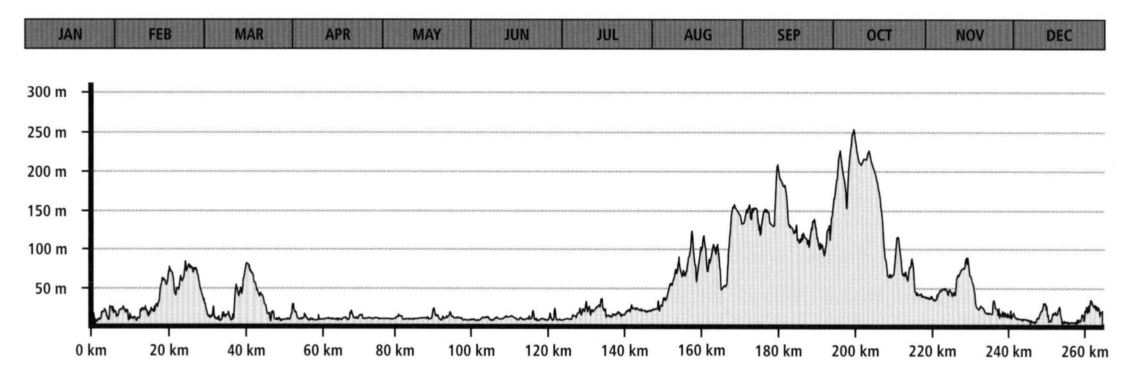

SCOTLAND
ENGLAND
North Sea
Solway Firth
Lockerbie
Dumfries
Annan
Gretna
Bowness-on-Solway
Drumburgh
Burgh by Sands
Anthorn
Silloth
Abbeytown
Carlisle
Wigton
Allonby
Maryport
Cockermouth
Workington
Whitehaven
Cleator Moor
Egremont
Seascale
Ravenglass
Keswick
Lake District
National Park
Ambleside
Windermere
Broughton in Furness
Ulverston
Grange-over-Sands
Kendal
Kirkby Lonsdale
Sedbergh
Penrith
Brampton
Birdoswald (Roman fort)
Gilsland
Greenhead
Haltwhistle
Vindolanda (Roman fort)
Bardon Mill
Irthing
Northumberland
National Park
North Tyne
Wall
Hexham
Corbridge
Tyne
Wylam
Prudhoe
Newcastle upon Tyne
Wallsend
Morpeth
Blyth
Cramlington
Sunderland
Stanley
Consett
Chester-le-Street
Durham
Allendale
East Allen
South Tyne
Alston
North Pennines AONB
Eden
Stanhope
Bishop Auckland
Barnard Castle
Darlington
Kirkby Stephen
Richmond
Northallerton
Leyburn
Hawes
Yorkshire Dales
National Park
A74(M)
A7
A6071
A689
A686
A68
A696
M6
A595
A596
A66
A593
A684
A1
A1(M)
N
0
10 Kilometres

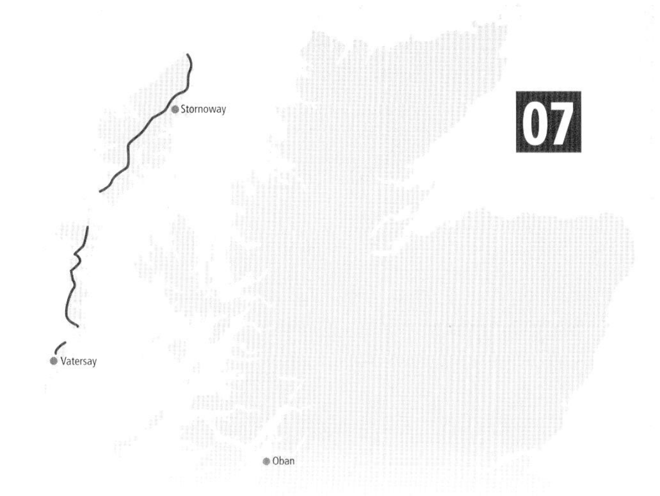

07 HEBRIDEAN WAY – 323km

The archipelago of the Outer Hebrides is a gold-fringed crocodile of islands that curves around the north-western tip of Scotland. The 323-kilometre Hebridean Way, once National Cycle Network (NCN) Route 780, stretches from the southern tip of Vatersay to follow quiet roads across ten islands, via two ferry crossings and six causeways, finishing at the Butt of Lewis, once declared the windiest place in Britain by Guinness World Records. Generally, you follow a coastal route besides the Hebrides's golden beaches, and past sea stacks and rippling sea lochs. Sometimes the road will rise before you over rock-strewn moorland or climb through rugged hills, but you never really lose sight of the sea on these Western Isles, the Islands of Strangers.

The Outer Hebrides consist of more than a hundred islands, most now deserted; your ride begins on Vatersay, the most southerly of the inhabited islands and Scotland's most westerly settlement. This serene, green island was a refuge for the Vatersay Raiders, landless cottars who were prosecuted in 1906 for illegally settling here and planting potatoes – their descendants still occupy the island crofts. A singletrack road winds through the dunes and along the shore of the tiny island before reaching the 200-metre-long causeway, built in 1991, which links Vatersay to Barra.

Beflowered Barra, with its grassy machair plains, white shell beaches and steep hills, has a reputation as the Hebrides's most beautiful island. Castlebay is the biggest village on the island, and you can catch a boat to the medieval Kisimul Castle, built on a rock in the bay – since 2001, the castle has been donated to the nation by the Clan MacNeil for a bottle of whisky and rent of £1 a year. After Castlebay, an undulating road through gentle hills will surprise you as sandy bay after sandy bay appear on the horizon.

Your first ferry crossing connects Barra to Eriskay; there are services every day, although generally only one morning and one afternoon crossing on winter Sundays. Not so long ago, everything shut on the Sabbath, particularly in the northern islands, and you may still struggle to find a shop or somewhere to eat. It was off the treacherous coast of Eriskay that the whisky-laden *SS Politician* foundered in 1941; local resident Compton Mackenzie was inspired to write *Whisky Galore!* as he watched the authority's attempts to thwart the locals' enthusiastic salvage attempts. Bottles still occasionally emerge from the sand dunes or gardens of the crofts. It was on Eriskay that Bonnie Prince Charlie, raised in Italy and France, first stepped on to Scottish soil.

South Uist is one long beach, with a thin strip of grassy machair next to it, backed by a high mountain ridge. The Way here takes you here on a gently climbing road across the green machair duneland rather than the beaches. The route passes the Kildonan Museum, where you can learn more about croft-living and see Celtic and Viking artifacts from the island. The museum is close to Flora Macdonald's birthplace, although there is no clear evidence for where exactly on the island she was born.

◀ CYCLING TOWARDS LUSKENTYRE BEACH.
© BARNEY VAUGHAN-KNIGHT

On the causeway to Benbecula, you may see a 'Caution: Otters Crossing' sign – although provision is generally made for otters to cross under the islands' causeways, they often scamper over the road. Another eight-kilometre causeway, the North Ford, links Benbecula to North Uist, crossing over the tiny island of Grimsay. Until the causeway was built, the island could only be reached by boat at high tide, so it is not surprising that traditional boatbuilding is an island tradition. North Uist's loch-dotted landscape is one of the richest archaeological sites in the Hebrides; cairns and roundhouses have been excavated on the island.

Many rush across the small island of Berneray to reach the ferry port, but the five-kilometre West Beach is so beautiful that the Thai tourist authorities used a photo of it in 2009 to promote holidays in Thailand. The ferry crossing between Berneray and Harris takes approximately one hour and there are several every day, except from Sunday which has just a morning and afternoon crossing.

The Way follows the Golden Road through villages, hamlets and past sapphire sea lochs through Harris. The road is named not for the sandy beaches but because it was the first tarmacked road on the island – locals complained it must be paved with gold for the cost of building it. Harris's cottage industry still thrives, and in these roadside homes, you may find weavers of Harris tweed or small local art galleries. While Harris and Lewis are both described as islands, with their own distinct heritage, they are one landmass, so you face no causeway or ferry crossing to reach the last island on the way. Instead the islands are separated by a hilly range, over which you must cycle, to emerge near the Callanish Stones, an impressive stone circle that dates back to between 2900 and 2600 BC.

CYCLING THE HEBRIDEAN WAY IN NORTH UIST, ISLAND SEVEN ON THE HEBRIDEAN WAY. © OUTER HEBRIDES TOURISM/SEAN MCFARLANE

One of the delights of the islands is their fresh seafood, and you can enjoy scallops, langoustines and lobsters as well as kippers smoked at the Stornoway Smokehouse in one of the last brick kilns in the world. Stornoway's other delicacy is the eponymous black pudding, which finally won PGI protected status in 2013 and is now only produced on Lewis. As you follow the windy, exposed road that climbs to the islands' most northerly point, the lighthouse at the Butt of Lewis, you may be grateful for these island delicacies.

Although there are no monster climbs on the Hebridean Way, there are long hauls on some of Britain's windiest roads that can be a challenge with a fully laden bike. You are unlikely to require a map or strong navigational skills: the Way is well waymarked and there are few other roads to stray on to. There are flights to the islands from Manchester and Scottish cities, but on these small planes there is unlikely to be room for your bike, even in the hold. You can hire a bike on the islands, but if you prefer your own you can travel to the islands on the CalMac Ferry; bikes are carried for free, although you may have to wait for the next boat if the crossing is busy. The Hopscotch ticket is a return ticket to the islands from the mainland, which also covers your ferry crossings between the islands.

Island life runs at a slower pace, and you would be hard pushed to race to complete this route, if only because you must wait for the ferries. The Hebrides are on the edge of the Atlantic, and first to experience any storm that blows in. In summer, the days will be impossibly long and the islands dotted with sea campions, bog asphodel, harebells and milk wort. At the end of a challenging day in the saddle, you can enjoy a refreshing swim on one of the island's near-deserted golden beaches before wild camping in the dunes under the dark, star-studded skies of the Western Isles.

THE BEACH BY VATERSAY AT THE START OF THE HEBRIDEAN WAY. © NICK HUBBLE

07 HEBRIDEAN WAY: ESSENTIAL INFORMATION

RIDE ESSENTIALS

Start: **Vatersay, Scotland**
End: **Butt of Lewis, Isle of Lewis, Scotland**
Distance: **323km**
Ascent/descent: **2,350m/2,340m**

HOW TO GET THERE

Vatersay can be reached most easily by a ferry from Oban. Vatersay is approximately ten kilometres from the ferry port. Oban's train station links to Glasgow on the West Highland Line, which has introduced increased capacity for bikes. Vatersay can also be reached by flights from the Scottish mainland to Barra, although you are more likely to transport your bikes on the ferry than the aeroplane.

The **Butt of Lewis** can be reached by ferry from Ullapool – the ferry port is approximately fifty kilometres from the Butt of Lewis. Ullapool is approximately fifty kilometres from a train station, although private taxis and minibuses can be used to make the connection. Stornoway Airport is served by direct flights from Manchester and Scottish cities.

TIME TO COMPLETE

Minimum days: **3 days/22 hours**
Maximum days: **5 days/28 hours**

PROS

- **Sandy beaches** – from the wide curves of Harris's Luskentyre to the flower-bedecked Halaman Bay on Barra, the Outer Hebrides offer some of the sandiest, and quietest, beaches in Great Britain.

- **Island living** – the islands have very low crime rates – there is no need to lock your bike. Although shops may be few and far between and close early, you'll often find shops welcome to open their doors a little late or locals happy to pick up supplies for you.

- **Seafood** – the Outer Hebrides are famous for their seafood, particularly shellfish – which is still landed and processed on the islands. You can enjoy langoustines, lobsters, scallops, crabs and mussels. The herring industry is also still active.

CONS

- **Bad weather** – stormy weather may blow in on the prevailing south-west wind with little warning at any time of year. This not only makes cycling difficult but may leave you stranded on the islands if the seas are too rough for ferries, although it may blow away midges in summer.

- **Transport** – the islands are not easy to reach, and planning your trip may be logistically challenging. There are lengthy rides from the ferry ports to the start and end of the route, and Ullapool – where the Lewis ferry departs/arrives from – is not on the national rail network.

VARIATIONS

There are few route variations, although plenty of opportunities for short diversions from the route, to visit beaches, ruins or cafes. You might choose to follow the road to Stornoway and then take the wild moor road across Lewis, should you want to end your ride with a challenge. In addition to the Hebridean Way, there is an off-road Hebridean Trail across the islands.

GOOD TO KNOW

Mark Beaumont, holder of a world record for cycling around the globe, launched the Hebridean Way in 2016 by cycling the entire route in under twenty-four hours.

FURTHER INFORMATION

www.visitouterhebrides.co.uk/hebrideanway/cycling; www.sustrans.org.uk/find-other-routes/the-hebridean-way

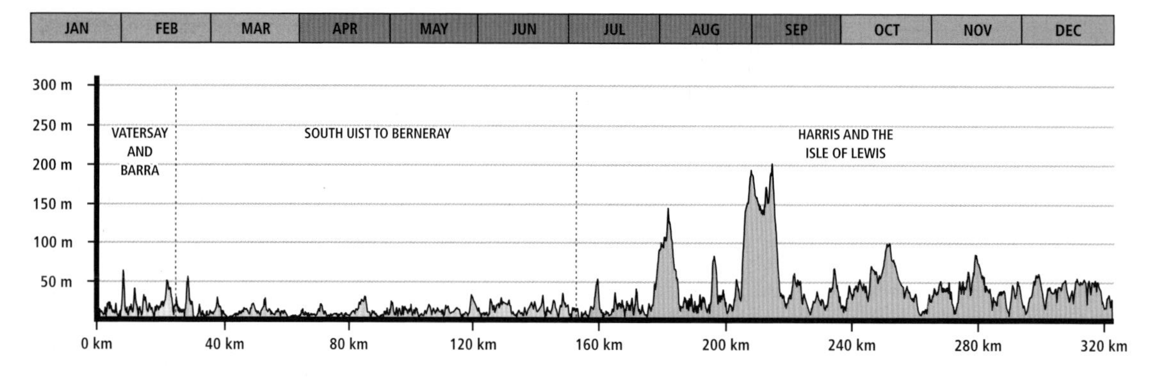

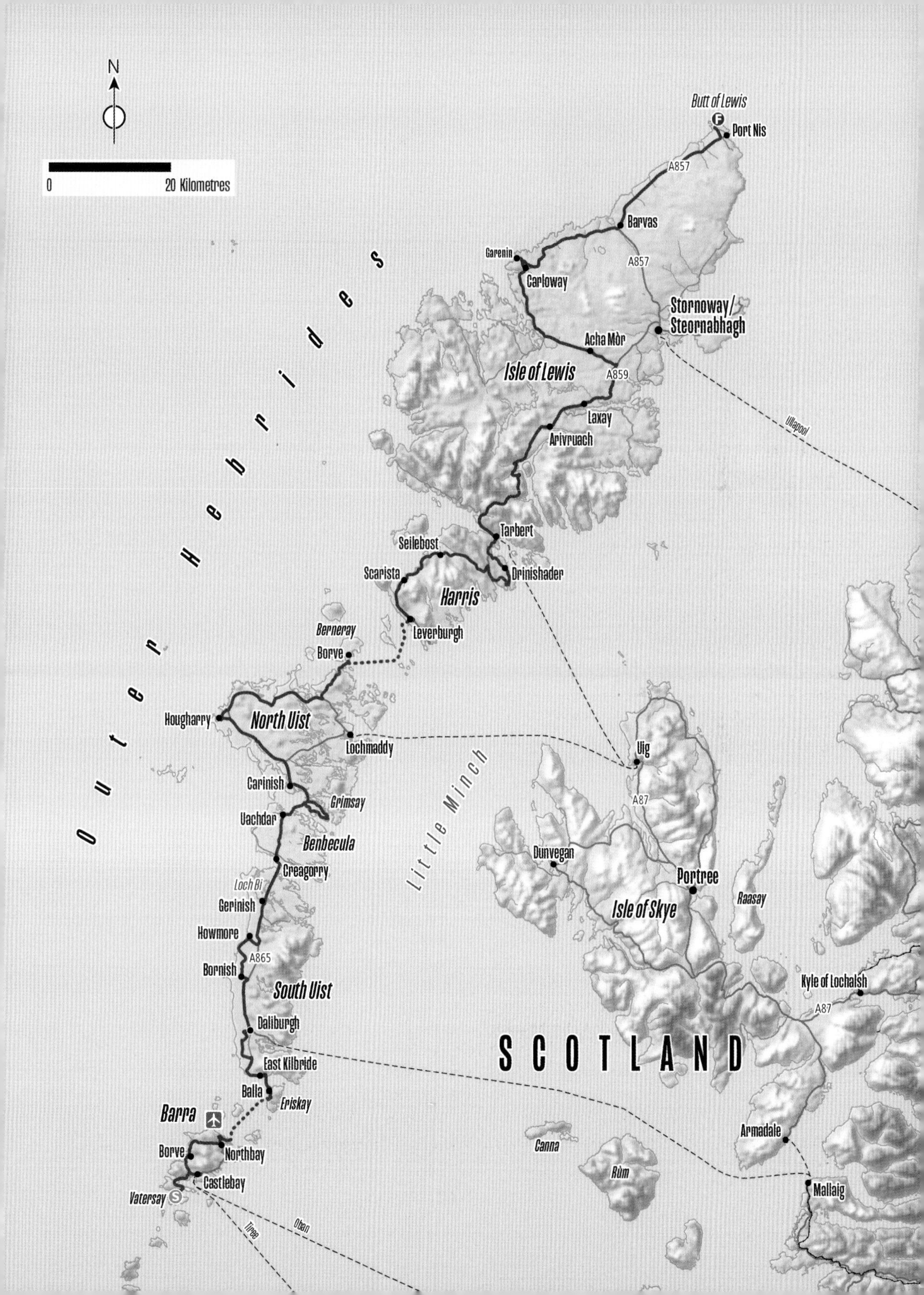
N
0
20 Kilometres
Outer Hebrides
Butt of Lewis
Port Nis
A857
Barvas
Garenin
A857
Carloway
Stornoway/
Steornabhagh
Acha Mòr
Isle of Lewis
A859
Laxay
Arivruach
Ullapool
Tarbert
Seilebost
Scarista
Drinishader
Harris
Leverburgh
Berneray
Borve
North Uist
Hougharry
Lochmaddy
Uig
Carinish
Grimsay
Uachdar
Benbecula
Little Minch
A87
Dunvegan
Creagorry
Loch Bi
Portree
Gerinish
Raasay
Isle of Skye
Howmore
A865
Bornish
South Uist
Kyle of Lochalsh
A87
Daliburgh
SCOTLAND
East Kilbride
Balla
Eriskay
Barra
Armadale
Borve
Northbay
Canna
Castlebay
Rùm
Mallaig
Vatersay
Tiree
Oban

CAPITAL
TRAIL

08

08 HIGHLAND TRAIL 550 – 884km

The 884-kilometre (550-mile) Highland Trail 550 is a rugged trail of three connected loops through Scotland's remotest landscapes. Inspired by the Colorado Trail Race, one of the first self-supported bikepacking races, Alan Goldsmith devised the route as an independent time trial (ITT) in 2013. First a 400-mile loop, the route has evolved since then. The route described here is the latest version of the trail from 2019, but using part of the route from previous years from Fionn Loch to Poolewe and on to Loch Maree. It takes you on stony singletracks, gravel tracks, forestry roads, narrow country lanes and quieter country roads. The route is a navigational and technical challenge; even though much of it is rideable, the stony tracks, thousands of metres of ascent and descent and limited facilities along the way make it a tough ask for even the best endurance cyclists.

The route heads north out of Tyndrum on the West Highland Way, and then follows a four-by-four track around Loch Lyon, on which rivers need to be forded a few times. From the eastern end of the loch a small tarmac road takes you to Innerwick, and from here the next tough climb on the Old Kirk Road through Rannoch Forest follows. After a short section of tarmac on the western end of Loch Rannoch, a technical singletrack takes you past Loch Ericht and over the shoulder of Ben Alder, with another technical descent to Loch Pattack, from where the riding gets a bit easier. Shortly after joining the main road from Inverness to Fort William you pass the purpose-built mountain biking trails at Laggan Wolftrax.

At Spey Dam Reservoir the route takes a minor road to Melgarve Bothy – from here it continues on the Corrieyairack Pass, one of General Wade's Military Roads, as it zigzags towards its highest point and on towards Fort Augustus. The small town on the shores of Loch Ness is the northern tip of the first loop, and you start the second loop on the Great Glen Way above the shores of the loch. The route follows tracks through Glenmoriston and on to the beautiful Loch ma Stac, where you follow the route along the rocky eastern shores, pushing your bike for the most part.

Passing Corrimony, a tiny hamlet famous for Mony's Stone and Corrimony Chambered Cairn, you soon join a road towards Cannich, proceeding further on quiet country roads along Strathglass past Struy. Near the white-walled, seventeenth-century Erchless Castle, you climb on hydro tracks to the Orrin Reservoir – although the Hydro bothy, once a cement store for the reservoir, has been demolished. It's a long downhill from here to Contin, which contains the last shop to replenish supplies until Drumbeg Stores a further 200 kilometres away.

Good forestry tracks take you to Garve, and from here the route takes you past Loch Vaich and Gleann Mor, giving you ample opportunity to enjoy the panoramic views across the Ben Wyvis National Nature Reserve. The remote Oykel Bridge Hotel, a fishing lodge with simple rooms, will be a welcome sight for adventurers in need of food or accommodation. Here you join the top loop. The route follows the A837 along the course of the River Oykel and then on a small tarmac road along the River Cassley north, and still on roads towards Loch Shin.

◀ CLIMBING ON THE WEST HIGHLAND WAY OUT OF TYNDRUM ON THE HIGHLAND TRAIL 550. © MARKUS STITZ

THE PATH INTO FISHERFIELD FOREST WITH STRATH NA SEALGA IN THE VALLEY. © MARKUS STITZ

The trail continues on lochside roads and then on tracks over the Bealach nam Meirleach to the northern point of the route. The trail passes down Glen Golly on gravelly, rutted four-by-four tracks and snakes towards your western return route. This is one of the hardest sections of the route, with a long and boggy hike-a-bike section to An Dubh-loch and a very steep track up to Bealach Horn. Your rewards are stunning views of the flanks of Arkle and a tricky, stony descent before more challenging ups and downs to Kylesku on the Cape Wrath Trail.

The route takes the undulating coast road to the white-walled cottages at Drumbeg, and then leaves the road for another technical singletrack to the beautiful beach and hostel at Achmelvich. Skirting lochans, you take a narrow, grass-clumped trail to the fishing village of Lochinver, famous for its pies. You head for the gap between the imposing Suilven and Canisp Marilyns, passing the Suileag bothy. Another tough hike-a-bike section follows to Cam Loch, with parts on stony technical singletracks and often very boggy tracks. The road to reach Oykel Bridge will be a relief and completes the top loop.

On trails that pass the edge of woodland, you reach the bothy at Duag Bridge and then follow good, wide tracks along Strath Mulzie. A stony singletrack undulates over the glen's sides as you head for Ullapool, a bustling ferry port. You tackle a steep climb up over the Coffin Road towards Dundonnell. You now face another challenging, but spectacular, section on the route as you cross the remote, treeless expanse of Fisherfield Forest, in the shadow of munros. Near Loch na Sealga you reach the Shenavall bothy. You also have to ford the Abhainn Srath na Sealga here, which can be impossible after heavy rainfall, so take extra food for this section. The route contours on stony singletracks, with challenging ascents as the Letterewe ridge looms in front of you. Poolewe provides a welcome change from the remoteness.

Above Loch Maree you come to another likely hike-a-bike section on a track to a road that follows the loch's shore down to Kinlochewe. The route continues on the road along Glen Torridon to Loch Clair. You face more climbs on the fire road to Coire Lair. Crossing the Torridon mountains, you pass the Easan Dorcha bothy, affectionately nicknamed 'the Teahouse'. Tricky descents on steep, stony singletracks follow before you reach well-surfaced forestry roads.

LOOKING TOWARDS BEING DEARG MOR FROM THE SHORES OF LOCH NA SEALGA IN THE REMOTE FISHERFIELD FOREST. © MARKUS STITZ

After a brief road section to Loch Carron, you climb on forestry tracks through the Attadale Estate, and then follow Glen Ling down to Killilan. You hit tarmac and take a narrow road along the shores of Loch Long. After Dornie the route contours on a road that undulates up and down the loch banks, offering good views of the thirteenth-century Eilean Donan Castle. From Morvich, you take the Affric Kintail Way as it climbs over the watershed, passing the Camban bothy and a beautiful, remote youth hostel. From Loch Affric you cycle through Dundreggan Forest and then join the Old Military Road towards Fort Augustus, where you complete the middle loop.

The trail follows the easy, and well waymarked, Great Glen Way from Fort Augustus to Fort William, on lochside tracks and canal paths. You complete the Highland Trail 550 on one of Scotland's most popular trails, the West Highland Way, although in the opposite direction to most hikers. Passing in the shadow of Ben Nevis, you head over the Devil's Staircase and cross the bleak Rannoch Moor, passing the remote Kinghouse Hotel and making use of the Old Military Road again to close the third loop and return to your starting point in Tyndrum.

The Highland Trail 550 is an extremely challenging route that often defeats experienced mountain bikers. You must be self-sufficient, prepared to bivvy down on the mountainside for the night in the company of midges, carry ample provisions and plan for bad weather. Even some road sections present sharp ascents and descents. This is a wild, largely off-road adventure for those that want to push themselves to the extreme and who are capable of dealing with emergencies. Sections of the route may become impassable at any time of year, but are likely to be extremely challenging in winter. Some estate trails may be used during red deer stalking season, which lasts from July to February, so the best time to tackle the Highland Trail 550 is spring. And if you fail on your first attempt at the Highland Trail 550, the scenery will lure you back.

08 HIGHLAND TRAIL 550: ESSENTIAL INFORMATION

RIDE ESSENTIALS

Start: **Tyndrum, Stirling, Scotland**
End: **Tyndrum, Stirling, Scotland**
Distance: **884km**
Ascent/descent: **13,010m/13,010m**

HOW TO GET THERE

Tyndrum has two railway stations, Tyndrum Lower and Upper Tyndrum, both of which are on the West Highland Line with services to Glasgow and Oban or Fort William. Upper Tyndrum is also served by the Caledonian Sleeper overnight service from London. Glasgow is the closest international airport.

TIME TO COMPLETE

Minimum days: **8 days/78 hours**
Maximum days: **18 days /108 hours**

PROS

- **Wildlife** – you may glimpse golden eagles, red squirrels, capercaillie, highland cattle and red deer in the wild highlands.
- **Bothies** – the 550 passes several remote bothies – the Old Schoolhouse, the Teahouse, the Suileag and Carnmore.
- **Fisherfield** – Scotland's Great Wilderness is one of the most beautiful and remotest sections on the Way, and there are two bothies where you can watch the sunset over the mountain ridges.

CONS

- **Navigation** – the route is not waymarked or obvious. It is easy to miss your turn and choosing the wrong trail in forests or estates, criss-crossed with unsigned tracks, may take you kilometres off-route.
- **Relentless** – there are very few easy sections of the trail. Gnarly descents follow long uphills, and there are hard road climbs and wide tarmac roads that quickly give way to stony singletracks or tricksy gravel trails.
- **Remote** – there are few facilities on the route. The first resupply point on the 550 is Fort Augustus, 160 kilometres from the start.

VARIATIONS

There are no variations to the official route.

GOOD TO KNOW

The route is ridden with a group at the start of every May. Neil Beltchenko holds the course record of three days ten hours and twenty-two minutes; Lee Craigie holds the women's record (three days twenty hours and fifty-three minutes). Tom Seipp is the youngest rider to complete the course in 2018, aged thirteen – he rode in the company of his dad. He had previously completed the route in 2017, but had not carried all his own kit.

FURTHER INFORMATION

highlandtrail550.weebly.com; *bikepacking.com/routes/highland-trail-550*

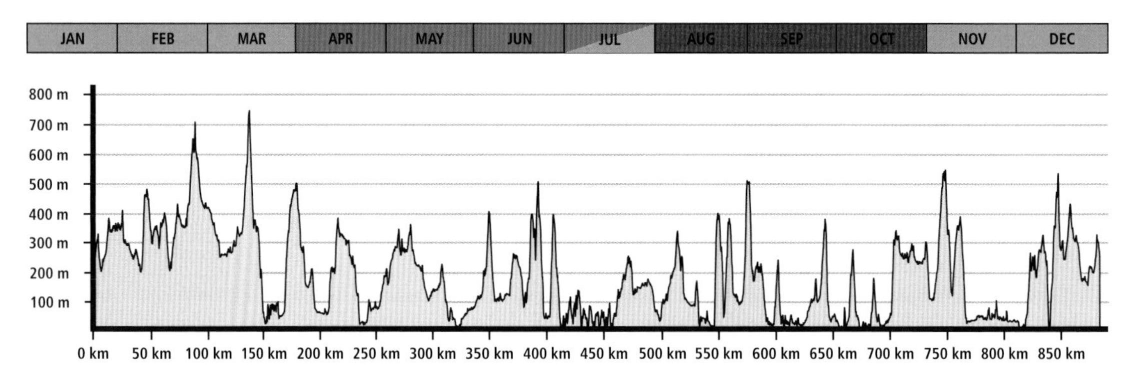

Kinlochbervie
Isle of Lewis
Scourie
Meall Horn
Loch More
Stornoway
Drumbeg
Kylesku
Stoer
Achmelvich
A837
Inchnadamph
Loch Shin
Lochinver
Suilven
Canisp
Ben More Assynt
The Minch
Assynt-Coigach
Cam Loch
A838
A835
Oykel Bridge
Lairg
Rosehall
Ullapool
Laide
Dundonnell
Dornoch
Ardgay
An Teallach
Inverlael
Gleann Mor
Poolewe
Tain
Easter Ross
Gairloch
Loch Vaich
A835
Loch Maree
Alness
Invergordon
Wester Ross
Kinlochewe
A832
Achnasheen
Garve
Dingwall
Fortrose
Nairn
Contin
Marybank
Loch Orrin
Muir of Ord
Portree
Craig
Strathcarron
Inner Sound
Inverness
Struy
Isle of Skye
Strathglass
Cannich
Killilan
Kyle of Lochalsh
Tomich
Corrimony
Loch Beinn a' Mheadhoin
Loch Ness
Dornie
Broadford
Inverinate
Loch Affric
Glenelg
Morvich
Glen Affric
Invermoriston
Aviemore
Fort Augustus
The Great Glen
A9
SCOTLAND
Kingussie
Invergarry
Mallaig
Loch Nevis
Laggan
A86
Bunarkaig
Loch Lochy
Gairlochy
Fort William
Ben Alder
A9
Ben Nevis
Loch Ericht
Salen
Strontian
Blackwater Reservoir
Kinlochleven
B846
Loch Rannoch
Pitlochry
Glen Coe
Rannoch Moor
Loch Linnhe
N
Aberfeldy
Bridge of Orchy
Loch Lyon
Glen Lyon
0
20 Kilometres
Oban
Tyndrum
S
F
A85
Crieff
Perth

09

09 JOHN MUIR WAY – 209km

Helensburgh
GLASGOW
EDINBURGH
Dunbar

Opened in 2014, the 209-kilometre John Muir Way is a coast-to-coast route named for the Scottish naturalist and environmentalist, the 'Man of the Mountains'. It traverses Scotland from Helensburgh, where Muir set sail for the United States, to Dunbar, his birthplace, on trails that stay low in the shadow of mountains, allowing anyone to cross the country on bike. On much of the Way, walkers and cyclists share the trail. However, there are separate cycling and walking braids on some sections; Scotland's open access laws mean that cyclists can still choose the walking rather than cycling options, which are often a more scenic choice for those on gravel or hybrid bikes.

The John Muir Way begins on the waterfront at Helensburgh, at a stone plinth and seat carved from Scottish oak and decorated with a John Muir quote. As you leave town, you pass the Mackintosh's Hill House – you can enjoy views of the town from walkways around and over the roof. Cyclists and walkers part company at Daligan, where cyclists are recommended a road route to Loch Lomond. However, you might prefer to stick with the hikers on a gravel track that climbs over Gouk Hill, a tough ascent that is rewarded with views over the long loch. You may have to push your bike on the gnarly, stony singletrack Stoneymollan Road through the forest. Cyclist and walkers' braids reunite on the tarmac road into Balloch at the foot of Loch Lomond, Britain's largest lake by area.

You pass the now derelict, grey, nineteenth-century Balloch Castle as you cross the Castle Country Park and join quiet roads. Walkers and cyclists again quickly diverge – cyclists follow roads through Croftamie and Gartness and join the West Highland Way on disused railway tracks, passing the Glengoyne Distillery at Dumgoyne. Cyclists rejoin the walkers near Carbeth Loch. Again, you might prefer to stick with walkers and make the ascent on tarmac then gravel forestry tracks to Burncrooks Reservoir in the Kilpatrick Hills, and then descend past the hutters' community at Carbeth.

The Way leaves the remotest section of the route behind as it reaches low tracks and canal towpaths under the backdrop of the green ridges of Campsie Fells. At Strathblane you take the disused Strathkelvin Railway Path, now NCN 755, through the old mill town of Lennoxtown to Kirkintilloch, the 'Canal Capital of Scotland'. Kirkintilloch was once the site of a Roman fort on the Antonine Wall, and traces of the Wall can still be seen throughout the town. You join the canal towpath by the Firth and Clyde Canal to Auchinstarry, and the walkers leave the canal to make a detour to the Antonine Wall. The route passes near the Roman fort at Bar Hill, but if you want to explore this site you will have to leave your bike behind and continue along the walkers' route.

Walkers and cyclists both follow the towpath from Auchinstarry to Bonnybridge, where you pass under the canal using a tunnel, nicknamed the Radical Pend for the Radicals who fought Hussars at the Battle of Bonnymuir in 1820. You can either splash through the ford or cycle the narrow, raised pathway. You join the road to visit the Antonine Wall at Rough Castle Roman fort. Cyclists are encouraged to follow good forestry tracks near the railway,

◀ JOHN MUIR COUNTRY PARK, EAST LOTHIAN.
© BARNEY VAUGHAN-KNIGHT

rather than the grassy paths through the archaeological site. The routes rejoin at the world's only rotating boat lift, the Falkirk Wheel, built to connect the Forth and Clyde and Union canals. You can either remain on the canal towpath, now on the Union Canal, or detour to tackle the gravel tracks through Callendar Woods, a popular mountain biking area.

After the twelve-arched, 250-metre-long Avon Aqueduct, the walkers leave the canal to follow the River Avon towards Linlithgow, parts of which might be hike-a-bike – you can stay on the canal path and then follow roads into the town centre instead. You can visit the ruins of Linlithgow Palace, birthplace of Mary, Queen of Scots. The route follows the Fisherrow, a historic fisherwomen's path towards the shores of the Firth of Forth as well as Kinneil, where the only visible Antonine Wall fortlet can be seen. The sixteenth-century Kinneil House was where James Watt worked on his steam engine in the 1770s. On good tracks and paths, you follow the shore past Blackness Castle, 'the ship that never sailed', and the stately home of Hopetoun House. On the Shore Road into Queensferry, you can enjoy views of the three bridges that span the Firth of Forth.

The Way turns past Cramond's fields of wheat and rapeseed to head for Scotland's capital. On steep, grassy sections, such as Corstorphine Hill, or where steps have to be negotiated on the Water of Leith, alternative cyclist braids are well signed. The route passes the international rugby stadium at Murrayfield and the Union Canal towpath takes you towards the city centre. You cycle through the Meadows and under the shadow of Arthur's Seat and Salisbury Crags, eventually following the Innocent Railway cycletrack towards the coast near Musselburgh, home to one of the world's oldest golf courses. You hug the

LEAVING THE FALKIRK WHEEL BEHIND, ONE OF THE FASCINATING MAN-MADE STRUCTURES ON THE JOHN MUIR WAY IN FALKIRK. © GAVIN MORTON

coast through Prestonpans; this shoreline is famous for its wading birds, and you may see redshanks, dunlin and in winter, eider ducks.

You follow roads through Longniddry, although you might choose to join the walkers on the sandy coast path instead. The trail follows gravel singletracks towards Gullane where you pass the championship Muirfield golf course on the road. Near the extinct volcano of North Berwick Law you can enjoy rolling forest trails through Craigmoor Wood. Singletracks and quiet roads take you towards the red cliffs of Dunbar. The walker's route between East Linton and Dunbar, along the River Tyne and through fields, can be muddy and slippery in wet weather. If you do not want to push your bike you might prefer the nearby roads. The Way ends in Dunbar, Muir's boyhood home, by his statue outside the John Muir's Birthplace museum.

The John Muir Way is an easy-going trail on gravelled tracks, quiet lanes, cycle paths and walking trails. It is well waymarked and there are plenty of bike repair shops en route for emergencies. It is the ideal family adventure, or a great ride for those new to cycling. The trails may be muddy but are never exposed, and you are always close to the next town or teashop.

John Muir believed that everyone should explore the wilderness, and the John Muir Way is a trail that allows everyone to discover Scotland's green beauty. There is adventure to be had in traversing an entire country coast-to-coast, and you will encounter Loch Lomond, the Campsie Fells, the Firth's iconic bridges and North Berwick's sandy shoreline. The John Muir Way is a rare example of a Great Trail where cyclists were not an afterthought, and all the better for it. Canals and railways were once the highways through Scotland's central belt, and now provide green corridors which are perfect for cyclists and walkers to escape from the city on.

ABOVE: EAST LOTHIAN COUNTRYSIDE, JOHN MUIR WAY. © LIZZIE VAUGHAN-KNIGHT
BELOW: THE SMALL SEASIDE TOWN NORTH BERWICK WITH BASS ROCK IN THE BACKGROUND, HOME TO A LARGE COLONY OF GANNETS. © MARKUS STITZ

09 JOHN MUIR WAY: ESSENTIAL INFORMATION

RIDE ESSENTIALS

Start:	**Helensburgh, Dunbartonshire, Scotland**
End:	**Dunbar, East Lothian, Scotland**
Distance:	**209km**
Ascent/descent:	**1,630m/1,610m**

HOW TO GET THERE

Helensburgh has train services to Glasgow, which has an international airport. Helensburgh is also on the Caledonian Sleeper route, an overnight rail service from Fort William to London.

Dunbar has a train station on the East Coast Main Line, offering connections to Edinburgh and other Scottish cities. Edinburgh is the closest international airport.

TIME TO COMPLETE

Minimum days:	**2 days/17 hours**
Maximum days:	**4 days/24 hours**

PROS

- **Birds** – Berwick's shores attract many feathered visitors, and you may see puffins, razorbills, guillemots and eider ducks. To find out more, you could visit the Scottish Seabird Centre at North Berwick.

- **Views** – the John Muir Way offers some great views – Loch Lomond, the Campsie Fells, Arthur's Seat and Dunbar's red cliffs – without gruelling hill climbs or exposed sections.

- **Waymarking** – the Way is well waymarked, particularly where there are walker and cyclist alternatives.

CONS

- **Obstacles** – if you choose to follow the walkers' routes, you may encounter the occasional stile or steps, as well as muddy trails. Even on the cyclists' trail, you may encounter cycle gates that are not easy to negotiate on non-standard bikes or bikes with packed panniers.

- **Busy** – the route coincides with many other local cycling routes and can become crowded.

- **Urban** – if you're searching for wild moorland then this isn't the trail for you – this is a route that passes through towns and villages in Scotland's Central Belt. You will often find yourself on the road, and passing through industrial estates or residential streets.

VARIATIONS

There are several suggested cyclist 'braids' on the Way, generally on sections that might be challenging on a road bike or for a novice cyclist, although some are to avoid damage to archaeological sites on the Antonine Wall.

GOOD TO KNOW

The Callendar Estate is a great place to try out mountain biking. There are purpose-built easy and moderate trails, suitable for most cyclists, such as the easy-going Canada Trail, which takes you past the Battle of Falkirk Muir site. More experienced riders might tackle the Kilbean Trail, or the Auchingean Trail which has an optional extreme section with gap jumps. Bicycle hire is available.

FURTHER INFORMATION

bikepackingscotland.com/johnmuirway; johnmuirway.org

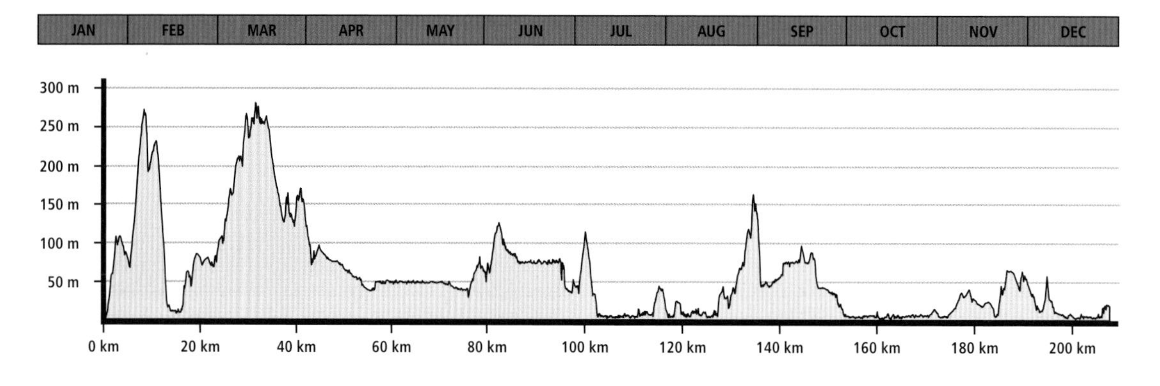

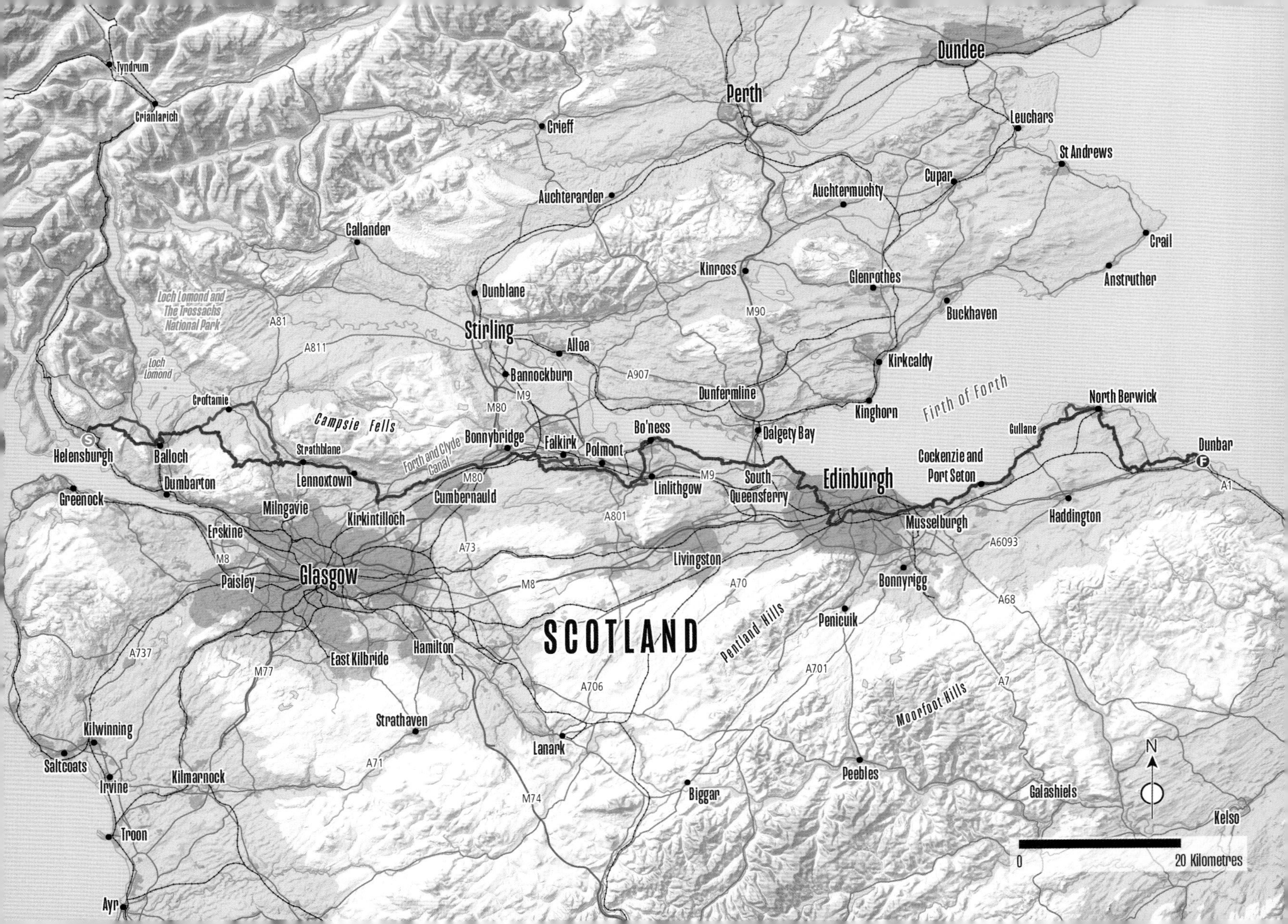

SCOTLAND
Dundee
Perth
Tyndrum
Crianlarich
Crieff
Leuchars
St Andrews
Cupar
Auchtermuchty
Auchterarder
Callander
Crail
Kinross
Glenrothes
Anstruther
Dunblane
Loch Lomond and The Trossachs National Park
Buckhaven
Stirling
Alloa
Loch Lomond
Kirkcaldy
Bannockburn
Dunfermline
Firth of Forth
Croftamie
Campsie Fells
Kinghorn
North Berwick
Bonnybridge
Falkirk
Polmont
Bo'ness
Dalgety Bay
Gullane
Dunbar
Helensburgh
Balloch
Strathblane
Forth and Clyde Canal
Cockenzie and Port Seton
Lennoxtown
Linlithgow
South Queensferry
Edinburgh
Dumbarton
Greenock
Cumbernauld
Milngavie
Kirkintilloch
Musselburgh
Haddington
Erskine
Livingston
Glasgow
Paisley
Bonnyrigg
Penicuik
Pentland Hills
Hamilton
East Kilbride
Moorfoot Hills
Strathaven
Kilwinning
Saltcoats
Lanark
Kilmarnock
Irvine
Peebles
Biggar
Galashiels
Kelso
Troon
Ayr
A1
A6093
A68
A7
A701
A70
A706
A71
A74
M74
M77
A737
M8
A73
A801
M80
M9
A907
M90
A81
A811
N
0
20 Kilometres
S
F

10

10 KING ALFRED'S WAY – 352km

The 352-kilometre King Alfred's Way starts in the historic city of Winchester and traces a grassy, sometimes muddy route through some of England's greenest rolling downs, along old paths and past ancient monuments. Though the Way is not easy, there is always a beautiful view or historical site to distract you from sore legs. The trail is a mix of terrains, from good bridleway and quiet lanes to grassy singletracks and tree root-rutted woodland paths. It is well suited to gravel bikes, although might be tackled on a hybrid or even a tourer with wide, off-road tyres. The trail is not waymarked, but it makes extensive use of other trails that are.

You leave Winchester on suburban roads, before taking a narrow track between hedges near Sparsholt. The route meanders through the chalky Test Valley on quiet roads and gravelly tracks, and then on a busier main road past the thatched cottages of King's Somborne. You are now on the Clarendon Way, as it climbs over Broughton Down on a wide, sometimes muddy, hollow way; your effort is rewarded by views of the Iron Age hill fort at Danebury. The route joins a Roman road to descend into Middle Winterslow, where you may glimpse the spire of Salisbury's cathedral.

On chalk and gravel tracks, which are often rutted, you skirt the military research laboratories at Porton Down to reach the archaeologically rich Old Sarum fort on the outskirts of Salisbury. The route bypasses the city, although it is a convenient stopping point, and turns north on a stone track towards the prehistoric sarsen circle of Stonehenge. You rejoin the roads at Lake, although there is an off-road alternative that takes you past the Normanton Down barrows but involves a short push along a permissive footpath and a tricky crossing of the busy A303 main road.

The routes rejoin south of Larkhill to follow a tarmacked trail across Salisbury Plain, an area still used for military training – you should be wary of army vehicles and unexploded ordnance and not cross past any red flags. The route takes you on hard trails next to the tank roads before a narrower track takes you through Orcheston. On good trails, you enjoy an often tranquil ride through a landscape rich in wildlife and Neolithic remains. If open to the public, it is worth a detour to the abandoned village of Imber, evacuated during World War II – the Way follows part of the Imber Range Perimeter Path.

On occasionally muddy tracks, you reach the edge of the plain near Gore Cross and take advantage of old military roads to climb up to the White Horse Trail – you can glimpse the Alton Barnes White Horse. After a brief road section through the villages of Chirton and All Cannings, you take a potholed track over the canal and face a long climb up Tan Hill. The area is rich in historic sites – you may glimpse the barrows as you enjoy the descent into Beckhampton. Two long stones – Adam and Eve – mark the start of an ancient avenue that once linked the village to Avebury. You will have instead to follow quiet country lanes to Avebury, the village that stands inside the world's largest stone circle. As you cycle through the circle on the High Street you pass the haunted Red Lion, the only pub inside a stone circle.

◀ ABOUT TO DESCEND OLD WINCHESTER HILL LOOKING OVER TO WEST MEON. © PAUL RAINBOW

An Anglo-Saxon military herepath leads you up a green byway to the chalky Ridgeway National Trail. This ancient route takes you above the Hackpen White Horse, carved to commemorate the coronation of Queen Victoria in 1838, but you will have to detour from the route if you want to see it. The grassy trail passes through the middle of the concentric Barbury Castle, an Iron Age hill fort and the site of the Battle of Beran Byrig, where the West Saxons defeated the Britons. The Ridgeway skirts the pretty village of Ogbourne St George as it climbs on to the Wessex Downs to reach the Bronze Age Liddington Castle.

You ride over the M4 motorway and past the Wayland's Smithy long barrow. It is worth a detour for a good view of the Uffington White Horse, which is at least 3,000 years old, making it the oldest in Britain. This is a horse-dominated section of the trail, passing through the Gallops on Ilsley Downs. You might choose to make a lunchtime detour to Wantage, Alfred's birthplace. The Ridgeway follows the Grim's Ditch Iron Age earthwork before taking advantage of the disused Didcot, Newbury and Southampton Railway to reach Goring-on-Thames.

The trail leaves the Ridgeway behind to follow the Thames as it snakes south, and you ride briefly on the Thames Path. Pleasant, hard-surfaced bridleways undulate by the river through Coombe Park and Whitchurch-on-Thames, and through Mapledurham, with its twelfth-century hall and working watermill. The gentle arc of the New (suspension) Bridge leads you into Reading, the halfway point of the Way. You ride through the town on well-signed, largely-traffic free routes, and leave again on a path that runs next to the A33 main road.

You follow the Devil's Highway, a Roman road to London, out of Riseley and gravel tracks give way to sandy trails as you reach Hazeley Heath and Odiham Common, passing concrete reminders of the World War II GHQ defence line. Minor roads take you into Farnham, by the red-bricked, twelfth-century castle, although there is a longer alternative by the Basingstoke Canal. Grassy, tree-lined bridleways lead you around the outskirts of the market town, but you are forced on to quiet roads at Moor Park (it is hoped that

ABOVE: HEADING TO KING'S SOMBORNE IN THE AFTERNOON SUN. © PAUL RAINBOW
BELOW: CLIMBING UP THROUGH DURFORD WOODS AT GOLDEN HOUR. © PAUL RAINBOW

cyclists will eventually be permitted to use a route through the park).

After a descent past the ruins of the Cistercian Waverley Abbey, you face a hilly section of the route. You follow a narrow tarmac track that becomes rougher as you cycle up Beacon Hill, south of Thursley – you may be rewarded by distant views of London on the horizon. Near Hindhead, you pass the natural amphitheatre of the Devil's Punch Bowl, scooped out by the Devil, who was infuriated by Surrey's surfeit of churches.

You leave Hindhead on busy main roads, but soon pick up the tranquil, shaded Shipwrights Way at Liphook. At Liss, you leave the Shipwrights Way for the broad tracks of an old military railway. Contouring around Combe Hill, you might divert to the Rogate mountain biking B1kepark. Near South Harting, you join the well-signed South Downs Way (see page 105) to return to Winchester, although you should take care to follow the bridleway rather than footpath where the routes diverge. The ups and downs of the Way, often on chalky or grassy trails form a challenging end to King Alfred's Way, particularly the steep climb over Butser Hill. From the summit, you may be able to see the Hampshire coast and the Isle of Wight.

King Alfred's Way is the perfect gravel bike adventure; an up-and-down route with loads of variation in terrain, you will encounter muddy tracks, bumpy towpaths, grassy trails and slippery chalk or rutted bridleways, but rarely busy roads. It is a route that meanders between small towns and villages, offering plenty of opportunities for slap-up lunches or cream teas, but one that escapes into beautiful, wildlife-rich countryside and passes some of the most fascinating archaeological sites in Southern England.

THE ROLLING RIDGEWAY ABOVE STREATLEY. © *CYCLE.TRAVEL*

10 KING ALFRED'S WAY: ESSENTIAL INFORMATION

RIDE ESSENTIALS

Start: **Winchester, Hampshire, England**
End: **Winchester, Hampshire, England**
Distance: **352km**
Ascent/descent: **3,510m/3,510m**

HOW TO GET THERE

Winchester has direct rail services to London, where connections may be made to London's international airports and national and international rail services. The Sustrans Thames Valley/NCN 4 off-road route connects London to the route at Reading.

TIME TO COMPLETE

Minimum days: **3 days/31 hours**
Maximum days: **7 days/42 hours**

PROS

- **Prehistoric sites** – there is perhaps no other route that packs in so many prehistoric sites in so few days – not only the stone circles at Stonehenge and Avebury, but also long barrows, hill forts, ancient roads and the 3,000-year-old Uffington White Horse.

- **Villages** – although you are often rolling through green countryside, you are never too far from the next town or village should you need a pitstop.

- **Views** – King Alfred's Way has its fair share of hills, but rewards these climbs with stunning views across the wide-skied South Downs, distant London and the glimmering sea on the horizon.

CONS

- **Military areas** – King Alfred's Way goes through several military areas. You should check for closures, be wary of straying from the trail or picking up unexploded ordnance and expect to encounter tanks and other large military vehicles.

- **Navigation** – the route is not waymarked, and makes use of other trails. You should pay attention when the Way leaves one trail for the next, and when making your way through the cities and larger towns on the route.

- **Slippery** – grassy tracks over chalky hills may be particularly slippery in wet weather.

VARIATIONS

You sometimes have a choice between off-road and on-road routes (for example, near Stonehenge and by the Basingstoke Canal) and there are plenty of opportunities to divert off-route to nearby towns and villages. King Alfred's Way is perhaps one of the best-connected trails in the country – it is easy to extend your ride on the Ridgeway, South Downs Way or the North Downs Way riders' routes.

GOOD TO KNOW

You can take a detour to cycle the new fifty-kilometre Imber Range Perimeter Path, which offers fine views of the Westbury White Horse. It encircles Salisbury Plain's abandoned village of Imber. In 1943, villagers were given just forty-seven days' notice to evacuate to make way for American troops, leaving forever on 17 December. Blacksmith Albert Nash died just six months later, purportedly of a broken heart. Despite promises, the villagers were never allowed to return to their homes, although the church still holds an annual service and the village is occasionally open to the public.

FURTHER INFORMATION

www.cyclinguk.org/king-alfreds-way; Cycling UK also produce a print guidebook.

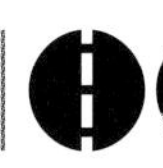

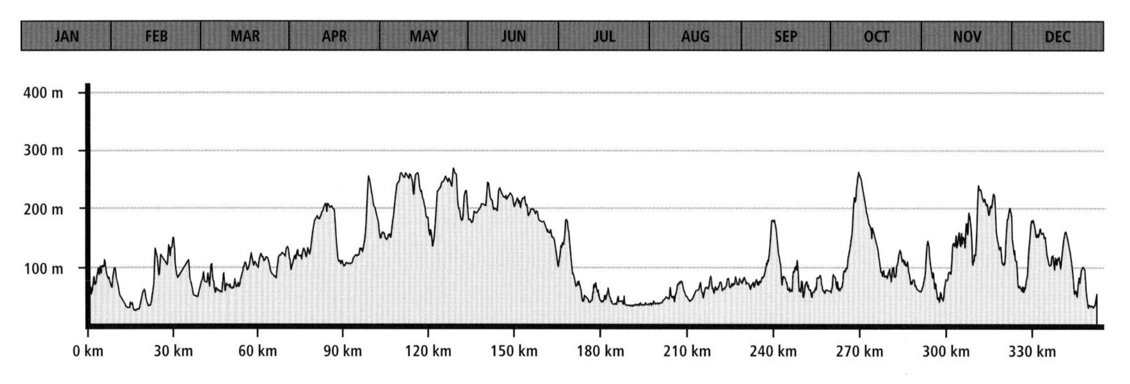

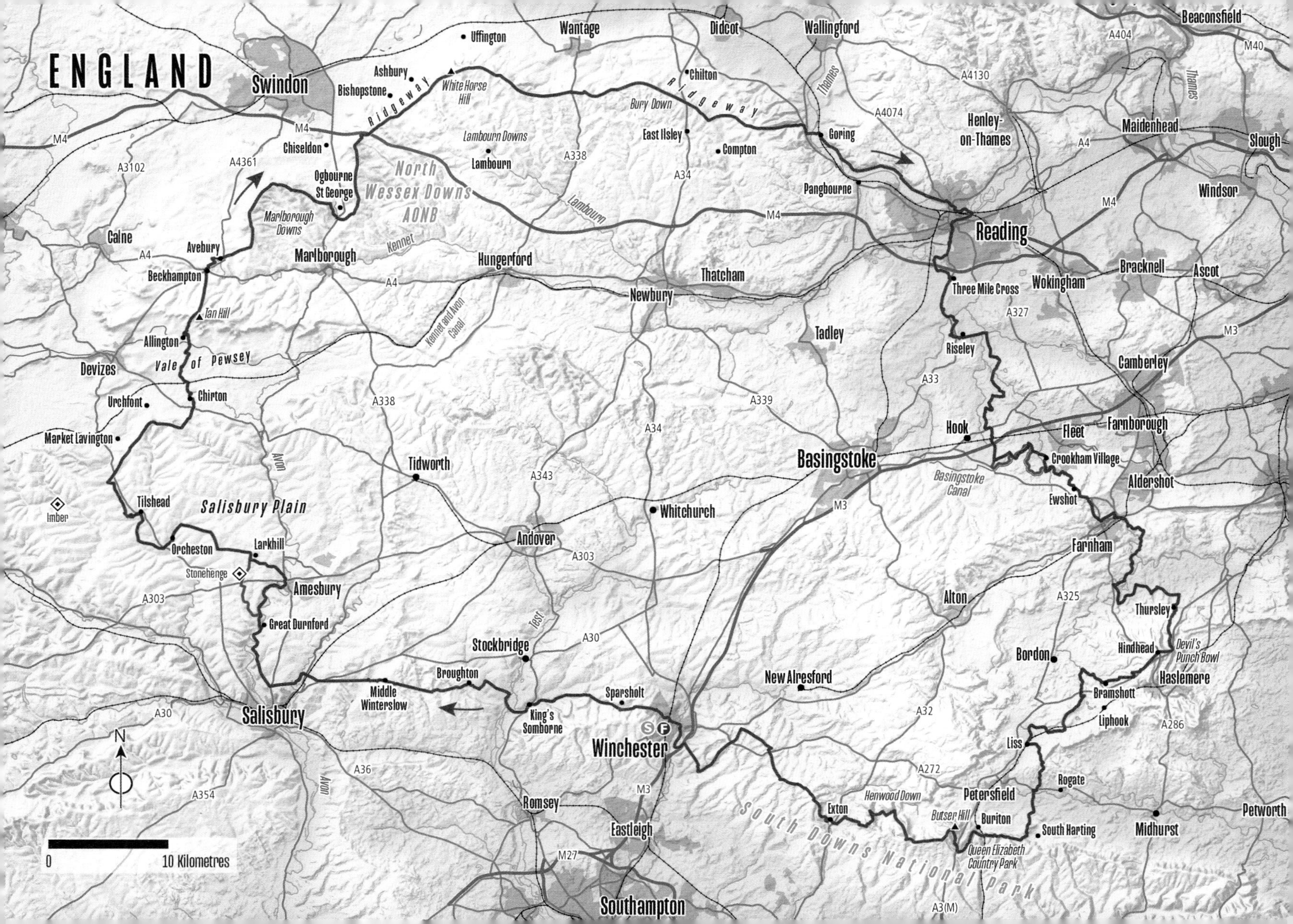
ENGLAND
Swindon
Wantage
Didcot
Wallingford
Beaconsfield
Uffington
Ashbury
Bishopstone
White Horse Hill
Ridgeway
Bury Down
Chilton
East Ilsley
Compton
Goring
Pangbourne
Henley-on-Thames
Maidenhead
Slough
Windsor
Reading
Bracknell
Ascot
Wokingham
Three Mile Cross
Riseley
Tadley
Thatcham
Newbury
Hungerford
Marlborough
Lambourn Downs
Lambourn
Chiseldon
Ogbourne St George
North Wessex Downs AONB
Marlborough Downs
Kennet
Kennet and Avon Canal
Calne
Avebury
Beckhampton
Tan Hill
Allington
Vale of Pewsey
Devizes
Chirton
Urchfont
Market Lavington
Imber
Tilshead
Salisbury Plain
Orcheston
Larkhill
Stonehenge
Amesbury
Great Durnford
Salisbury
Tidworth
Andover
Whitchurch
Basingstoke
Hook
Fleet
Farnborough
Camberley
Crookham Village
Basingstoke Canal
Ewshot
Aldershot
Farnham
Alton
Thursley
Hindhead
Devil's Punch Bowl
Haslemere
Bordon
Bramshott
Liphook
Liss
New Alresford
Stockbridge
Broughton
Middle Winterslow
King's Somborne
Sparsholt
Winchester
Test
Avon
Lambourn
Thames
Romsey
Eastleigh
Southampton
Exton
Henwood Down
Butser Hill
Buriton
Queen Elizabeth Country Park
Petersfield
Rogate
South Harting
Midhurst
Petworth
South Downs National Park
M4
M40
M3
M27
A404
A4130
A4074
A4
A3102
A4361
A338
A34
A327
A33
A339
A343
A303
A30
A36
A354
A32
A325
A286
A272
A3(M)
N
0
10 Kilometres

11 LAKELAND 200 – 206km

The Lakeland 200 is a 206-kilometre route over Wainwrights, high mountain passes and down valleys. It is a technically challenging off-road route that takes singletracks, rutted gravel trails, boggy bridleways and muddy, bouldered tracks up and down through the best of the Lake District's green beauty. Even the short road sections are often breathtakingly steep and bendy; off-road you should anticipate hiking with your bike as much as riding, and you will encounter some knuckle-clenching descents. The route was devised by Alan Goldsmith, founder of the Highland Trail 550 race (see page 45), as an independent time trial (ITT) but it passes several youth hostels, making it the ideal choice for mountain bikers who want to spend a few days enjoying the Lakes.

The route starts in Staveley, a popular destination for cyclists as it's home to Wheelbase, the UK's largest bike shop, which is next door to Hawkshead Brewery with its beer hall that offers food and drink. You leave Staveley on a lane by the River Kent before taking a slightly damaged tarmac lane on an easy climb past High Borrans. The trail rejoins the road through Troutbeck, and on good gravel tracks you contour around the wooded Jenkins Crag above Lake Windermere, then down to Ambleside.

The bridleway over Loughrigg Fell is sometimes gravel, sometimes rocky and grassy, but never too technical. You pass Loughrigg Tarn on hard-surfaced tracks and skirt around Elterwater on the road to reach Langdale. After Chapel Stile, with its little village stores, you take hard-surfaced, gritty tracks and tarmac past disused quarries.

A wooded byway passes Tarn Hows, followed by roads to High Wray and a hard-topped trail over Three Dubs Crags to pop out next to Hill Top, Beatrix Potter's farm. You have to book to visit the cottage, which Beatrix bequeathed to the National Trust, but might seek refreshment at the neighbouring Tower Bank Arms. You take a stony track by the forest, past the Red Sandstone Fox, to reach Grizedale, where you could pause for a different type of adventure at Go Ape, the high ropes centre.

The route soon reaches the shores of Coniston, and then the town. You take the gravelly Walna Scar Road as it climbs around the Old Man of Coniston and Brown Pike, followed by a handlebar-gripping descent. The rutted track at Stephenson Ground is often boggy as it delivers you down towards Seathwaite. You should enjoy the easy road climb as it ascends besides the river, with England's highest mountain, Scafell Pike, looming ahead of you, because the route begins to get tougher.

You climb over Harter Fell and then descend into Boot in Eskdale and then you face a tough, unrideable boggy slog past Burnmoor Tarn. The trail reaches Wasdale, a popular departure point for the walk up Scafell Pike. From Wasdale Head, you take the grassy, stony trail over Black Sail Pass, descending past the remote youth hostel, built as a shepherd's hut and only accessible by bike or foot. You now face one of the toughest climbs on the trail, almost certainly a hike-a-bike section, up the Scarth Gap Pass in the shadow of Hay Stacks, the fell where Wainwright chose to have his ashes scattered. You have a tricky and stony

◀ LOOKING DOWN ON WINDERMERE FROM THORNTHWAITE BEACON. © CALLUM JAMES – *WWW.EXPLOREEVERYTHING.CO.UK*

technical descent along a bouldered path towards Gatesgarth on the shores of Buttermere.

A steep climb up the snaking Honister Pass road follows, often busy with traffic, and you pass the Honister Slate Mine. You join the route of the Borrowdale Bash, a bracken-fringed gravel singletrack that stays beneath the crags to head to Derwent Water. You contour around the water in the shadow of the Cat Bells to reach Keswick. The route skirts the town centre but it's worth the short detour because there are not only plenty of cafes and pubs, but also lots of bike and outdoors shops should you need repairs or replacement kit. On a stony, bumpy route, you climb above Glenderaterra Beck as it flows between Skiddaw and Blencathra – this is a popular way to reach Skiddaw House Hostel and is part of the Cumbria Way so you may struggle to pass walkers on the narrow track.

You return on the other side of the Beck on a wider, lower track that passes the Blencathra Field Centre. After crossing the A66 main road at Threlkeld you take the easy Old Coach Road to High Row. Here you reach the northern fringe of the Lake District where the landscape gets gentler, and so you have a break from the biggest climbs and most demanding trails. You face a short section on the narrow, busy A592 road along the shores of Ullswater to reach Pooley Bridge. The eighteenth-century stone bridge across the River Eamont was washed away during Storm Desmond in 2015, and you now cycle across the 2020 replacement, the first stainless steel road bridge in the UK.

You climb up to the Cockpit Stone Circle, briefly joining the High Street Roman road before turning down to contour above Ullswater beneath Barton Fell and Bonscale Pike. The route passes through Martindale on the roads. The road up Boredale Beck gives way to bridleway and you

RIDING TOWARD BLACK SAIL HUT, ENNERDALE. © TOM MCNALLY PHOTOGRAPHY

may find yourself pushing your bike up the grassy track to Boredale Hause, but you will be rewarded with stunning views of the giant Helvellyn. You have a slippery, skiddy descent down into Hartsop before facing another challenging climb.

The stony, gritty climb up to High Street will see you on and off your bike to reach the high Roman road on the ridge which you follow over the summit of High Street. You pass the imposing cairn of Thornthwaite Beacon and have a long, fast descent along Hagg Gill into Troutbeck. After climbing up Garburn you face a knuckle-clenchingly technical descent through bowling-ball boulders. You have one final ascent up the slopes of Kentmere Park before you descend to the River Kent. An easy descent on roads by the river leads you back into Staveley.

Only the hardiest and most experienced of mountain bikers will tackle this route in winter – the route may well be covered in snow and ice. In addition, many facilities en route will be closed and accommodation may be hard to find. Even in summer, the high passes may be drenched by heavy rain or wreathed in mist, and the finest of sunny days can quickly turn into bad weather. However, even under grey skies the Lake District's green beauty astounds, and the Lakeland 200 will offer mountain bikers the chance to take their bikes high into the hills and to enjoy spectacular views of the mountain giants and shimmering lakes.

DESCENDING SCARTH GAP, TOWARDS BUTTERMERE. © CALLUM JAMES – *WWW.EXPLOREEVERYTHING.CO.UK*

11 LAKELAND 200: ESSENTIAL INFORMATION

RIDE ESSENTIALS

Start:	**Staveley, Cumbria, England**
End:	**Staveley, Cumbria, England**
Distance:	**206km**
Ascent/descent:	**6,080m/6,080m**

HOW TO GET THERE

Staveley has a rail station on the Windermere Branch Line, which connects with mainline services at Oxenholme. The closest international airport is at Manchester.

TIME TO COMPLETE

Minimum days:	**2 days/22 hours**
Maximum days:	**5 days/30 hours**

PROS

- **Hostels** – although time trailers may wild camp, for those tackling the route as a leisure ride, the Lakeland 200 passes youth hostels at Keswick, Honister, Black Sail, Ambleside, Coniston and Boot. The detour to the high Skiddaw House Hostel is recommended.

- **Peaks** – the route takes you around the flanks of the Old Man of Coniston, over the pass beneath Hay Stacks, between Skiddaw and Blencathra, and along High Street.

- **Varied** – this not only takes you past the Lakes' iconic peaks, but past quarries, through forests and across the gentler countryside near Pooley Bridge and Staveley.

CONS

- **Remote** – the route takes you into the Lakes' high hills, and even when you are on roads or reach villages there are often no shops, cafes, pubs or places to stay.

- **Hike-a-bike** – most people will find that they have to push or carry their bikes over some of the most technical sections of the route.

- **Weather** – even in summer, the weather may make this route challenging. In bad weather, you will be exposed and should ensure that you have sufficient safety kit – you will be well-advised to carry an emergency shelter.

VARIATIONS

There are no variations to the route, although if pressed for time you might choose to omit the loop out to Staveley or the excursion up Glenderaterra Beck.

GOOD TO KNOW

The route record of sixteen hours, forty-five minutes was set by local mountain bike adventurer Chris Hope in 2014. To be considered an Independent Time Trail completer, you must complete in forty hours, be completely unsupported and not prebook accommodation, use caches or stay in private accommodation.

FURTHER INFORMATION

www.selfsupporteduk.net/lakeland200

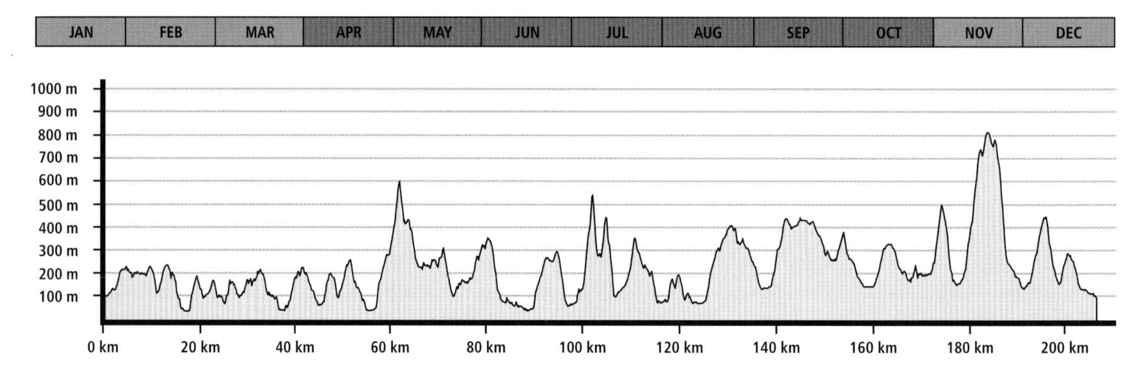

Knott
Embleton
ENGLAND
A66
Bassenthwaite Lake
Skiddaw
Skiddaw House Hostel
Blencathra
Lonscale Fell
A66
Troutbeck
A591
Threlkeld
A592
A66
Matterdale End
Pooley Bridge
Portinscale
Keswick
Old Coach Road
The Cockpit Stone Circle
High Brow
Dockray
Derwent Water
A591
Grasmoor
Great Dodd
Cat Bells
Borrowdale
Ullswater
Howtown
Martindale
Crummock Water
Grange
Thirlmere
Martindale Common
Buttermere
Glenridding
Boredale Hause
Patterdale
Buttermere
Dale Head
Helvellyn
Rosthwaite
High Stile
Scarth Gap Pass
Stonethwaite
Haweswater Reservoir
Honister Pass
Seatoller
A591
Lake District
Black Sail Hut
Hayeswater
Pillar
National Park
Fairfield
High Street
Black Sail Pass
Great Gable
Glaramara
Thornthwaite Beacon
Harter Fell
A592
Wasdale Head
High Street
Grasmere
Scafell Pike
Kent
West Water
Loughrigg
Chapel Stile
Ambleside
Burnmoor Tarn
Garburn Pass
Elterwater
Sallows
Kentmere
Little Langdale
Skelwith Bridge
Troutbeck
Hodge Close
Eskdale
Boot
High Wray
Harter Fell
Swirl How
Windermere
A591
The Old Man of Coniston
Claife Heights
Hawkshead
Staveley
S
F
Windermere
Coniston
Esthwaite Water
Grizedale Forest
Dunnerdale
Seathwaite
Walna Scar Road
Hill Top
Caw
A593
Coniston Water
N
A592
0
5 Kilometres
High Nibthwaite

LANDS
END
2011
NEW YORK 3147
JOHN O'GROATS 874

12 LAND'S END TO JOHN O' GROATS – 1,897km

John o' Groats

Land's End

12

The 1,897-kilometre Land's End to John o' Groats (LEJOG) or John o' Groats to Land's End (JOGLE) is the route that you choose to make it. Will you ride from Cornwall to Scotland (the direction described here) with the prevailing wind behind you but a challenging, hilly start for unseasoned legs? Should you stay to the wetter west of the Pennines or criss-cross the country? Do you want to speed along sometimes busy roads, take a meandering route on country lanes or seek the muddy, rocky off-road alternatives? Unless you join a charity challenge or book an organised LEJOG, your trip will probably begin with winter afternoons spent poring over maps or reading other riders' blogs, pondering these choices, as you begin the hours of planning that will create your personal adventure of a lifetime.

From its very beginning, LEJOG is not straightforward – both Land's End and John o' Groats are some way from public transport, adding distance to your ride unless you have a car or minibus at your disposal. Your LEJOG will probably begin with a ride out from Penzance to Land's End, the shopping complex at Cornwall's tip, which is not Britain's most westerly, southerly or south-westerly point. You retrace your route back past Mousehole, famous for the sardine heads poking out of its stargazey pies, as well as the fishing town of Newlyn and on through Penzance.

The NCN 3 (often traffic-free) route offers a good alternative to the busy A30 main road. You can follow quiet roads on the St Piran Trail through Newquay and Padstow to reach the traffic-free ex-railway Camel Trail, or take the hillier southern Coast and Clay trails past the Eden Project and Lost Gardens of Heligan. The trails reunite in Bodmin, and you skirt the moor on quiet country roads. You join the West Country Way (see page 135) in Bude, which has a gentle start on the flat Tarka Trail (a former railway) before crossing the wild, remote Exmoor and then taking advantage of the easy Bridgwater and Taunton Canal path. Sustrans, the charity responsible for the National Cycle Network, was founded in Bristol in 1977; this perhaps explains why the city is easy and pleasant to traverse by bike.

With the worst of the hills behind you, you face a scenic road meander through chocolate-box villages on the NCN 41. Near Worcester, you join the NCN 5 – the completed sections offer usually well-surfaced off-road alternatives along canal paths and rail paths and across Cannock Chase, but there are gaps that will force you back on the road. Near Stoke-on-Trent, if you prefer an off-road route, the Great North Trail (see page 21) offers a great but often technical alternative from the southern Peak District to John o' Groats.

If the grassy, hilly tracks of the Great North Trail are not for you, once you have escaped the roads of the sprawling Greater Manchester area the Lancaster Canal offers a good off-road route between Preston and Manchester. There is no perfect route from southern Cumbria through the Scottish borders. You face busy, honeypot roads through the Lakes, although there are rocky, technical trails over high passes (for example, from Grasmere to Patterdale via Grisedale Tarn) to take you off-road if you are an experienced mountain biker. You may instead choose to ride through the Yorkshire Dales by picking up the Pennine Cycleway

◀ THE ICONIC SIGNPOST AT LAND'S END.
© MARKUS STITZ

or the Great North Trail at Austwick – both lead along the Ribble and Eden valleys towards Appleby, but the Pennine Cycleway adheres more closely to the roads while the Great North Trail prefers more challenging off-road routes. From the Scottish borders, you follow roads through Gretna and Moffat to reach the underwhelming NCN 74 as it wends its often muddy way to Glasgow.

Sustrans suggest the Loch and Glens Way as a picturesque route between Glasgow and Inverness that is largely on quiet roads as it passes through the Loch Lomond and the Trossachs National Park. You leave Glasgow on the good, tarmacked and traffic-free NCN 7, following the banks of the Clyde, and then turn north to Loch Lomond. Past Balloch, you follow gentle, hawthorn-lined lanes through the Trossachs, with spectacular views of Ben Lomond. The climbs get harder after Drymen, but the scenery also gets wilder – you are now crossing the Highland Boundary Fault.

Near Aberfoyle, you rejoin rough gravel tracks that lead along the shores of Loch Venachar. The route stays largely off-road on tarmac and gritty tracks through glens and along lochs to Killin, where you climb up and down on lumpy roads through Pitlochry. At Blair Atholl you can visit Blair Castle, the last castle in the British Isles to be besieged (during the Jacobite Rising in 1746). You are now inside the Cairngorms National Park – General Wade's Military Roads provide some convenient, hard-surfaced, off-road routes as you follow Scotland's watershed through the national park; they take you over the high Pass of Drumochter that marks the boundary between the southern and northern Highlands. For most, this (at 460 metres) is the highest point on the route.

Near the outdoor adventure hub of Aviemore, you return to the roads to reach Inverness, and the last, remotest stage of LEJOG. However you proceed, you are likely to find yourself often on-road for the last kilometres of your journey.

REWARDING VIEWS OF THE RIBBLE VALLEY. © JOOLZE DYMOND

The suggested Sustrans route takes you inland along the A386, but do not let its designation as an A road deceive you – this is a remote, singletrack road whose surface clearly bears the brunt of brutal Highland winters. By the Kyle of Tongue, you join the North Coast 500 route (see page 81) to follow Scotland's northern coast to John o' Groats.

Your alternative, longer and more challengingly off-road route from Glasgow is to follow the West Highland Way to Fort William and then join the Great Glen Way, both of which are among Scotland's Great Trails. They are primarily walkers' routes; cyclists will either need good mountain bike skills or must be prepared to walk short sections or follow road diversions. On the shores of Loch Ness you can rejoin the Great North Trail for an alternative route to John o' Groats. The route follows muddy military roads and hydroelectric tracks through Scotland's pine forests. From Oykel Bridge, most follow the singletrack roads to John o' Groats although there are technical, off-road mountain biking alternatives.

Those choosing to cycle LEJOG in a fast time will be forced on to unpleasant and dangerously busy main roads, including the A30 in Cornwall, A38 near Bristol and A1 through Northumberland. Even on country lanes you will face the hazard of fast cars on narrow roads with poor visibility. There is no good entirely off-road LEJOG route, although Cycling UK are working hard to create one, and options improve the further north you travel. The route choices you make will determine whether you need a tourer, gravel or mountain bike but it is worth choosing the quieter, longer routes if you want to enjoy this adventure.

LEJOG is the challenge of a lifetime, the perfect route for those that like to plan a big trip. The adventure is in the journey, not the destination; those who take the slow route will explore a country from end to end – from the Cornish cliffs and the canals of the Midlands to cycling in the shadow of the Pennine spine, past castles and lochs, and eventually keeping company with red deer in the Scottish Highlands.

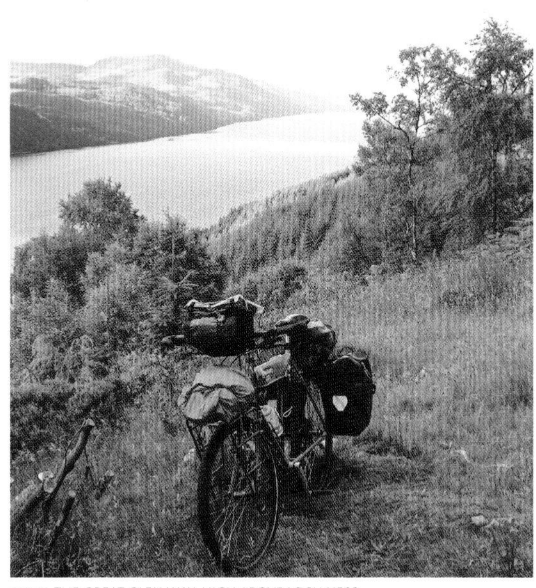

ABOVE: THE GREAT GLEN WAY, HIGH ABOVE LOCH NESS.
© GRAHAM BLAND – *AWAYWANDERING.BLOGSPOT.COM*
BELOW: BEAUTIFUL COUNTRY LANES BETWEEN TONGUE AND LAIRG.
© GRAHAM BLAND – *AWAYWANDERING.BLOGSPOT.COM*

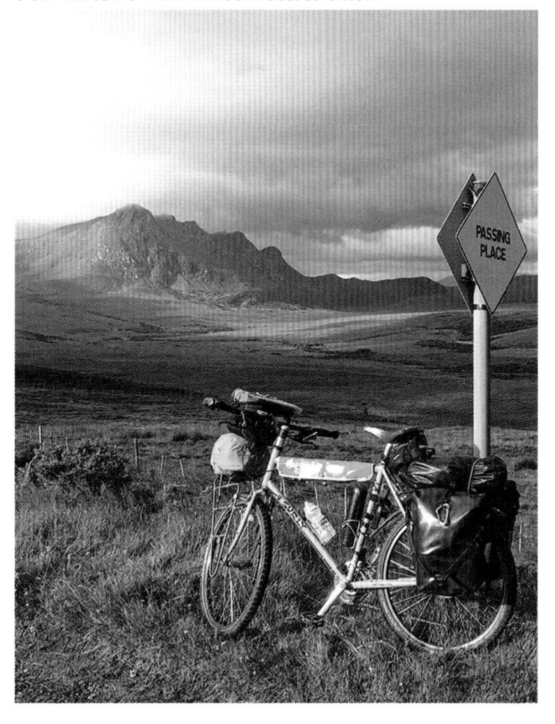

12 LAND'S END TO JOHN O' GROATS: ESSENTIAL INFORMATION

RIDE ESSENTIALS

Start: **Land's End, Cornwall, England**
End: **John o' Groats, Caithness, Scotland**
Distance: **1,897km**
Ascent/descent: **13,720m/13,760m**

HOW TO GET THERE

Land's End is approximately twenty kilometres from Penzance. Penzance offers high-speed rail connections to London, where international connections can be made by air or Eurostar. Land's End Airport only offers connections to the Isles of Scilly. Bristol and Exeter are the closest international airports.

John o' Groats is approximately thirty kilometres from Wick and thirty-five kilometres from Thurso, which both have local train stations that connect to Inverness. Bus services link John o' Groats with Wick and Thurso, but will not transport bikes; there are several local courier operators. Inverness is the closest international airport.

TIME TO COMPLETE

Minimum days: **12 days/122 hours**
Maximum days: **28 days/170 hours**

PROS

- **Scenery** – you can enjoy some of Britain's best scenery, from the Cornish coast and the green heartlands of the Midlands to Scotland's forests, lochs and mountains.
- **Camaraderie** – you are likely to meet fellow LEJOGERs or JOGLERs en route, and even more online before you leave, who will be happy to offer advice.
- **Food** – you have the opportunity to enjoy the best of British food – Cornish pasties, Grasmere gingerbread, and in Scotland stovies, haggis, clootie dumplings and, of course, porridge.

CONS

- **Roads** – whatever route you choose, you are likely to face at least some short sections on busy roads. On country lanes, expect to encounter fast-moving traffic that may not be looking out for bike riders.
- **Terrain** – unless you choose a road route, there are a lot of different terrains on a LEJOG, from gravelly trails and muddy and sometimes rutted paths to grassy trods and rocky limestone trails. Conditions under-wheel will vary considerably depending on season and weather. This variation makes choices about bike and tyres challenging.
- **Sightseeing** – although it is possible to make short diversions to explore Britain's castles, Roman remains, stately homes or museums, this is not a tour of Britain's best tourist attractions. Routes generally skirt Glasgow and Edinburgh and pass close to Hadrian's and the Antonine walls, but do not linger.

VARIATIONS

There are as many ways to ride LEJOG (or JOGLE) as there are cyclists to ride it. Choices include whether to take the south or north coast of Cornwall, which side of the Welsh border to travel, whether to choose the Lakes or the Dales and which way to travel from Glasgow.

GOOD TO KNOW

In July 2019, teacher Richard Thoday broke a 133-year-old Guinness World Record – previously set by George Pilkington Mills in 1886 – by cycling from Land's End to John o' Groats in four days and twelve hours on a penny farthing (that he had designed himself).

FURTHER INFORMATION

www.cyclinguk.org/routes/lands-end-john-o-groats; www.sustrans.org.uk/national-cycle-network/lands-end-to-john-ogroats-lejog

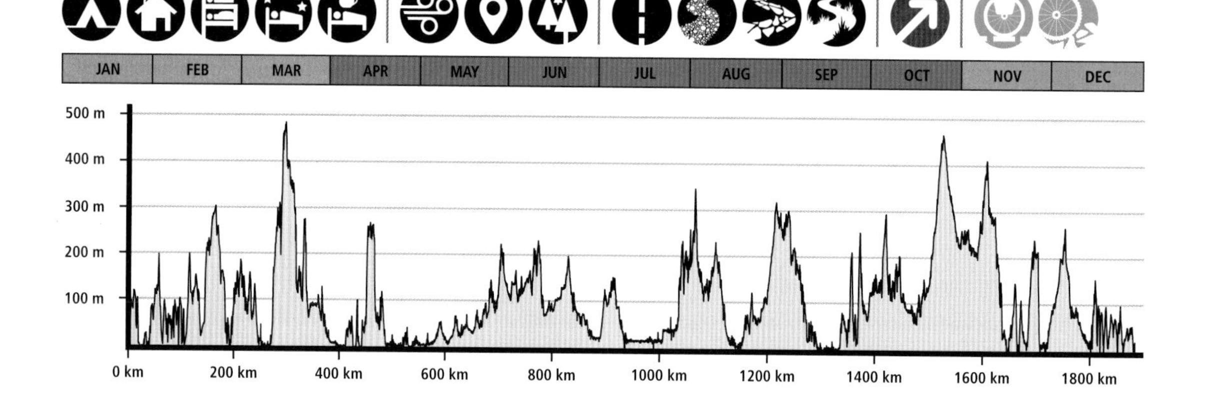

Orkney Islands
John o' Groats
Duncansby Head
Thurso
Bettyhill
Wick
Kinbrace
Lairg
Outer Hebrides
Alness
Garve
Inverness
Tomich
Fort Augustus
Aviemore
Kingussie
Cairngorms National Park
Aberdeen
SCOTLAND
The Great Glen
Fort William
Pitlochry
Aberfeldy
Perth
Dundee
North Sea
Loch Lomond & The Trossachs National Park
Callander
Atlantic Ocean
Stirling
M90
Drymen
Balloch
Dumbarton
M8
Edinburgh
Glasgow
Stonehouse
M74
Southern Uplands
Ayr
Moffat
Lockerbie
Ballycastle
Gretna
Dumfries
Newcastle upon Tyne
Larne
Carlisle
NORTHERN IRELAND
Penrith
Belfast
M1
Keswick
Lake District National Park
M6
Middlesbrough
Ambleside
Kendal
Yorkshire Dales National Park
A1(M)
Lancaster
York
Blackpool
Leeds
Preston
Irish Sea
Bolton
M62
ENGLAND
IRELAND
Dublin
Liverpool
Manchester
Holyhead
Altrincham
Sheffield
Peak District Nat. Park
Lincoln
Bangor
Chester
Congleton
M9
Stoke-on-Trent
M1
Nottingham
M8
Stafford
Shrewsbury
M54
Burntwood
Leicester
Peterborough
Norwich
Wolverhampton
Birmingham
Wexford
Aberystwyth
Redditch
Cambridge
WALES
Worcester
M5
Stratford-upon-Avon
Evesham
M1
M11
Haverfordwest
Gloucester
Cheltenham
M40
Harwich
The Cotswolds
Oxford
M25
Swansea
Cardiff
London
Bristol
M4
M5
Ostend
Exmoor National Park
Wells
M20
A18
Barnstaple
Bridgwater
Street
M3
Dover
Calias
BELGIU
Taunton
N
A25
Tiverton
Bude
Exeter
Southampton
Brighton
FRANCE
Padstow
Dartmoor National Park
Weymouth
A26
A16
Newquay
Bodmin
Channel
Truro
Mevagissey
Plymouth
English
Land's End
Penzance
0
100 Kilometres

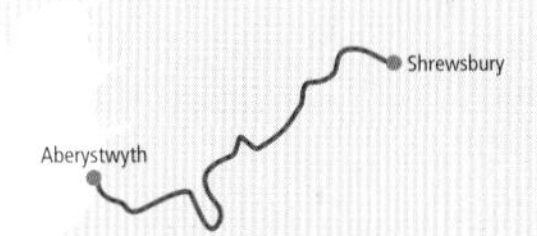

13 LON CAMBRIA – 181km

The 181-kilometre Lon Cambria, part of the NCN 81, is a route that traverses Wales from east to west. It starts in the market town of Shrewsbury on the banks of the Severn, and climbs through the green centre of Wales along the beautiful Elan Valley to reach the coast at Aberystwyth. The Lon Cambria would make a great adventure for a long weekend, with a few leg-warming climbs, panoramic views over green Welsh hills, pleasant stretches along wildlife-rich canals and gentle roads through sheep-dotted pastures.

You begin the Lon Cambria on the banks of the River Severn, behind Shrewsbury Castle, built by Roger de Montgomery in the 1070s. Lon Cambria follows the NCN 81, which also links Shrewsbury to Wolverhampton if you want an alternative starting point. The route follows the river on popular riverside tarmac trails, passing under the low stone arches of the English Bridge and then the metal-arched Kingsland Bridge, a privately-owned toll bridge. In the Quarry, a park area created in 1719, you ride in front of the eighteenth-century lead statue of Hercules, who has been subject to many indignities since being gifted to the town in the nineteenth century – he has been painted in football colours, had his arms wrenched off, been feathered and painted by local schoolboys and had his fig leaf stolen. You cross the river on the Porthill suspension bridge to meander through Shrewsbury's suburbs on residential roads and roadside cycle paths.

The route crosses the Severn again over Montford Bridge, the first bridge designed by Thomas Telford in the 1790s. Heading for the Welsh border on quiet, flat country lanes, the trail crosses into Wales near Crewgreen, although promptly returns to England and then enters Wales again. The route climbs over the ominously named Long Mountain on narrow country lanes that were once a Roman road. You face a fast descent on the narrow, bendy, hawthorn-edged Hope Road into Welshpool. You skirt the thirteenth-century Powis Castle, with its attractive formal gardens.

The trail takes towpaths along the Montgomery Canal to Newtown; the canal was built to carry limestone from Llanymynech to canal-side kilns, and then lime to agricultural land. The canal, which is a green haven for wildlife, fell into disrepair but has undergone significant restoration, including improvements to the towpath in the last ten years. Newtown was the birthplace of Robert Owen, the textile manufacturer and social reformer who campaigned for children's education and the eight-hour working day, advocating for eight hours' work, eight hours' leisure and eight hours' rest.

Flat towpaths are left behind for hilly country roads through Caersws and high, sheep-grazed pastures. The route continues to undulate as you follow lanes to the market town of Llanidloes, the first town on the River Severn. The trail briefly joins the NCN 8 Lôn Las Cymru route, which crosses Wales from Holyhead to Cardiff. You face a tough climb from Llanidloes to cross the watershed – you are close now to the sources of the Severn and the Wye on the slopes of Plynlimon. You descend on quiet lanes along the River Wye to the first town on that river, Rhayader, which has some claim to having the most pubs per head of population than anywhere else in Britain. There is a red kite

◀ CRAIG GOCH DAM, ELAN VALLEY.
© SHUTTERSTOCK/BILLY STOCK

QUIET COUNTRY LANE ON THE WAY TO RHAYADER. © RICHARD GOWER, @GROWLEROUTDOOR

feeding centre near Rhayader, so you should keep your eyes to the skies as you climb up the Elan Valley.

The route leaves NCN 8 at Rhayader to join the Elan Valley Trail. On well-surfaced gravel and tarmac tracks, the Trail follows the line of the Birmingham Corporation Railway, built to service the building of the reservoirs that were constructed here from the late nineteenth century onwards to provide clean water to the rapidly growing metropolis of Birmingham. You join the Trail at the Rhayader Tunnel Nature Reserve, but cycle over the top of the tunnel because it has been bricked up as an important habitat for bats – five species (whiskered, lesser horseshoe, Daubenton's, Natterer's and brown long-eared) are known to roost here. The route climbs gently, on tree-lined tracks that run parallel to the River Elan, to reach Caban-coch, Garreg-ddu and Penygarreg Reservoirs. The Elan Valley was closed and evacuated during World War II, and the Nant-Y-Gro Dam was used to test Barnes Wallis's bouncing bombs.

Leaving the reservoirs behind, you follow the River Elan down towards Cwmystwyth on gently undulating, quiet roads. On shale-sided, deserted hills, you can see the crumbling remains of the lead mines that thrived here in the eighteenth century. You leave Cwmystwyth, the geographical centre of Wales, on bumpy, stonewalled lanes through farmland before turning on to traffic-free trails through the Hafod estate. The estate once formed part of the lands of the Strata Florida Cistercian abbey, but was gifted to the Herbert family after the dissolution of the monasteries. The mansion that once stood here was demolished in 1958, but you can still enjoy the landscaped, picturesque grounds. After taking a trail through woods, you pass the Hafod Walled Garden, a kitchen garden that is now managed by a local community group.

You return to the roads and follow the River Ystwyth along the valley. At Pont-rhyd-y-groes you pass a water wheel, another reminder of the area's mining history – the village pub is still called the Miners Arms. The route climbs through woods as the road contours on the hillside above the river, and you enjoy a brief traffic-free stretch of road. Near Abermagwr, you join the well-surfaced cycletrack along the disused railway to Llanilar, still by the River Ystwyth. After a brief section on narrow lanes, you return to the railway path that leads you into the centre of

ABERYSTWYTH CASTLE. © SHUTTERSTOCK/BILLY STOCK

Aberystwyth, the town on Cardigan Bay where the route ends. You finish on the seafront, by the ruins of Aberystwyth Castle, built by Edward I from 1277.

The Lon Cambria can be completed at any time of year. It is largely on country lanes, although it also follows disused railway trails, forest roads, on- and off-road cycle lanes, riverside tracks and towpaths, usually on good, firm surfaces. It should not be difficult on a tourer but gravel or hybrid bikes are also a good choice. The route is never particularly high or exposed, but facilities along the route are few and far between. The Lon Cambria is generally well waymarked, usually as NCN 81, although this may change with Sustrans's re-evaluation of road sections of the National Cycle Network.

The Lon Cambria is a gentle, meandering route through the tranquil, green heart of Wales. It is a route that will take you over hills, not mountains, and along Wales's great rivers, the Wye and the Severn. It is a route too good to be rushed – make time to sit by the giant, shimmering reservoirs high in the Elan Valley and enjoy the mountain backdrop, or look to the sky and spot red kites.

RIDING THROUGH THE QUARRY, BY THE RIVER SEVERN IN SHREWSBURY.
© KATHY ROGERS

13 LON CAMBRIA: ESSENTIAL INFORMATION

RIDE ESSENTIALS

Start: **Shrewsbury, Shropshire, England**
End: **Aberystwyth, Ceredigion, Wales**
Distance: **181km**
Ascent/descent: **2,080m/2,120m**

HOW TO GET THERE

Shrewsbury has a rail station offering direct services to Birmingham, Manchester, Cardiff, London and Holyhead. The closest international airport is Birmingham, although Manchester is also close.

Aberystwyth has direct train services to Birmingham and Birmingham Airport, which pass through Shrewsbury. Birmingham is the closest international airport.

TIME TO COMPLETE

Minimum days: **2 days/12 hours**
Maximum days: **3 days/17 hours**

PROS

- **Off the beaten track** – the route avoids the tourist hotspots of the North Wales coast (Snowdonia and the Brecon Beacons), preferring a green route through Wales's farmlands and abandoned mines.

- **Red kites** – a red kite feeding station was established at Gigrin Farm near Rhayader in 1992 to combat the declining breeding population. Hundreds of red kites visit the feeding station every day now, and the birds are commonly seen in the Elan Valley.

- **Elan Valley** – the Elan Valley, the 'Welsh Lake District', is one of Mid Wales's most scenic areas. Its remoteness made it a strategically important military site during the world wars. The Elan Valley Trail offers a well-surfaced, easy way to explore this isolated region.

CONS

- **Facilities** – although you often pass small villages, these often have no pub, no shop and no place to stay. Where there is a pub or cafe, its opening hours may be short.

- **Waymarking** – the NCN 81 is generally well waymarked, but markers may be missing at junctions or may have disappeared into the undergrowth. Some waymarkers may be removed due to the re-evaluation of the road sections of the National Cycle Network.

VARIATIONS

There are no route variations, although many choose to extend their ride by continuing on to the Lon Teifi, which runs from Aberystwyth to Fishguard. You can start in Wolverhampton and follow the NCN 81 to Shrewsbury.

GOOD TO KNOW

Between 2005 and 2011, the Cycling (Demonstration) Towns initiative ran – selected towns received funding to encourage increased cycling through promotion, education and investment in infrastructure. Shrewsbury acquired Cycling Town status in 2009, and its legacy can be seen in the good-quality cycle path provision along the river and the suburban stretches of the NCN 81.

FURTHER INFORMATION

www.sustrans.org.uk/find-a-route-on-the-national-cycle-network/lon-cambria-aberystwyth-to-shrewsbury

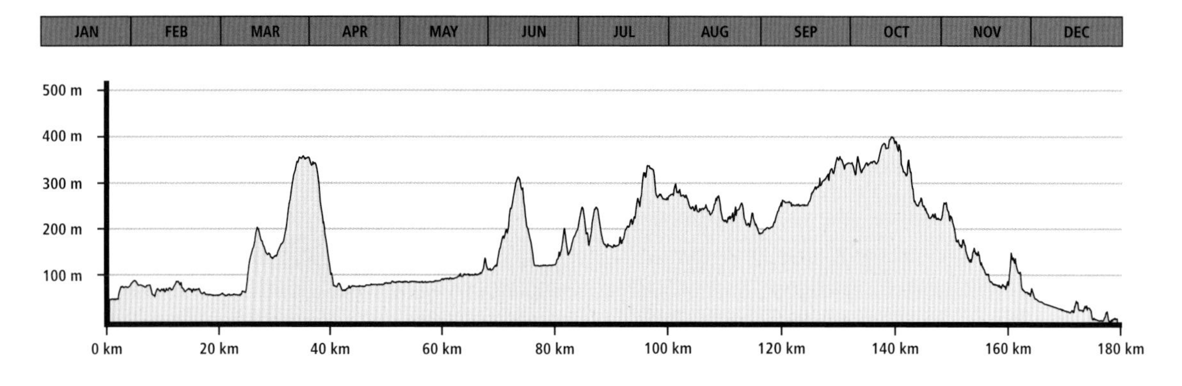

WALES
ENGLAND
Harlech
Rhinogydd
Y Llethr
Dolgellau
Barmouth
Cadair Idris
Mallwyd
Lake Vyrnwy
Oswestry
Wem
Crewgreen
Montford Bridge
Shrawardine
Severn
Shrewsbury
Welshpool
Long Mountain
Tywyn
Machynlleth
Berriew
Montgomery
Cardigan
Bay
Abermule
Caersws
Newtown
Stepaside
Church
Stretton
Borth
Plynlimon
Bishop's
Castle
Shropshire Hills
AONB
Aberystwyth
Llanidloes
Ponterwyd
Cambrian
Mountains/ Elenydd
Llangurig
Clun
Craven Arms
Rhydyfelin
Ystwyth
Pontarfynach
Wye
Llanilar
Pont-rhyd-y-groes
Ludlow
Lledrod
Craig Goch
Reservoir
Rhayader
Knighton
Caban-coch
Reservoir
Llandrindod
Kington
Leominster
0
10 Kilometres
Builth Wells
Llanwrtyd
Wells
Lampeter
N
A496
A470
A494
A483
A49
A5
A528
A458
A488
A489
A487
A44
A483
A4113
A4110
A485
B4343

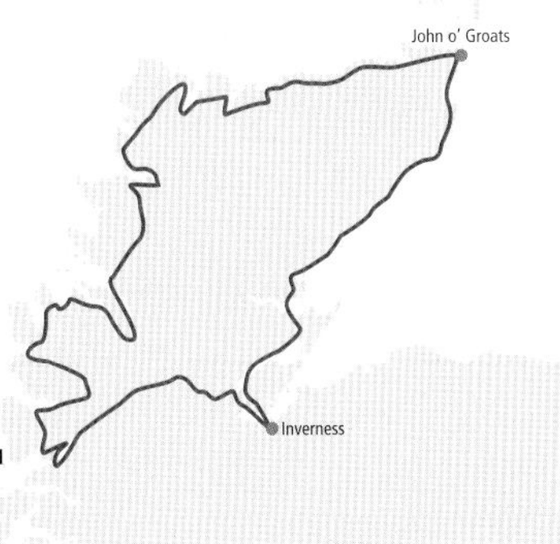

14 NORTH COAST 500 – 816km

The North Coast 500 is an 816-kilometre (or just over 500-mile) loop around the Scottish Highlands, offering the very best views of the northern Scottish coast. This challenging road route, with plenty of climbs and fast-wheeling descents, takes you from Inverness past castles, lochs and beaches to Scotland's most northerly town and most north-western point before closing the loop. Launched in 2015, the North Coast 500 is primarily a driving route, but choosing quieter routes on minor lanes and using NCN trails will keep you away from busy roads and the worst of the traffic, and let you experience an adventure that takes you further than a car could.

Many choose to attempt the loop in a clockwise direction due to the wind blowing more in your favour. You start at Inverness's nineteenth-century, red sandstone castle, although you might choose to begin with coffee and cake at the Velocity Cafe, which was voted Scotland's cyclist cafe of the year in 2018 and 2020; there is an attached workshop where you can book a stand if you need to make some last-minute adjustments to your bike. Rather than busy roads, you can take traffic-free tracks along the shores of Beauly Firth towards Marybank, although you might stop en route at the Glen Ord Distillery. You can enjoy a largely traffic-free route on tarmac tracks, with the occasional residential road, to Contin.

From Contin to Garve, you have little choice but to join the traffic on the narrow, busy A835 main road as it snakes across the country. Those on a hybrid or gravel bike might follow the Great North Trail instead on muddy forestry tracks. At Garve, you must dismount to cross the railway – the lines cut across the road at a dangerous angle. You follow a low route, along rivers and lochs, to reach Loch Carron on the western coast.

You now face the longest road climb in Britain, up the narrow Bealach na Ba (or Pass of the Cattle), although you can cut cross-country to Sheildaig to avoid this leg-burning ascent, which tops out at 626 metres. The climb is made even more difficult as you may have to pause in the passing places to allow motorists to overtake you on this switch-back road. You face an up-and-down route along the coast, with fine views across to the islands of Skye, Rona and Raasay. The route turns inland at Torridon on roads that roll between munros, through the Beinn Eighe National Nature Reserve – you may see golden eagles soaring above the pinewoods.

Following the shores of Loch Maree, you return to the coast, reaching shining white beaches fringed by an impossibly blue sea, where you may see humpback and minke whales. The ferry port of Ullapool is a good overnight stop, with a reputation for traditional music.

The trail leaves the driving route to follow Loch Lurgainn towards Lochinver. Although this does mean that you miss Loch Assynt and Ardvreck Castle, it does take you directly through Lochinver where you can sample the Lochinver Larder's renowned pies, a good idea given the steep climb that you face north of Lochinver.

◀ DESCENDING TOWARDS DUNDONNELL ALONG LITTLE LOCH BROOM.
© AMY JURRIES

At Kylesku, a curved, white bridge takes you over the loch towards Scotland's northernmost coast, which you reach at Durness. You can rest a while in the John Lennon Memorial Garden – the Beatle spent his childhood holidays here, and last visited with Yoko Ono in 1969 – or marvel at the adventurers preparing to set out on foot or bike to reach Cape Wrath, Scotland's remote north-western point. Your route, however, takes you along the shores of Loch Eriboll and then over the Kyle of Tongue to Bettyhill, a town named for the Countess of Sutherland who built it as a resettlement town during the Highland Clearances.

Thurso is the northernmost town on the British mainland; once a Norse port, it is now a popular surfing and kayaking destination. You are now riding through the north-east's wild landscape of blanket bog and crumbling clachans – a short detour will take you to Dunnet Head, the most northerly point on the mainland. On the horizon, you can see the Orkney Islands.

You now reach John o' Groats, the end destination on the iconic Land's End to John o' Groats route (see page 69), but can continue further north-west still to the lighthouse that overlooks the stacks of Duncansby, before you turn down the eastern coast to head back towards Inverness. The route passes the ruins of old Keiss Castle, teetering on the edge of the east coast's sheer, striated cliffs. At the southern end of Sinclair's Bay, you travel past the haunted Ackergill Tower – the abducted Helen Gunn flung herself from the tower, her death provoking a long feud between the Gunns and the Clan Keith.

The trail arrives at the royal burgh of Wick, now a popular destination for boating holidaymakers thanks to its three harbours. You can visit Ebenezer Place, the world's shortest

A VIEW OF BEINN EIGHE FROM LOCH COULIN IN TORRIDON. © NORTH COAST 500

street at just a door's width long. After Dunrobin, you face a route choice (although you will have to follow the drivers briefly at least if you want to visit the Glenmorangie Distillery). You can follow NCN 1 on a quieter road route through Dingwall that runs parallel to the motorist's route. The NCN 1 also offers an alternative route that takes you across the Cromarty Firth to the beautiful peninsula of the Black Isle. However, the Cromarty–Nigg Ferry across the firth only runs during the summer. The two routes join back together just north of Beauly Firth, and offer quieter roads as an alternative to the traffic-heavy A9 main road back towards Inverness – cyclists cross the firth with the main road, but the bridge has a shared path for riders and pedestrians.

The North Coast 500 is the perfect tourer's route, but you might choose instead a gravel or hybrid route if you want to leave the road behind you occasionally or explore Scotland's bogs and forests. The Highlands are remote, with long distances between small villages – you may have to cover long distances to reach accommodation. With Scotland's open access laws, this would be the ideal bikepacking adventure, with plenty of idyllic wild beach campsites.

The North Coast 500 is a challenging ride with long days in the saddle, but you will be rewarded with stunning views of the Highlands and, as you look out to sea, the islands. You can whale watch on the west's sandy coast, look out for dolphins from the Black Isle and spot golden eagles in nature reserves.

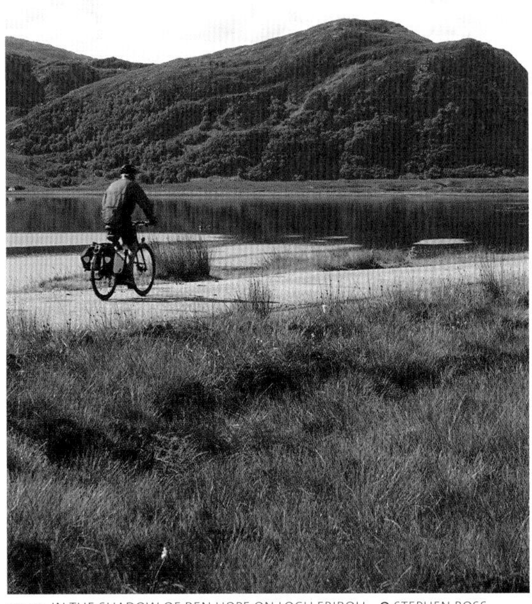

ABOVE: IN THE SHADOW OF BEN HOPE ON LOCH ERIBOLL. © STEPHEN ROSS
BELOW: THE A832 WINDING THROUGH GLEN DOCHERTY WITH A VIEW OF LOCH MAREE. © NORTH COAST 500

14 NORTH COAST 500: ESSENTIAL INFORMATION

RIDE ESSENTIALS

Start: **Inverness, Scotland**
End: **Inverness, Scotland**
Distance: **816km**
Ascent/descent: **8,150m/8,150m**

HOW TO GET THERE

Inverness's railway station has direct services to London including a sleeper train; a booking must be made for bikes at least a day in advance. Inverness also has an international airport.

TIME TO COMPLETE

Minimum days: **6 days/52 hours**
Maximum days: **12 days/73 hours**

PROS

- **Castles** – the trail starts at Inverness Castle and offers many castles to spot along the way. Dunrobin, in the style of a French chateau, is the seat of the Clan Sutherland. Castle Varrich is believed to date from the fourteenth century but may be older. You can treat yourself to a stay in Dornoch Castle, now a hotel.

- **Distilleries** – the Highlands are home to some of Scotland's best whisky distilleries. Pultney in Wick produced the world's best whisky in 2012. GlenWyvis in Dingwall, established in 2015, is the first community-owned distillery. Glen Ord, founded in 1838, is the only remaining distillery on the Black Isle. If you don't like whisky, you might prefer Black Isle Brewery's Spider Monkey IPA or the Dunnet Bay Distillers' gins and vodkas.

- **Highlands and islands** – there are plenty of stunning scenes on the route, from the rugged beauty of Torridon to the golden sands of Sandwood Bay. You'll have great views of Scotland's islands and could take a detour to the Outer Hebrides or Orkney Islands.

CONS

- **Cars** – the trail has been heavily promoted as a tourist driving route, and cyclists will sometimes have to share the route with motorists.

- **Hilly** – this is a route with plenty of climb, some on narrow roads, often busy with cars. The Bealach na Ba is the biggest road ascent in Britain, but the western coast stretch is bumpy.

- **Winter** – weather in the northern Highlands can be extreme in the winter. As hospitality services will be limited, you may find yourself stranded by snow or inclement conditions.

VARIATIONS

The North Coast 500 is a build-your-own adventure by bike – there are obvious diversions to be made from the driving route, but there are also off-road options and decisions about which roads and how many hills.

GOOD TO KNOW

The deserted landscape which the North Coast 500 explores owes its quietness to the Highland Clearances. Between approximately 1750 and 1860, an economic revolution took place in the Highlands as traditional farming tenants were resettled (often through eviction) to coastal crofting communities. The roofs of their homes were burnt to prevent them from returning. The Highland Potato Famine and failure of the kelp industry saw nearly a third of the population dispossessed, with many emigrating to America and Australia. The Clearances effectively signalled an end to the clan system after the Jacobite Rising, created a global diaspora of Scots and are still a source of sorrow and resentment for many even today.

FURTHER INFORMATION

www.northcoast500.com

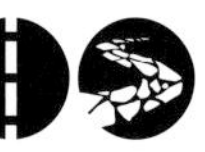

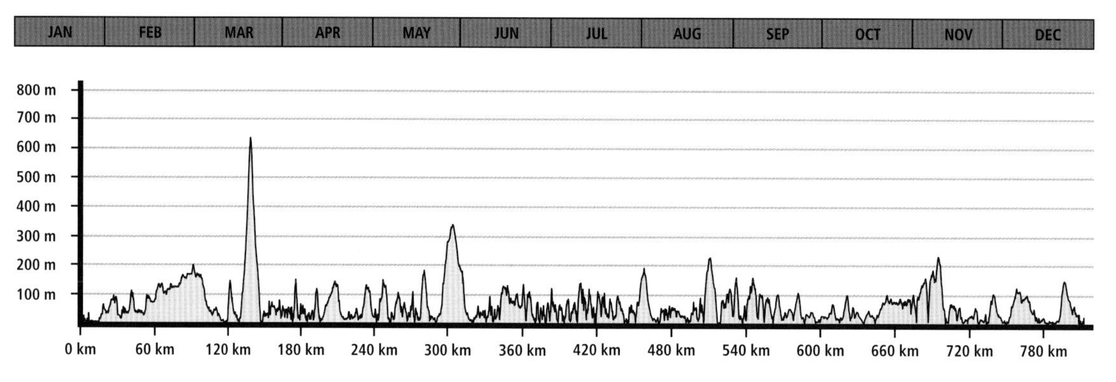

Cape Wrath
Durness
Whitten Head
Dunnet Head
John o' Groats
Strathy Point
Armadale
Strathy
Portskerra
Thurso
Bettyhill
Melvich
Reay
A' Mhòine
A836
Tongue
Noss Head
A838
Kyle of Tongue
Wick
Scourie
North West Sutherland
A897
A9
Loch More
A836
A894
Drumbeg
Kylesku
Stoer
Dunbeath
A837
Inchnadamph
Lochinver
A838
A9
The Minch
Loch Shin
Assynt
Helmsdale
Portgower
Lairg
A835
Brora
A837
Golspie
Ullapool
Dornoch Firth
Laide
Dornoch
A835
Aultbea
Dundonnell
Inverlael
Tain
Poolewe
Wester Ross
Easter Ross
Gairloch
A835
Balintore
A832
Loch Maree
Moray Firth
Alness
Lossiemouth
Loch Fannich
Buckie
Black Isle
Elgin
N
Garve
Kinlochewe
A832
A832
Dingwall
Loch Luichart
Torridon
Achnasheen
Nairn
Forres
Fortrose
Shieldaig
Keith
Craig
Muir of Ord
Beauly Firth
SCOTLAND
Applecross
Strathcarron
Inverness
0
20 Kilometres
Loch Carron
Loch Ness

15

15 NORTH NORFOLK COAST CYCLEWAY – 159km

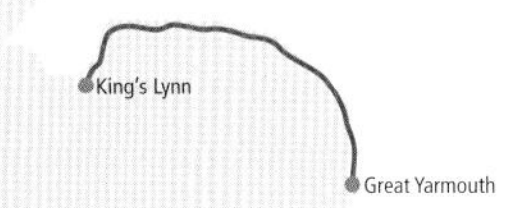

The 159-kilometre North Norfolk Coast Cycleway leads from King's Lynn to Great Yarmouth. It is a route on narrow, singletrack country lanes through fields and marshes, past castles and cafes. Although it is not comprehensively waymarked, it is difficult to get lost on these green-fringed roads. The route takes you past the Queen's beloved Sandringham, round Burnham's bird-rich marshes and through the crab town of Cromer before finishing with a coastal spin through the seaside resorts of Hemsby, Caister-on-Sea and Great Yarmouth. This is not a route to be raced; it is an opportunity to relax into the slow pace of Norfolk's coast.

In the fourteenth century, the now tranquil King's Lynn was once one of Britain's most important seaports. The town was bombed during World War I by a Zeppelin in January 1915, making it one of the first British mainland settlements to suffer aerial attack. You begin by the King's Lynn tourist information office, on the banks of the Great Ouse river. The route follows the NCN 1 out of King's Lynn, a fast start as you spin out of the town on tarmac tracks that run behind the railway station and through green parks. Near the King's Lynn golf course, you join quiet country roads. The trail passes the grey stone walls of the ruined Castle Rising, a twelfth-century castle that was once home to Edward II's widow, Isabella of France.

The Cycleway turns on to a shady, wooded road through the Sandringham estate. Sandringham House is a private royal residence, where both George V and VI died, and is the Queen's preferred Christmas residence. You can visit the house and its formal gardens during the summer months, and also the church on the estate, St Mary Magdalene, which the royal family attend on Christmas Day.

You skirt Dersingham, birthplace of Queen's Roger Taylor, and Snettisham through bird-rich nature reserves. At Sedgeford, you might choose to make a small diversion past the Norfolk Lavender fields to Hunstanton, with its stripy cliffs; it is one of the few places on the east coast where the sun sets over the sea. Across narrow lanes over the flat Ringstead Common, you head for the tranquil village of Burnham Market. You might choose again to detour to the sea to visit Brancaster, famed for its mussels – Brancaster Staithe is still a busy fishing port. Near the windmill at Burnham Overy, which is now owned by the National Trust and available as holiday accommodation, Lord Nelson learnt to sail – back on route, you pass his birthplace at Burnham Thorpe.

You cycle around the outskirts of the Palladian Holkham Hall, passing near the Triumphal Arch, although you might choose to pedal through the parkland on a loop that reaches the coast at Wells-next-the-Sea. The trail departs from the NCN 1 at Wighton to follow regional routes on country roads. At Binham, you pass the ruins of the eleventh-century priory and the medieval market cross. On Salthouse Heath, you can see prehistoric barrows.

The route passes Holt station, the western terminus of the heritage North Norfolk 'Poppy Line' Railway, and then turns to the coast at Cromer, the seaside resort famed for its crab. You head south between the railway and the coast,

◀ HORSEY WINDPUMP. © CHRIS COLES

veering back towards the coast at Mundesley with its multicoloured beach huts. The trail now hugs the coast more closely as it heads for Happisburgh, with its lighthouse, which is the oldest working lighthouse in East Anglia and the only privately operated one.

Past the sandy beaches of Sea Palling, you skirt Hemsby – during its heyday, the Pontins holiday camp could accommodate nearly 2,500 sunseekers. As you pass the quaint village of Ormesby St Margaret, you are now well within the Norfolk Broads. The Broads, although long believed to be natural, are a man-made landscape that results from the medieval excavation of peat. The peaceful rivers and lakes make this a popular boating holiday area.

You skirt the sprawling caravan parks at the busy seaside resort of Hemsby to reach Caister. On Ormesby Road you pass the East and West Caister Village Cemetery, where you can see the Grade II memorial to the nine men who died when the Caister lifeboat capsized while attempting to rescue a stricken vessel during the Great Storm of 1901. Only three crew survived – the incident gave rise to the saying 'Caister men never turn back'. You can also enjoy the golden sands of Caister's Georgian beach – tourists have been visiting the town since at least the 1790s.

Caister's suburbs now blend into its neighbour and your journey's end, Great Yarmouth. In *David Copperfield*, Charles Dickens called Great Yarmouth 'the finest place

GREAT YARMOUTH BEACH. © CHRIS COLES

in the universe'. However, the town suffered considerably during World War II – as the last significant settlement on the east coast passed by homeward bound German planes, it was subject to much bombing and postwar reconstruction has sometimes been more functional than aesthetic. Despite this, you can still reward your efforts with an ice cream on the Golden Mile, stroll along the newly restored Venetian Waterways and step out on to the town's twin piers.

The North Norfolk Coast Cycleway is a flat, easy road trail between Norfolk's villages and seaside resorts. It is the perfect first adventure on a tourer, although there are so many bed and breakfasts, cafes and seaside stops that you might attempt it on a road bike over a weekend with minimal baggage. You will cycle through woodlands and farmers' golden fields, along the coast and past castles, through bird-rich marshes and pretty villages. This is the perfect winter getaway – although the coast is occasionally subject to flooding and damage in extreme weather, generally the roads will be easily passable at any time of year. Sustrans is removing most on-road routes from the National Cycle Network, so waymarking may be removed from the route but navigation is straightforward.

Norfolk has sandy beaches, green fields and fresh seafood. The North Norfolk Coast Cycleway is a perfect opportunity to explore Norfolk's undiscovered treasures. It is the perfect weekend route for those who want to escape the urban bustle, but it is perhaps better suited to those who want to meander slowly and enjoy the views.

ABOVE: GREY SEAL PUP AT HORSEY GAP. © CHRIS COLES
BELOW: WAXHAM CHURCH AND BARN. © CHRIS COLES

15 NORTH NORFOLK COAST CYCLEWAY: ESSENTIAL INFORMATION

RIDE ESSENTIALS

Start: **King's Lynn, Norfolk, England**
End: **Great Yarmouth, Norfolk, England**
Distance: **159km**
Ascent/descent: **770m/780m**

HOW TO GET THERE

King's Lynn has rail connections to London via Cambridge. The closest international airports are London Luton and Stansted, and there are international ferry connections to the Netherlands from Harwich ferry port.

Great Yarmouth has a train station with services to Norwich, where connections can be made to London.

TIME TO COMPLETE

Minimum days: **1 day/10 hours**
Maximum days: **3 days/14 hours**

PROS

- **Seafood** – North Norfolk has several busy fishing ports, and its crabs and lobsters are highly prized for their sweet flesh – flavours that are often attributed to the underwater chalk ridge.

- **Flat** – the highest point in Norfolk is Beacon Hill near Cromer (103 metres) and the highest point en route is ninety-three metres. This is one of the flattest coastal rides in the United Kingdom, and perfect for those who don't enjoy pedalling a heavily laden tourer up and down bumpy lanes.

CONS

- **Coast** – the route does not hug the coast, but instead runs parallel on inland country lanes. If you want to make the most of the seaside, you will have to frequently detour from the Cycleway, often on busier roads.

- **Caravans** – Norfolk is a popular destination for holiday-makers and there are big campsites and caravan parks dotted along the coast. You may encounter caravans and motorhomes even on quiet country lanes.

- **The future** – the Cycleway is not a well-known route, and it relies heavily on the NCN 1 cycle route. The future of on-road routes like this is uncertain following Sustrans's decision to remove on-road routes from the National Cycle Network. The North Norfolk Coast Cycleway may disappear from public view (although the roads will still be there to enjoy) or spur local councils to provide better traffic-free alternatives and promote the routes themselves.

VARIATIONS

The route avoids the busy coast roads and runs parallel to the coast. There are several loops that you can follow to visit coastal resorts such as Hunstanton, Cromer and Brancaster.

GOOD TO KNOW

North Norfolk may be beloved for its beaches now, but in the early seventeenth century it was a hotbed of witchcraft. On the side of a house on the edge of Tuesday Market Place, you can still see the scorch mark left when the heart of witch Margaret Read exploded from her chest. In 1616 Alexander Roberts, a priest in King's Lynn, wrote *A Treatise of Witchcraft* and the town caught the attention of Witchfinder General Matthew Hopkins in the 1640s.

FURTHER INFORMATION

www.norfolkcoastaonb.org.uk/partnership/norfolk-coast-cycleway/388

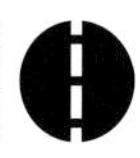

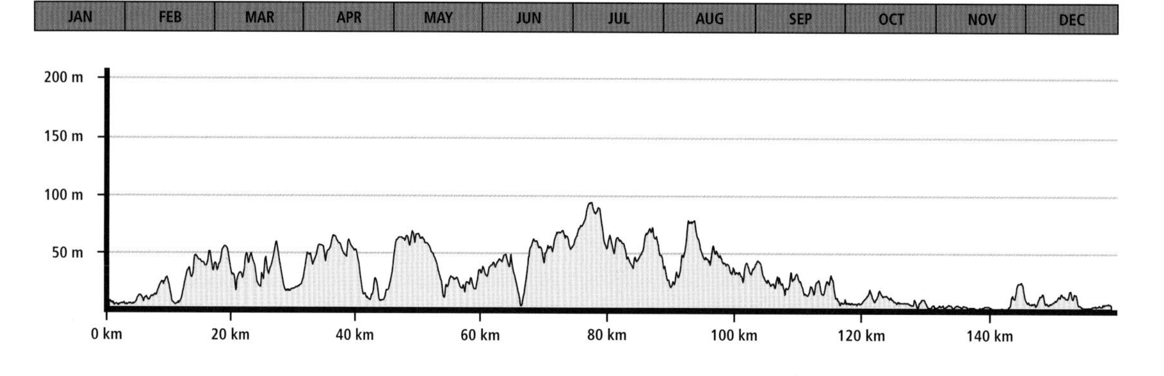

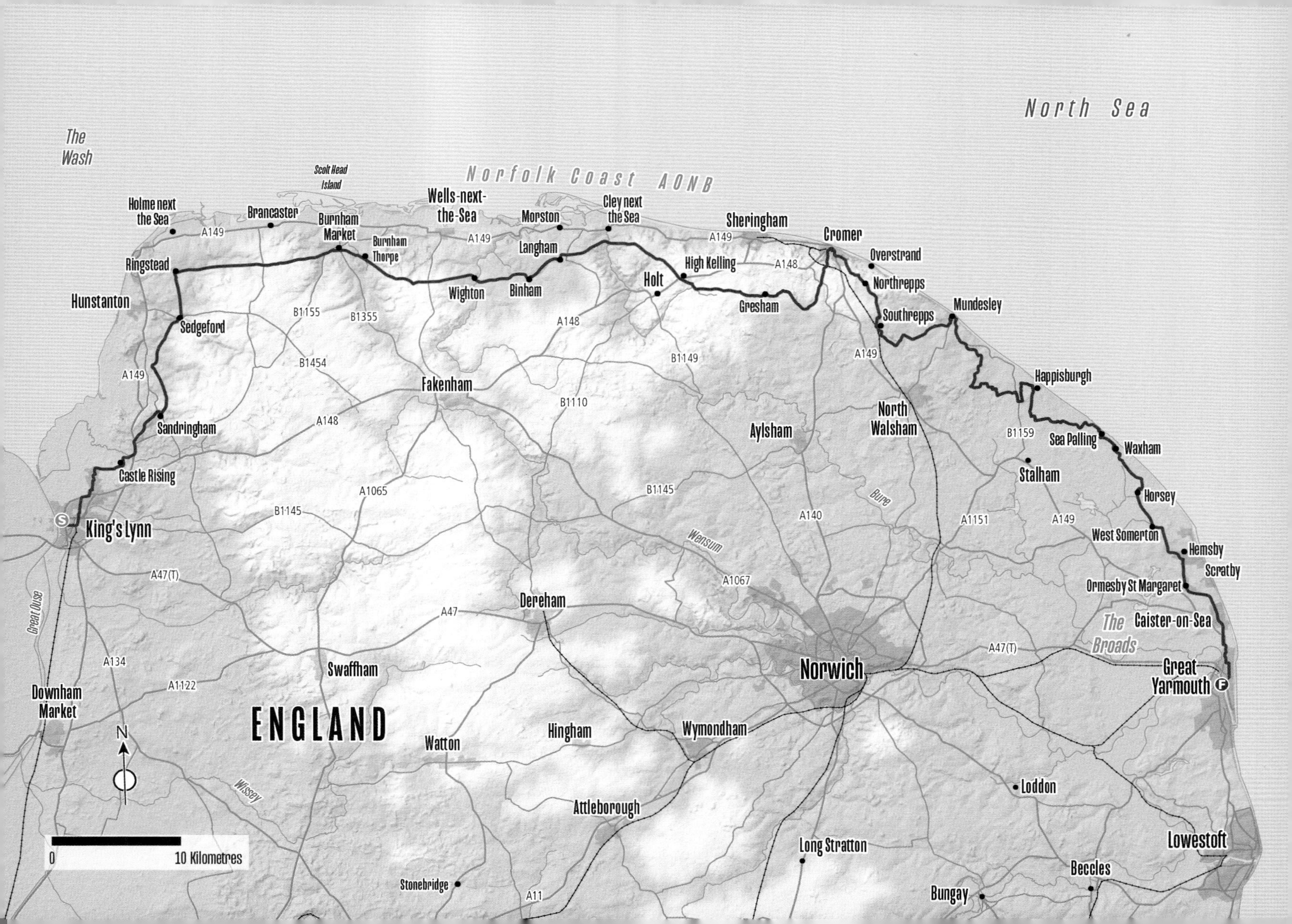

North Sea
The Wash
Norfolk Coast AONB
Scolt Head Island
Holme next the Sea
Brancaster
Burnham Market
Burnham Thorpe
Wells-next-the-Sea
Morston
Cley next the Sea
Sheringham
Cromer
Overstrand
Northrepps
Southrepps
Mundesley
Happisburgh
Sea Palling
Waxham
Horsey
West Somerton
Hemsby
Scratby
Ormesby St Margaret
Caister-on-Sea
Great Yarmouth
The Broads
Ringstead
Hunstanton
Sedgeford
Sandringham
Castle Rising
King's Lynn
Langham
Wighton
Binham
Holt
High Kelling
Gresham
Fakenham
Aylsham
North Walsham
Stalham
Dereham
Norwich
Swaffham
Downham Market
ENGLAND
Watton
Hingham
Wymondham
Attleborough
Long Stratton
Loddon
Lowestoft
Beccles
Bungay
Stonebridge
A149
A148
B1155
B1355
B1454
B1149
B1110
B1159
A1065
B1145
A140
A1151
A1067
A47(T)
A47
A134
A1122
A11
Great Ouse
Wissey
Wensum
Bure
N
0
10 Kilometres

16

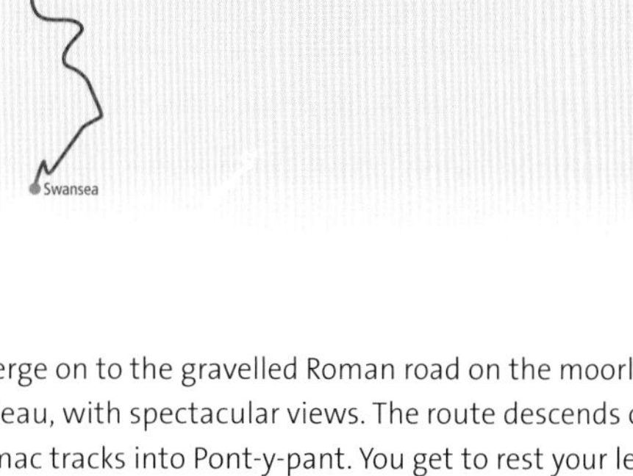

16 SARN HELEN – 342km

The Sarn Helen is a 342-kilometre route that traverses Wales from north to south, from Conwy to Swansea, taking in some most of beautiful Welsh scenery and offering technical riding on challenge ascents over tough terrain. The route was created by Mountain Bikes Routes UK in 1998, but Sustrans have also suggested less technical off-road alternatives. Wales has long been at the forefront of British mountain biking so there are plenty of route options – you can choose technical tracks across bouldered or slate-topped tracks, forestry tracks and grassy trods across open moor, or stick to quiet country lanes, good riverside trails and wide, easy gravel tracks – depending on your experience, tyres and the weather.

The Sarn Helen begins in Conwy, by Edward I's castle. On narrow roads you cycle under the town walls, past white-washed Victorian villas and through green farmland as you follow the River Conwy south. At Caerhun you pass the Canovium Roman fort, built around AD 75, at the river crossing. You have been tracing the edge of the Snowdonia National Park but now you traverse it. Near Dolgarrog's Surf Snowdonia, the world's first commercial artificial surfing lake, you turn on to gravel doubletracks that cross heathered moorland. On sometimes boggy, stony trails you follow the shores around Llyn Bowydd to reach the road again near Plas y Brenin, the popular National Outdoor Centre.

After Capel Curig, you pass the remains of the Roman fort Caer Llugwy before taking the Sarn Helen route through Gwydir Forest near Betws-y-Coed. You face a steep climb on bouldered, stony trails through the trees before you emerge on to the gravelled Roman road on the moorland plateau, with spectacular views. The route descends on to tarmac tracks into Pont-y-pant. You get to rest your legs on a road spin into Dolwyddelan, with its castle where Prince Llywelyn ap Iorwerth, Llywelyn the Great, is supposed to have been born. The trail climbs gently on doubletrack through the Cwm Penamnen Valley before navigating through an alien landscape of disused slate quarries to reach Llan Ffestiniog.

There is a brief road section to Bont Newydd, and you climb on narrow lanes beneath conifers contouring around Mynydd Maentwrog. You enjoy wide, gravel tracks to Llyn Trawsfynydd, built to provide water for hydroelectric power stations and Trawsfynydd nuclear power station, and here you are briefly on a busy main road. On tarmac lanes, you follow the route of the Roman road beneath the mountains to reach gravel tracks through the forest. You emerge at the valley bottom at Coed-y-Brenin, Britain's first purpose-built mountain-biking centre. The route follows wide, easy gravel tracks along the River Mawddach. On the outskirts of Dolgellau you pass the picturesque ruins of Cistercian Cymer Abbey.

The trail now leaves Snowdonia and heads for the ups and downs of the Cambrian Mountains. You have a steep climb up to Tabor, in the shadow of Cadair Idris, and then join NCN 8, the Lôn Las Cymru route from North to South Wales, into Machynlleth. The trail passes the Centre for Alternative Technology, which focuses on sustainable living. On rutted gravel tracks and slate-topped trails,

◀ RIDERS CLIMBING FFORDD DDU ON THE SLOPES OF CADAIR IDRIS. © PHIL STASIW – *WWW.MTB.WALES*

you climb high into the Cambrian Mountains. In the shadow of Plynlimon, the mountain where the Severn springs to life, you ride the shores of Nant-y-moch Reservoir towards Ponterwyd. You enjoy a ride along the pretty Rheidol Valley to Devil's Bridge, where there is an iron bridge built on top of a stone bridge built on top of a medieval bridge.

You cycle up roads to the Hafod Arch, on the edge of woods, to join the Trans Cambrian Way past the Cwmystwyth Mines and then take roads to Rhayader. Leaving Rhayader, you can enjoy the Elan Valley Trail as it heads high past the lonely reservoirs, with red kites soaring above you. The route climbs steeply on doubletrack gravel tracks between Drygarn Fawr and Gorllwyn. The tracks narrow as you conquer the pass and head for Beulah, where you take easy roads across the floodplain, past the Roman auxiliary fort at Caerau, to Llangammarch Wells.

ABOVE: WATERFALLS NEAR CLAERWEN DAM, ELAN VALLEY © PHIL STASIW – *WWW.MTB.WALES*
BELOW: GRAVEL RIDERS ON THE FFORDD DDU. © PHIL STASIW – *WWW.MTB.WALES*

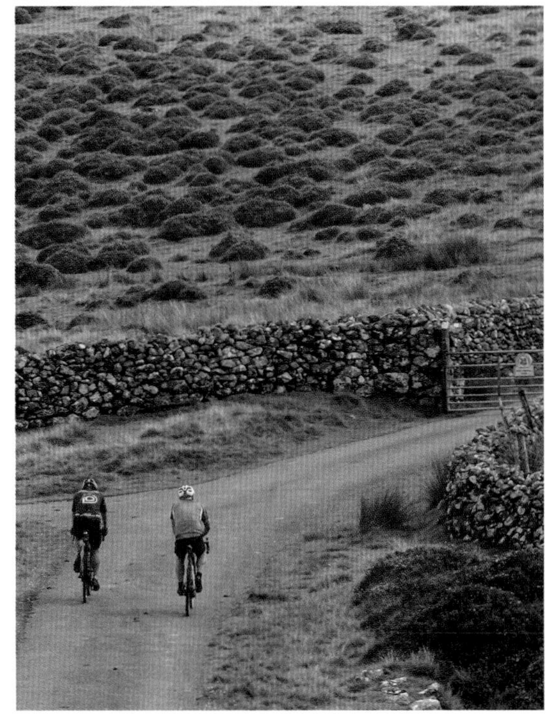

After a steep climb up Pennau Hill, you cross Mynydd Epynt – this is one of the UK's largest military training areas, so you should stick to the mountain bike trails if you do not follow the road. You will know that you are arriving at the Beacons as you climb to the summit of Pen-y-crug, with its hilltop Iron Age fort. The route descends to the gateway to the Beacons, Brecon. You cross the Beacons climbing on bendy, narrow lanes that turn into gravel tracks, beneath the giants of Fan Llia and Fan Nedd, then pass the Maen Madoc inscribed menhir stone that stands on the edge of the Roman road. You ride through the Fforest Fawr on rocky, gravelly technical tracks. Near Banwen the landscape is dotted with wind turbines, and you take advantage of tarmac tracks through the forest laid for the wind farms.

With the hills behind you, you follow the canal and then the River Tawe into Swansea. The trail follows the edge of the sandy Swansea Bay as it heads towards the Gower peninsula. Near the ruins of the twelfth-century Pennard Castle you climb the ridge of Cefn Bryn, the spine of the Gower. The route takes gravel tracks through rolling farmland before facing one last stiff climb over Rhossili Down, with glorious sea views. You join the tourists on roads near the tip of the peninsula, Worms Head. You can only access Worms Head by causeway at low tide; caution should be exercised as visitors are often cut off – poet Dylan Thomas was once stranded overnight on the island.

Wales is a land of green hills, rivers and plenty of rain, and on the hilltop tracks of the Sarn Helen you are exposed to the worst of the weather. Stony tracks are slippery in wet weather and firm tracks may become boggy. The Sarn Helen is challenging in good weather and may feel impossible in bad weather. It is best tackled in summer, with longer and sunnier days. The route offers plenty of ascent and descent, and your choice of technical trails. As you encounter boulders, tree roots and slippery slates, even the downhills will take longer than you anticipate.

Sarn Helen is a coast-to-coast adventure that takes you from Conwy through Snowdonia, the Cambrian Mountains and the Brecon Beacons. As well as the mountain tops, it offers rivers and streams, verdant farmland, sandy beaches, quiet country lanes and plenty of Roman ruins. It prefers quiet villages and outdoor centres to busy towns, and explores Wales's most remote countryside. Sarn Helen is a reminder that the Roman route through a landscape is not always the lowest or most straightforward line to follow.

RIDERS CLIMBING HIGH ABOVE DEVIL'S BRIDGE TOWARD THE HAFOD ARCH. © PHIL STASIW – *WWW.MTB.WALES*

16 SARN HELEN: ESSENTIAL INFORMATION

RIDE ESSENTIALS

Start:	**Conwy, Wales**
End:	**Worms Head, Swansea, Wales**
Distance:	**342km**
Ascent/descent:	**6,360m/6,320m**

HOW TO GET THERE

Conwy has direct train services to Cardiff, Birmingham and Holyhead. The closest international airports are at Liverpool and Manchester; Holyhead has ferry services to Ireland.

Worms Head is approximately thirty kilometres from Swansea's train station on the South Wales Main Line – the regional station at Gowerton is slightly closer. Cardiff is the closest international airport.

TIME TO COMPLETE

Minimum days:	**3 days/28 hours**
Maximum days:	**6 days/38 hours**

PROS

- **Mountains** – Sarn Helen traverses Wales's three great mountain ranges – Snowdonia, the Cambrian Mountains and the Brecon Beacons – and offers plenty of ascents and descents en route.

- **Terrain** – from rutted doubletracks and loose, slate-topped trails to muddy forest tracks, tarmac strips, grassy paths, easy granite, boulders and rocks, the Sarn Helen offers every possible terrain and plenty of technical challenge.

- **Roman ruins** – while the route of the Sarn Helen Roman road is disputed, you will pass several Roman forts on the trail: Canovium at Caerhun, Tomen-y-Mur and Brecon Gaer. There are many more forts to make short detours to.

CONS

- **Rain** – on high, exposed routes, you may find yourself unprotected from the worst of Britain's weather, and technical trails may become even more challenging in wet weather.

- **Navigation** – you will need your wits about you to follow this route. It often follows tracks and trails rather than public bridleways. Forests and quarries are criss-crossed with many tracks, and picking the right one may be challenging. Weather, forestry work or military manoeuvres may mean you have to make last-minute route changes.

VARIATIONS

There are many variations; some continue on-road to Betws-y-Coed, rather than cutting cross-country to Capel Curig. You may visit Builth Wells rather than Llangammarch Wells. You can stay on the roads around Mynydd Epynt or take newly opened trails across the military area. There is a coastal variation on the NCN 8 section of the route.

GOOD TO KNOW

The route is named for Saint Helen, or Elen, of Caernarfon. The wife of a fourth-century Roman emperor, Elen ordered a road-building program to facilitate the movement of troops. Unfortunately the sections of Roman road now associated with Elen's name predate her by several centuries. While much of the Roman road has now disappeared under modern highways, you can see the cobbles and ditches of the original Roman construction near the standing stone at Maen Madoc.

FURTHER INFORMATION

www.mbruk.co.uk/mbruk_SarnHelenTrail_details.htm

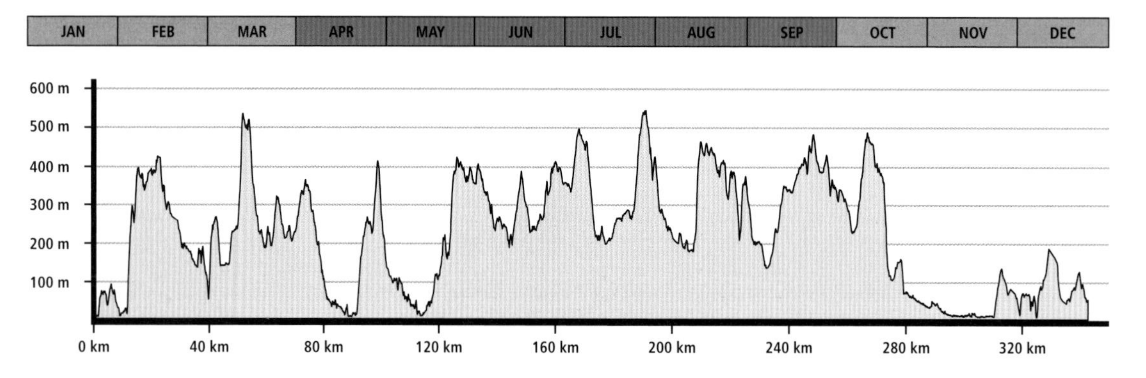

Liverpool
Runcorn
Ellesmere Port
M56
Llandudno
Rhyl
Colwyn Bay
Holyhead
Anglesey/
Ynys Môn
Conwy
A55
Holywell
A55
Bangor
Carnedd
Llewelyn
Dolgarrog
Chester
A5
Caernarfon
A470
Ruthin
Snowdon/
Yr Wyddfa
Plas y Brenin
Betws-y-Coed
Snowdonia
National Park
Dolwyddelan
A5
Clwydian Range and
Dee Valley AONB
Wrexham
Whitchurch
Llan Ffestiniog
Llangollen
Porthmadog
Chirk
Trawsfynydd
Bala
Cadair Berwyn
Harlech
Rhinogydd
Oswestry
Abersoch
Coed-y-Brenin
A494
A49
Dolgellau
Barmouth
A470
Shrewsbury
Cadair Idris
Aberllefenni
A458
Welshpool
WALES
ENGLAND
Cardigan
Bay
Tywyn
Machynlleth
Cambrian Mountains/
Elenydd
A470
Newtown
A487
Severn
Bishop's Castle
Pumlumon
Llanidloes
Aberystwyth
Ponterwyd
Pontarfynach
Knighton
Ludlow
A487
Llan Ddu Fawr
Rhayader
A485
A44
Aberaeron
Elan Village
Llandrindod
Leominster
Carnau
Kington
Llanwrtyd
Wells
Beulah
Builth Wells
Lampeter
Cardigan
Llangammarch Wells
A49
Hay-on-Wye
Mynydd
Epynt
Hereford
Fishguard
Llandovery
A483
Talgarth
Pwllgloyw
A40
Usk
Brecon
Black
Mountains
Llandeilo
Black Mountain
Carmarthen
Pen y Fan
A4067
Crickhowell
A40
Haverfordwest
Brecon Beacons
National Park
Abergavenny
Wye Valley
AONB
Monmouth
Gurnos
Banwen
Ebbw Vale
A465
Merthyr Tydfil
Pembroke
Tenby
Pontypool
N
Swansea
Neath
Gower
Rhossili
Southgate
Pontypridd
Newport
M48
F
S
Worms Head/
Penrhyn Gŵyr
Oxwich
Bay
M4
M4
Severn
0
20 Kilometres
Cardiff
Bristol
Barry

17 SEA TO SEA (C2C) – 219km

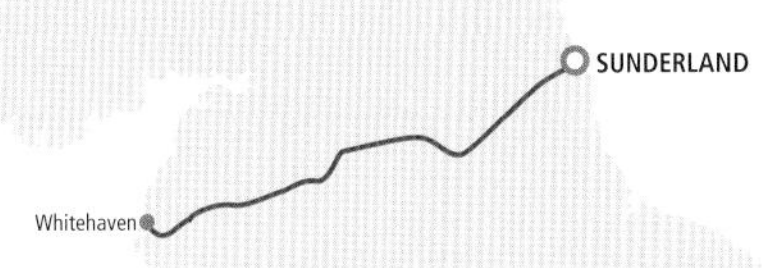

The 219-kilometre Sea to Sea (C2C) is the cyclist's retort to Wainwright's Coast to Coast. Beginning on the Cumbrian seashore, it takes a surprisingly low route through the Lake District and then clambers high over the Pennine spine of the country. You have a long descent through the farmland and industrial landscapes of County Durham to reach Sunderland in Tyne and Wear. You will often find yourself on high moorland with no one but sheep for company, and golden-green heath stretching as far as you can see.

The Sea to Sea begins at Whitehaven's inner harbour – it is traditional for riders to dip their back wheel in the water before setting off. After cycling the quayside roads, you turn off on to a tarmac, traffic-free cycletrack that meanders between car parks, shops and industrial units to reach the suburbs, occasionally popping out briefly on to a quiet residential road. The cycle path takes advantage of disused railway tracks past Cleator Moor and Frizington, gently climbing towards the Lake District.

After Rowrah, you take to quiet country lanes along the grassy, green borders of the national park. You face a pleasant descent after Lamplugh, which becomes steeper at Fangs Brow, to Loweswater. You cycle the length of the small lake and then follow the course of the River Cocker on a flat route. At High Lorton, you are reminded that you are now firmly within the Lakes as you face a challenging climb over Whinlatter Pass, and then descend sharply. The trail takes forestry roads through Whinlatter Forest to reach Thornthwaite.

The route skirts the foot of Cat Bells to reach Keswick, at the head of Derwent Water – these narrow roads may be busy with cars heading for the popular walk over Cat Bells. The Threlkeld railway track was washed away in Storm Desmond in 2015 but finally reopened in 2020, so you can enjoy an easy ride along the bottom of Blencathra. You ride undulated roads to Mungrisdale.

You cycle beside the busy A66 main road through Troutbeck and, leaving the Lake District National Park, turn off towards Greystoke – the village's castle was first built in 1129 but has been expanded and rebuilt several times since. The trail meanders through the verdant farmland of the Eden Valley as it descends towards Penrith, crossing under the M6 motorway on farm tracks. Penrith is a bustling market town and agricultural centre, and although you do not go through the town centre the roads may be busy and lined with parked cars.

You are soon on narrow lanes through farmland, but join the A686 main road to Langwathby; you cross the Eden on the single carriageway bridge that was put in place as a temporary measure when the 300-year-old sandstone bridge was washed away by a flood in 1968. The trail passes Long Meg and Her Daughters, one of England's largest stone circles, reputedly a coven of witches turned to stone.

You now have the challenge of crossing the Pennine spine of England, the hilliest section of the route. This begins with a steep, lengthy ascent over Hartside on hairpin bends.

◀ WHINLATTER PASS ON AN AUTUMNAL MORNING.
© SHUTTERSTOCK/JONTY M. SEXTON

THE QUIET LANES HEADED TOWARD LORTON IN ALLERDALE OVER THE WESTERN SIDE OF WHINLATTER'S WOODED SUMMIT. © TOBY CUMMINS

The road straightens out for your descent and you can enjoy views of the expanse of isolated moorland that stretch in front of you. Once you reach Garrigill, an old lead mining village, you are at about the halfway point.

The route climbs up and over Nunnery Hill and then on to the highest point on the route on Black Hill (609 metres). You have a curving descent along quiet roads to Allenheads and then ascend again through conifer plantations. This is a landscape scarred by mining, and you pass disused shafts and mine workings, including the Minehead at Grove Rake Mine, the North Pennine's last fluorspar mine. You may also glimpse crumbling stone arches on the moor; these are all that remain of the Rookhope Chimney, a horizontal flue built to carry poisonous gases from lead smelting works out on to the open moor.

From Rookhope you take a stony track following the grouse moor route of A Pennine Journey, for a brief respite from the roads. You have conquered the Pennine ridge now and have a long descent down towards the east coast. The route rejoins the road by the stoop boundary marker, Dead Friar's Stone. The gravelly Waskerley Way on a disused railway track soon offers you a traffic-free route towards Consett, freewheeling through sheep-strewn moorland and past sparkling reservoirs. On tarmac tracks now, you will need a head for heights as you cycle over the lofty Hownsgill Viaduct high above the treetops.

If you wish to finish in Newcastle upon Tyne, turn off on to NCN 14 just before Consett, which will take you to the Tyne on good traffic-free tracks. Otherwise, you continue on cycletracks that avoid the centre of Consett despite sometimes taking you beside busy roads. You leave the urban area behind you, still following disused tracks of the Consett and Sunderland Railway.

Near the village of No Place, it is a short detour from the route to visit the Beamish Open Air Museum, dedicated to recreating nineteenth- and early-twentieth-century everyday life in the North-East of England. The railway cycle path offers you a green corridor through Washington's busy streets and delivers you to the banks of the River Wear. The route passes the Nissan car manufacturing plant at North Hylton. On tarmac tracks by the river, you will be reminded that Sunderland was, in the nineteenth

ROKER PIER AND LIGHTHOUSE. © SHUTTERSTOCK/STUARTS PHOTOGRAPHY

century, possibly the world's greatest shipbuilding port. This was a city whose wealth was built on more than ships and coal – in the seventh century, Benedict Biscop brought French glaziers here, introducing glass-making to Britain, and Sunderland was a major glass producer in the nineteenth century, manufacturing most of the glass for the Crystal Palace. You pass the National Glass Centre on the harbour. The route follows the banks of the river to Sunderland's seafront, where the Sea to Sea ends at Roker Rocks, and you should dip your front wheel in the water.

The Sea to Sea has high, exposed sections which can be challenging at any time of year, but may be particularly difficult in winter. The lines of snow poles on the Pennines' highest roads should remind you that these ways are often cut off in winter weather. Accommodation is also often closed over winter. The majority of the well-waymarked route is on road or well-surfaced tracks; a gravel bike would be a good compromise to tackle the hilly roads and gravelly, occasionally muddy, off-road sections. There are mountain braids that can be chosen over some road sections.

There are many ways to cross a country, whether on roads or across mountains, but the Sea to Sea is one of the best. It offers you a classic Lake District pass, the bustling, outdoorsy Keswick on the shores of Derwent Water and the verdant Eden Valley. With your legs warmed, you have a challenging mid-section that climbs over the Pennine spine, England's watershed. You follow one of England's greatest rivers towards the seafront city of Sunderland. The Sea to Sea is a route that reminds you how diverse England's green countryside is, as well as showing you how a nation was built.

17 SEA TO SEA (C2C): ESSENTIAL INFORMATION

RIDE ESSENTIALS

Start: **Whitehaven, Cumbria, England**
End: **Sunderland, Tyne and Wear, England**
Distance: **219km**
Ascent/descent: **3,010m/3,000m**

HOW TO GET THERE

Whitehaven has a railway station on the Cumbrian Coast Line, which connects to the West Coast Main Line at Carlisle. Newcastle is the closest international airport.

Sunderland has regional train services to Newcastle, which is on the East Coast Main Line. Newcastle is the closest international airport. Newcastle also has international ferry services to the Netherlands.

TIME TO COMPLETE

Minimum days: **2 days/15 hours**
Maximum days: **4 days/21 hours**

PROS

- **Sunderland** – often overshadowed by its Tyneside neighbour, Sunderland is a great city to end your adventure in. With museums, riverside walks and sandy beaches, it has a fascinating history to explore (although it was also through Sunderland's port that the cholera epidemic arrived in Britain in the 1830s).

- **Industrial Revolution** – from mine workings to harbourside cranes, this route offers plenty of reminders that even the heathered moorland was at the heart of England's Industrial Revolution. You can learn more about Britain's industrial heritage at the Beamish Open Air Museum, National Glass Centre and Whitehaven's Beacon Museum.

- **Best C2C** – of the (non-MTB) routes, the C2C – which offers a gentle Lake District route, a spectacular Pennine challenge, great railway cycle paths, an iconic river and Sunderland's award-winning beaches – has something for everyone.

CONS

- **Pennines** – your ride over the Pennines is challenging, with steep ascents, difficult descents and exposed roads.

- **Remote** – the route often avoids towns and villages, even when it passes close to them. In the Lakes and on the Pennines you are often some distance from the closest shop or cafe, and you may need to divert off-route to find overnight accommodation.

VARIATIONS

There is an alternative start at Workington – the routes merge at Keswick. At Consett, you can take the NCN 14 to finish at Tyneside rather than Sunderland. There are road braid alternatives to the off-road sections as well as mountain bike braids, some of which might be tackled on a gravel or hybrid bike.

GOOD TO KNOW

Specially commissioned sculptures are scattered along the C2C route. You should look out for the scrap metal Beamish Shorthorns on the Consett and Sunderland Railway Path, David Kemp's Old Transformers near the site of the Consett Steelworks and Tony Cragg's Terris Novalis at Knitsley. Sculptures also stand at the start and end of each route.

FURTHER INFORMATION

www.sustrans.org.uk/find-other-routes/c2c-or-sea-to-sea

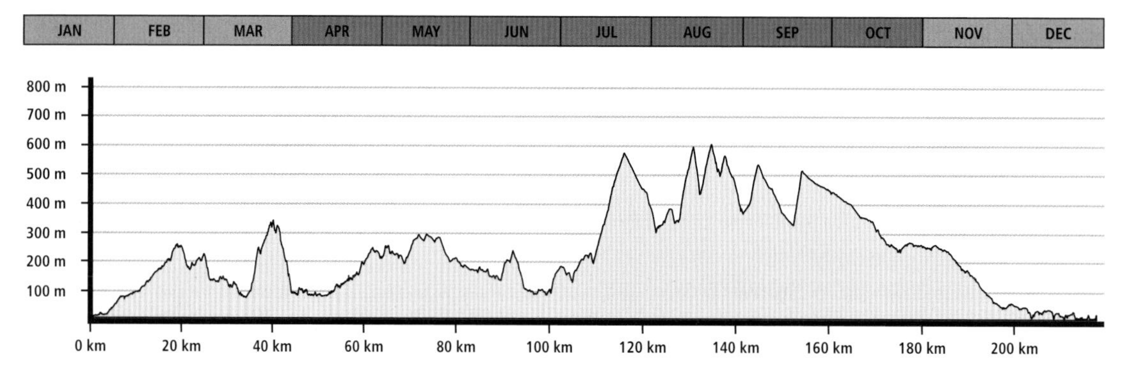

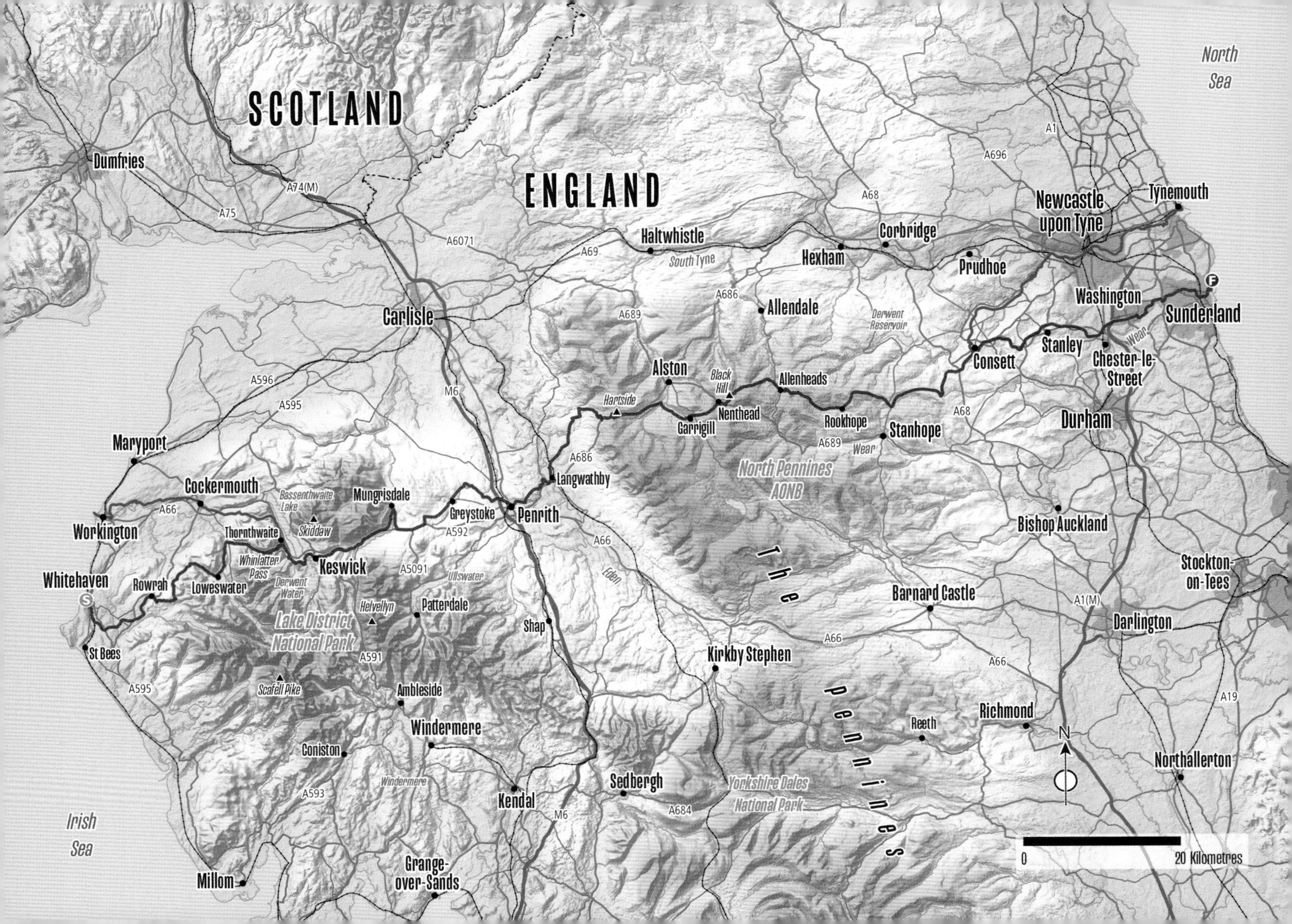

SCOTLAND
ENGLAND
North Sea
Irish Sea
Dumfries
Carlisle
Haltwhistle
South Tyne
Hexham
Corbridge
Prudhoe
Newcastle upon Tyne
Tynemouth
Washington
Sunderland
Allendale
Derwent Reservoir
Stanley
Chester-le-Street
Wear
Consett
Durham
Alston
Black Hill
Allenheads
Hartside
Garrigill
Nenthead
Rookhope
Stanhope
North Pennines AONB
Langwathby
Maryport
Cockermouth
Bassenthwaite Lake
Skiddaw
Mungrisdale
Greystoke
Penrith
Workington
Thornthwaite
Whinlatter Pass
Keswick
Derwent Water
Whitehaven
Rowrah
Loweswater
Ullswater
Helvellyn
Patterdale
Lake District National Park
Shap
Eden
St Bees
Scafell Pike
Ambleside
Windermere
Coniston
Kendal
Sedbergh
Grange-over-Sands
Millom
Bishop Auckland
Stockton-on-Tees
Barnard Castle
Darlington
Kirkby Stephen
The Pennines
Reeth
Richmond
Northallerton
Yorkshire Dales National Park
N
0
20 Kilometres
A74(M)
A75
A6071
A69
A68
A696
A1
A686
A689
A596
A595
M6
A66
A592
A5091
A591
A593
A684
A1(M)
A19

18 SOUTH DOWNS WAY – 160km

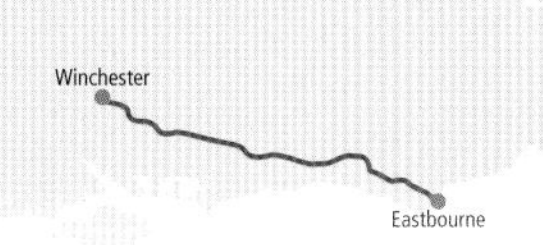

The 160-kilometre South Downs Way is the only National Trail that falls completely within a national park, and one of only two that can be followed by cyclists as a bridleway (the other being the Pennine Bridleway, which forms part of the Great North Trail – see page 21). The Way connects the historical cathedral city of Winchester with the south-coast seaside resort of Eastbourne. It follows old drovers' roads, historic bridleways and well-trodden routes over the chalk ridges of the rolling South Downs.

You begin your ride in Winchester – the official start is by the City Mill, which was once a YHA hostel, but many choose to start a few metres down the road by the statue of King Alfred. On busy paths by the river, you follow the Itchen to the outskirts of the city. The route crosses the river near the historic boys' school of Winchester College and the ruins of the bishops' palace of Wolvesey Castle, where Bloody Mary held her wedding reception to Philip of Spain in 1554. After crossing high above the M3 motorway, you separate from the walkers to skirt the sports ground rather than cut across it, but both routes rejoin through the traditional Chilcomb village.

Through poppied farmland, your peaceful ride may be interrupted by the sound of gunfire from the nearby Ministry of Defence's rifle range. The route takes a gravelly bridleway shaded by trees to reach the natural amphitheatre of Cheesefoot Head; General Eisenhower addressed American troops here on the eve of D-Day. The Way follows well-surfaced tracks through the corn fields of Temple Valley – this is home to the popular Boomtown music festival so the route may be diverted in August.

You emerge on to the road at the seventeenth-century The Milbury's pub, famous for its deep indoor well.

After a brief road section you take leaf-strewn lanes before contouring around the steep sides of Beacon Hill. You follow roads through Exton before joining the hikers on the chalky bridleway over the orchid-rich Old Winchester Hill – you may want to lock your bike up and explore the Iron Age hill fort and Bronze Age barrows. Your bumpy ride continues on grassy trails around the edge of Butser Hill, the highest point on the South Downs Way.

The route climbs on forestry tracks through the beech woods of Queen Elizabeth Park, a popular mountain biking destination. Near Buriton on tarmac tracks, you pass the disused chalk pits and encounter a rolling up-and-down section of the South Downs. Beneath the Vandalian Tower, where Emma Hamilton would wait for Lord Nelson, you face a tough climb – perhaps a hike-a-bike – over Harting Downs. You take wood-fringed paths to the five Bronze Age barrows at the Devil's Jumps – on Midsummer's Day, the barrows align with the setting sun. The route takes you across the high Downs, with panoramic views on occasionally rutted tracks.

Hawthorn-fragranced, hedgerowed tracks through farms on gentle gradients turn into steeper climbs as you leave Amberley, the halfway point of the route. You can detour into Washington if you fancy a pub lunch or need to stop at a shop. On stony, chalky trails, you reach Chanctonbury Ring. This prehistoric hill fort has a long association with

◀ THE SOUTH DOWNS WAY NEAR AMBERLEY. © STEPHEN ROSS

CLIMBING AWAY FROM WINCHESTER. © STEPHEN ROSS

the Devil, who is said to linger here to offer you a bowl of soup in exchange for your soul. You can watch the paragliders hovering over the rim of Steyning Bowl.

The Way passes the National Trust's Devil's Dyke Valley; now a tranquil Site of Special Scientific Interest, in Victorian times it hosted funfairs and cable cars. There is a wide, chalky bridleway along the valley if you want to explore further. Near Clayton you ride past the two white windmills, Jack and Jill, near the top of a breezy hill. You face a stiff climb up and over Ditchling Beacon, the final, elongated climb dreaded by road cyclists on the British Heart Foundation's annual London to Brighton sponsored cycle ride – you cross the charity route at the car park on the Beacon's summit, where there is often an ice cream van.

On the outskirts of Brighton, you cross over the busy A27 main road and pass under the railway. You reach Alfriston, where the South Downs Way divides. Most walkers take the southern route as it follows the River Cuckmere to the spectacular white cliffs of the Seven Sisters, but this is a footpath rather than a bridleway. As a cyclist, you must take the inland route, which passes the chalk figure of the Long Man of Wilmington. The sixteenth- or seventeenth-century monument, which is holding two staves and is also nicknamed the 'Green Man', is one of only two remaining human hill figures in England (the other being the Cerne Abbas Giant, although some horse figures include human riders).

At Jevington, the Hungry Monk restaurant, where banoffee pie was invented in 1971, has long since closed. The Way takes a well-surfaced, gritty bridleway that cuts a green path through fields and past the golf course, skirting Eastbourne. The route ends at an ice cream kiosk just off the Duke's Drive. If you wish to visit the Seven Sisters, you can continue on the often-busy coastal road to Birling Gap, near the Belle Tout clifftop lighthouse. Otherwise, you may want to continue east another three kilometres to reach Eastbourne's Victorian pleasure pier and celebrate your ride with fish and chips on the shingly beach.

You rarely find yourself on country roads on the South Downs Way, with the majority of the trail being off-road. Much of the bridleway is (sometimes rutted and puddly) chalky tracks, or granite or flint-topped trails.

CYCLING OVER THE CHALKY SOUTH DOWNS. © STEPHEN ROSS

You occasionally find yourself on grassy trods, muddy paths by farmers' fields or bumping over tree roots. You will find yourself opening and shutting a lot of gates along the trail, and may have to avoid sheep or cows. Sharp turns, tricky descents and boneshaking sections of trail will all be encountered. Although the South Downs Way often skirts the summits of hills, usually due to erosion, there is still a challenging amount of climbing on the route.

The South Downs Way can be cycled at any time of year, although facilities and accommodation may shut over the winter months. It can be cycled in either direction, and there is a train station at the midway point at Amberley if you want to tackle it as a ride of two halves. The Way prefers to stay high on the ridge, so you will have to detour from the route to find food and somewhere to sleep, although there are water taps on the trail.

The South Downs Way is not an easy ride, but it is one that rolls through the sun-strewn South Downs, offering panoramic green views, challenging descents, shaded wooded paths and hilltops of butterflies and flowers. This is not wild, rugged mountains or high, heathered moorland, but it is a verdant haven that offers you a glorious escape from the bustle of the urban south-east sprawl; these golden cornfields and gorsey, grassy tracks are unbelievably close to London, and are the perfect weekend escape from the city.

18 SOUTH DOWNS WAY: ESSENTIAL INFORMATION

RIDE ESSENTIALS

Start: **Winchester, Hampshire, England**
End: **Eastbourne, East Sussex, England**
Distance: **160km**
Ascent/descent: **2,820m/2,810m**

HOW TO GET THERE

Winchester has a direct rail connection to London (approximately one hour) where rail connections can be made to London's airports and to national and international rail services.

Eastbourne has direct rail connections to London Gatwick Airport, and to London.

TIME TO COMPLETE

Minimum days: **2 days/17 hours**
Maximum days: **4 days/23 hours**

PROS

- **Water taps** – there are water taps, often sponsored by local rotary organisations, on the route, so even on the hottest days you will not have to carry litres of water.

- **Flowers** – the chalk-rich fields encourage bee-heavy clover, carpets of buttercups, daisies and poppies, yellow rattle, cowslips, orchids and the purple round-headed rampion. The sweet-scented flowers attract hordes of butterflies.

- **Sunshine** – Eastbourne has some claim to being the sunniest town in Great Britain, and the South Downs enjoys more hours of sunshine and less rain than most other areas of Britian.

CONS

- **Events** – the South Downs Way is a popular route, and several charity and endurance events take place on it each year. You should check the calendar before planning your trip, and also try to avoid clashing with the Boomtown festival en route near Winchester.

- **Livestock** – you may encounter sheep and cows on the route, and with them plenty of gates to pass through.

- **Stones** – the route is often topped with loose stone that can make descents tricky, and can make you feel like you are slipping back with each turn of the pedal on uphills.

VARIATIONS

There are no variations, but many riders choose to make short detours into towns and villages.

GOOD TO KNOW

Attempting to cycle the Way in twenty-four hours is a popular endurance challenge, but some attempt the double – Winchester to Eastbourne and back again. Ian Leitch set the men's record (fifteen hours thirty-five minutes) in 2016; Ian is also believed to have ridden the fastest South Downs Way (seven hours three minutes). Amanda Brooks set the women's record for the double (twenty-one hours forty-four minutes) in 2014.

FURTHER INFORMATION

South Downs Way Guidemap (Vertebrate Publishing, 2020); *www.nationaltrail.co.uk/en_GB/trails/south-downs-way*

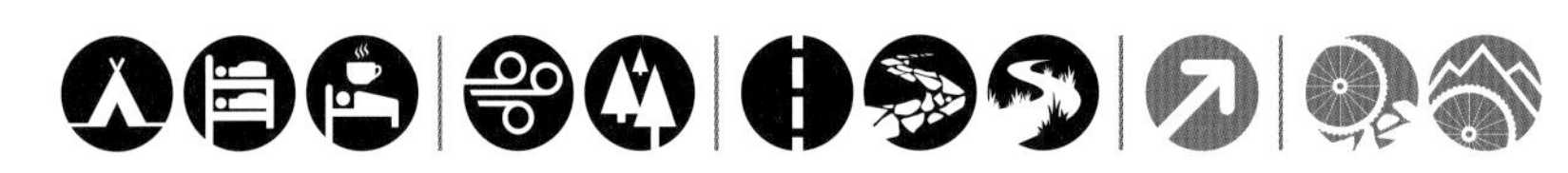

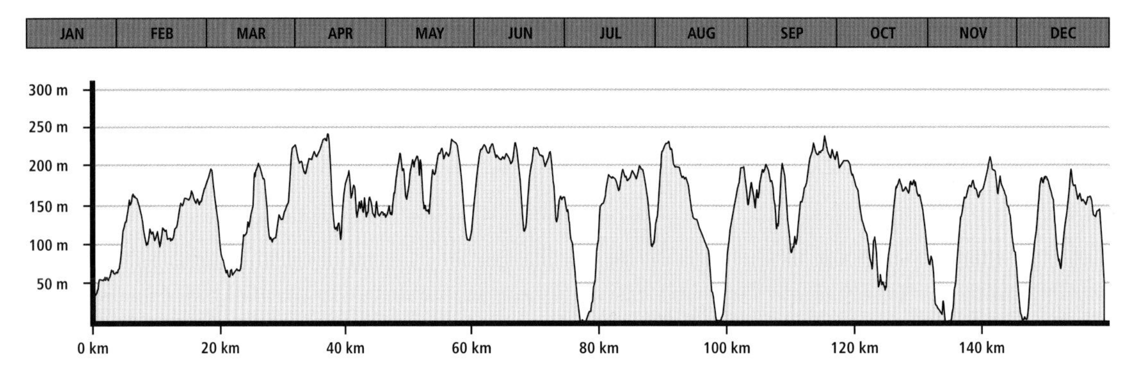

ENGLAND
English Channel
South Downs National Park
North Downs
Surrey Hills
Winchester
Southampton
Eastleigh
Bishop's Waltham
Whitchurch
Basingstoke
New Alresford
Alton
Farnham
Aldershot
Farnborough
Woking
Guildford
Cobham
Coulsdon
Redhill
Oxted
Sevenoaks
Tonbridge
Royal Tunbridge Wells
East Grinstead
Crawley
Horsham
Haslemere
Billingshurst
Midhurst
Petersfield
Buriton
South Harting
Cocking
Haywards Heath
Burgess Hill
Uckfield
Crowborough
Heathfield
Hailsham
Henfield
Storrington
Washington
Amberley
Houghton
Steyning
Pyecombe
Plumpton
Lewes
Rodmell
Southease
Alfriston
Jevington
Eastbourne
Beachy Head
Seaford
Peacehaven
Brighton
Worthing
Littlehampton
Bognor Regis
Chichester
Waterlooville
Fareham
Portsmouth
Exton
Beacon Hill
Henwood Down
Butser Hill
Hyden Hill
Linch Down
Heyshott Down
Glatting Beacon
Chantry Hill
Truleigh Hill
Ditchling Beacon
Castle Hill
Arun
Ouse
Cowes
Ryde
Newport
Isle of Wight
Sandown
Ventnor
A34
M3
A32
A3
A283
A272
A23
M23
A264
A267
A22
A27
A3(M)
M27
M25
M20
N
0
20 Kilometres

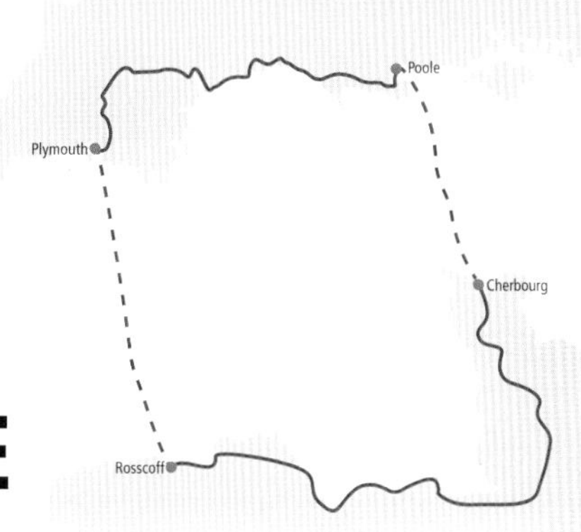

19

19 TOUR DE MANCHE – 1,005km

The 1,005-kilometre Tour de Manche is a route that follows the shores of the English Channel, or La Manche. It begins at the ferry port in Plymouth and follows part of Devon's Coast to Coast route as it skirts Dartmoor. After travelling cross-country to Exeter, the route follows the Devon coast before heading inland through Dorset. You return to the coast near Sandbanks and the ferry port of Poole. After crossing the channel you reach Cherbourg-en-Cotentin and follow green cycleways and quiet roads along the Normandy coast, passing the abbey island of Mont Saint-Michel. The French segment takes you through Normandy's bocage wood and farmland and along the Emerald and Pink Granite coasts to finish at Roscoff.

The route begins at Plymouth on NCN 27, or the Drake's Trail. The cycleway goes along the port roads and you follow the trail on-road around the Hoe, where Sir Francis Drake is reputed to have played bowls before sailing off to fight the Spanish Armada. The lighthouse on the green is John Smeaton's, relocated from Eddystone Rocks, and is one of the first modern lighthouses. You pass the beautiful art deco Tinside Lido which juts out towards the sea. These roads offer great seaside views but may be choked by motorists in the summer and have little in the way of cycling infrastructure.

You leave the traffic behind you as you cross the River Plym and join the riverside West Devon Way – a treelined, tarmac track. The route takes you past the grounds of the Georgian Saltram House; there is a tearoom in the chapel. You take a disused railway track north on traffic-free trails to Tavistock, a gentle route through dark tunnels, across bridges and along tree-lined cuttings. The route takes briefly to the roads through Peter Tavy and Mary Tavy before returning to the railway, for a spectacular section that offers great views of Dartmoor.

Leaving Okehampton, you take lumpy roads that are often busy with overflow traffic from the A30 main road to Exeter; you have to negotiate a tricky crossing of the main road. After cycling through the suburbs, you reach the River Exe near the Fat Pig Brewery. Here you take the excellent, wide and traffic-free paths by the river and then the canal, past the waterside Double Locks pub. Near Countess Wear you join roadside cycle paths to reach Topsham. You cycle past the town's pretty quayside to reach the Exe Estuary Trail, a modern, well-surfaced and largely off-road cycle path that follows the river past Lympstone, and the marine camp, to the seaside resort of Exmouth.

You are now on NCN 2, the route that will take you all the way through to Poole; plans are in place to extend it still further to Dover. The disused railway line offers an off-road route to Budleigh Salterton, where you must cycle slightly inland to cross the River Otter. You should be cautious on the steep descent into Sidmouth on bendy, thin roads, past the tourist hotspot of Jacob's Ladder. After an easy ride along Sidmouth's long, stony seafront, you face a hilly road section that becomes steeper after the Donkey Sanctuary.

Following the River Axe to Axminster the route becomes gentler, if not entirely flat. The trail takes hedgerowed lanes over rolling hills, with panoramic views of green fields to

◀ A GREENWAY FOLLOWING THE RIVER VIRE THROUGH NORMANDY.
© GRAHAM BLAND – *AWAYWANDERING.BLOGSPOT.COM*

Dorchester, entering the town via a bridleway that skirts the Iron Age fort of Maiden Castle. On flatter roads that trace the route of the River Frome you reach the white sands of Studland Bay, where you must take the chain ferry to reach Poole. There is a daily sailing to Cherbourg and one return – the crossing takes four and a half hours.

The French section of the route takes advantage of La Vélomaritime, France's 1,500-kilometre Atlantic coast route. You arrive at Cherbourg's harbour, one of the largest artificial harbours in the world. Near the sixteenth-century Château des Ravalet, you leave the city on gentle roads that take you across the Cotentin peninsula. Near Rocheville you join the wide, gravelly Voies Vertes, greenways that often take advantage of disused railway tracks. The trail passes the tall walls of the ruins of the fortified Château de Saint-Sauveur-le-Vicomte. At Carentan, you return to country roads.

You take traffic-free towpaths along the River Vire through the historic city of Saint-Lô before returning to hilly roads through Normandy's bocage. Back on greenways, you pass the ruins of the La Souleuvre Viaduct, built by Gustave Eiffel; you can now bungee jump from the top of one of the five pillars. The route follows cycle paths to the coast at Pontaubault where it takes quiet country roads to Mont Saint-Michel.

The abbey-topped tidal island of Mont Saint-Michel has been a garrison, a prison and a place of pilgrimage. Monks have lived on the island since the sixth century, but the Benedictine abbey was founded in 966. At the busiest summer times you have to walk or take the shuttle bus across the causeway, but at quieter times you can cycle across to the island on the wooden plankway. You continue along the coast on greenways.

ONE OF MANY VARIED TRAFFIC-FREE CYCLE TRAILS ACROSS DEVON, BETWEEN SIDMOUTH AND OKEHAMPTON. © GRAHAM BLAND – *AWAYWANDERING.BLOGSPOT.COM*

Near Saint-Malo, now a busy port, known for its corsairs, you return to the roads. The Tour passes through Rothéneuf, famous for its rock sculptures carved by the hermit monk Abbé Fouré. You take the seabus boat to Dinard to avoid a busy section of road – the seabus does not operate in the winter. You travel along the Emerald Coast on-road, but the route is often slightly inland. The sea views get better after Erquy, but the ascents and descents get steeper too. On spectacular clifftop roads you reach Paimpol, with its ruined thirteenth-century abbey. You enjoy one final seaside stretch along Brittany's Pink Granite Coast to reach Roscoff, where there are one or two daily crossings to Plymouth; overnight crossings take eleven and half hours, but daytime crossings are quicker.

If the 1,005 kilometres of the Tour are too much of a challenge, there is a 440-kilometre Petit Tour that goes from Weymouth to Dorchester, and then follows the Tour to Poole. You follow the Tour route from Cherbourg to Saint-Malo, via Mont Saint-Michel, and then return to England via Jersey.

The Tour de Manche is a unique loop route that takes in the coastline of two neighbours, France and Britain. It is still a work in progress and some sections are provisional. It often relies too heavily on roads, which are frequently busy in the summer season. It is, however, a route that includes some of the best coastal views the two countries have to offer – Devon's Jurassic Coast, the unique island of Mont Saint-Michel and Normandy's Pink Granite Coast. It also meanders inland through historic cities, past castles, cathedrals and chateaux and through rural farmland. If you want a Big Ride that is an opportunity to travel and one that provides sea breezes, stiff cliff climbs and seafood fresh off the boats, the Tour de Manche is the trip for you.

A GREENWAY THROUGH BRITTANY, ON THE WAY TO FREHEL. © GRAHAM BLAND – *AWAYWANDERING.BLOGSPOT.COM*

19 TOUR DE MANCHE: ESSENTIAL INFORMATION

RIDE ESSENTIALS

Start:	**Plymouth, Devon, England**
End:	**Roscoff, Brittany, France**
Distance:	**1,005km**
Ascent/descent:	**7,360m/7,370m**
	England: 2,870m/2,880m;
	France: 4,490m/4,490m

HOW TO GET THERE

Plymouth has high-speed train services to Bristol and London. The closest international airport is at Exeter. Plymouth has ferry services to Roscoff and, in the summer, Santander.

Roscoff has local train stations, with connections to high-speed services at Morlaix. Roscoff has ferry services to Plymouth. The closest international airport is Paris, and there are also international train services, including the Eurostar to London.

TIME TO COMPLETE

Minimum days:	**England 2 days/19 hours**
	France 8 days/50 hours
Maximum days:	**England 5 days/26 hours**
	France 12 days/69 hours

PROS

- **Seafood** – Dorset's coast is famous for its sweet, juicy scallops, and the Cotentin peninsula for its fresh oysters. You can also try clams, mussels, whelks and Brittany's blue lobsters.

- **Coast** – from the fossil-rich Jurassic Coast to the high cliffs of the Emerald Coast and the sculpted Pink Granite Coast, the route offers diverse and beautiful coastal views.

CONS

- **Roads** – the route makes extensive use of minor roads; although not main roads, sections such as Okehampton to Exeter on the edge of Dartmoor and coastal roads past France's busy ports may be congested, particularly in summer.

- **Prevailing winds** – you cycle the English and French segments in opposite directions. If you cycle the route clockwise from Plymouth, you will generally have the wind in your favour in England and against you in France.

VARIATIONS

There is a shorter Petit Tour de Manche, from Weymouth to Poole, and from Cherbourg to Saint-Malo and on to Jersey. There are link routes to nearby towns and historical sites.

GOOD TO KNOW

The French section of the Tour de Manche takes advantage of La Vélomaritime, a cycle route that runs along the French coast of the channel from Dunkirk to Roscoff. At Roscoff you can continue on to Vélodyssée, France's Atlantic coast route that will take you all the way to the Spanish border. La Vélomaritime is part of the longer EV4, one of seventeen long-distance European cycle trails that have been under development since 1995. EV4 links Roscoff to Kiev in Ukraine.

FURTHER INFORMATION

www.freewheelingfrance.com/where-to-go/the-tour-de-manche-bike-route.html

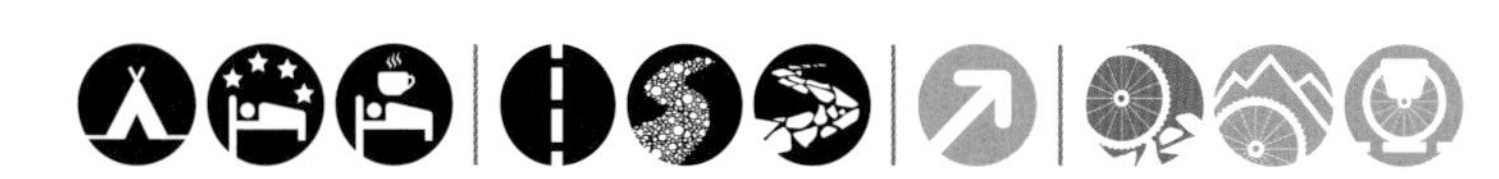

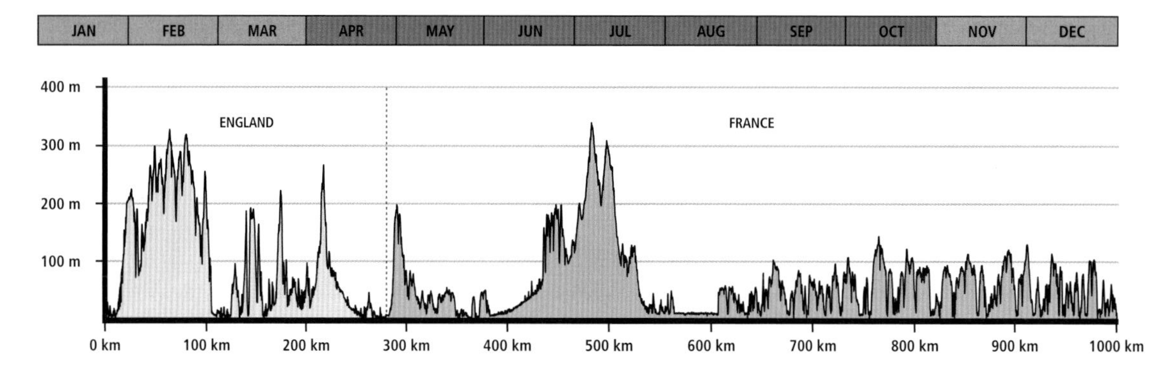

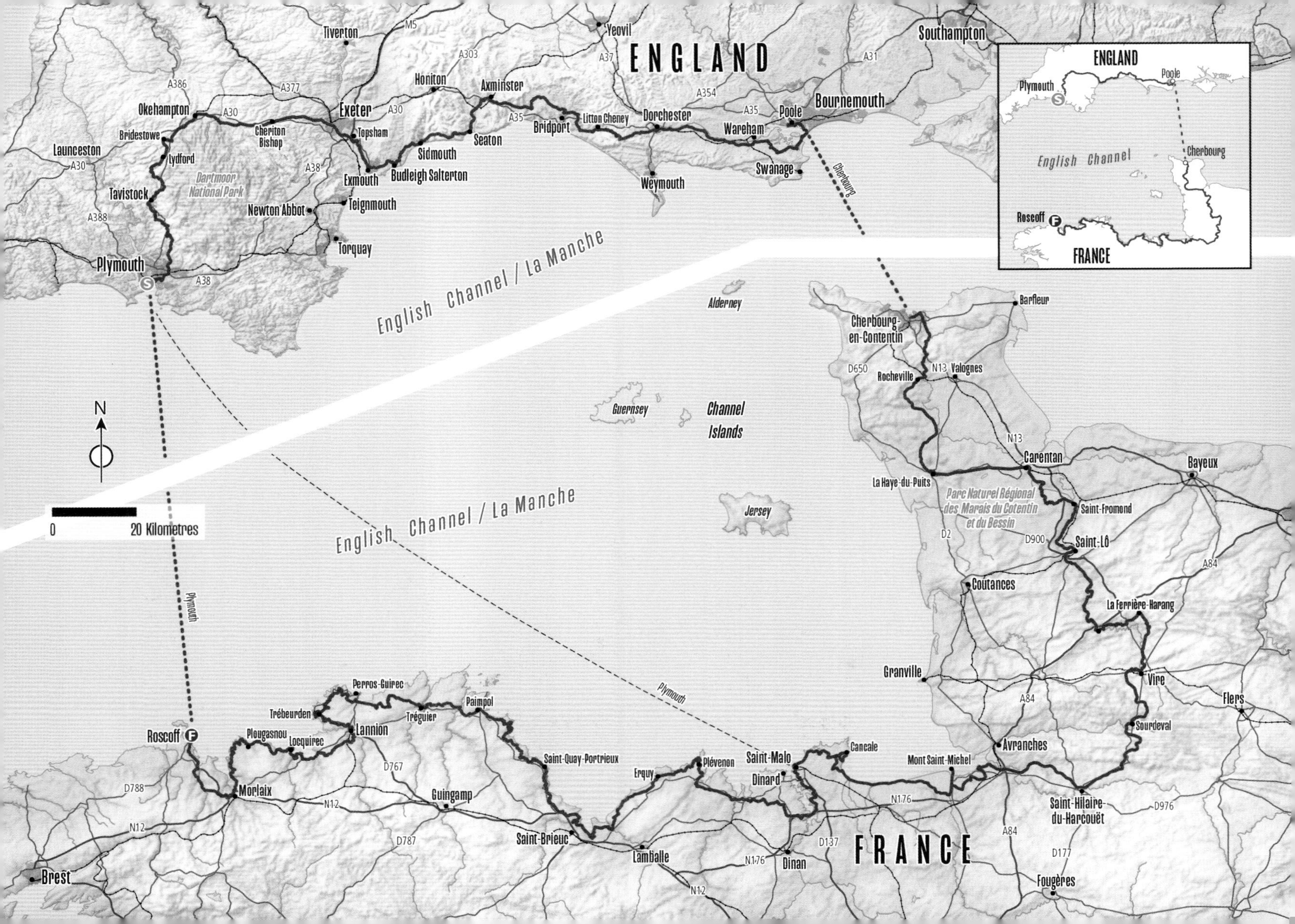
ENGLAND
Tiverton
Yeovil
Southampton
M5
A303
A37
A31
A386
A377
Honiton
Axminster
A354
Okehampton
Exeter
A30
Bournemouth
Poole
A35
Cheriton
Bishop
Topsham
Bridport
Litton Cheney
Dorchester
Wareham
Bridestowe
Seaton
Launceston
Lydford
Sidmouth
A30
Dartmoor
National Park
A38
Exmouth
Budleigh Salterton
Swanage
Weymouth
Tavistock
Newton Abbot
Teignmouth
A388
Torquay
Plymouth
A38
Cherbourg
English Channel / La Manche
Alderney
Barfleur
Cherbourg-
en-Contentin
D650
Rocheville
N13
Valognes
Guernsey
Channel
Islands
N13
Carentan
Bayeux
La Haye-du-Puits
Parc Naturel Régional
des Marais du Cotentin
et du Bessin
Saint-Fromond
Jersey
0
20 Kilometres
English Channel / La Manche
D2
D900
Saint-Lô
A84
Coutances
La Ferrière-Harang
Plymouth
Granville
Vire
Flers
A84
Perros-Guirec
Paimpol
Trébeurden
Tréguier
Sourdeval
Roscoff
Lannion
Plougasnou
Locquirec
Cancale
Avranches
Saint-Malo
Mont Saint-Michel
Saint-Quay-Portrieux
Plévenon
D767
Erquy
Dinard
D788
Morlaix
Guingamp
N12
N176
Saint-Hilaire-
du-Harcouët
D976
N12
D787
Saint-Brieuc
D137
FRANCE
A84
Lamballe
N176
Dinan
D177
Brest
N12
Fougères
ENGLAND
Plymouth
Poole
English Channel
Cherbourg
Roscoff
FRANCE

20

20 TOUR DE PEAK DISTRICT – 252km

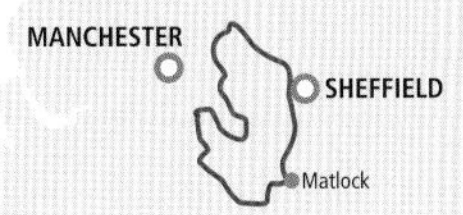

The 252-kilometre Tour de Peak District is a route that loops around the edge of the Peak District National Park. It is a route created by outdoor writer and photographer Chiz Dakin, who has written a route guide (*Cycling in the Peak District*). While there are long stretches on quiet country roads, the Tour also takes advantage of the Peak District's best railway tracks, towpaths, reservoir roads and riverside trails. By circling rather than going through the Peak, the Tour offers panoramic views while avoiding the busy honeypot Peak District villages.

The Tour starts in the (often congested) quaint spa town of Matlock. You have a gentle climb out of town past the popular fishing spot of Cawdor Pond, a disused quarry. The trail passes the medieval manor house of Snitterton Hall, its fishing pond perhaps associated with seventeenth-century angler Isaak Walton. The route takes advantage of the pleasant Derwent Valley Heritage Way as it follows the river towards Rowsley, where you have to negotiate a busy, challenging junction with the A6 main road.

The Tour follows roads close to the River Derwent through Beeley, on the Chatsworth estate, followed by a rolling route through heathered moors and green farmland on the very edge of the Peak District National Park. On undulating, hawthorn-fringed lanes, you reach Smeekley Wood. You have to tackle the busy, elongated roundabout at Owler Bar on the outskirts of Sheffield, and the often traffic-heavy B6064 between Totley and Big Moor. The situation does not improve with a short section on the A625 main road near Fox House, a key through-route into the Peak.

You can remain on busy, popular roads to reach Ringinglow or take the stony Houndkirk Road over Burbage Moor. On undulating roads, with views of Sheffield on the horizon, you pass Redmires Reservoirs. After the Three Merry Lads and Sportsman, home to the Dark Peak Fell Runners, you face a steep descent with blind bends on a busy road to the Rivelin Valley bottom. You might reward yourself on the steep climb towards Dungworth by a short detour to the ice cream parlour at local farm Our Cow Molly. The route passes the Royal Hotel, famous for its pies and Christmas carols, and goes on to a challenging, curved descent down to Damflask with a difficult reverse-angle road junction.

The trail climbs on narrow tarmac lanes to Holdworth, and reaches Kirk Edge Road near the Carmelite Monastery of the Holy Spirit; the Tour de France tackled Kirk Edge Road on its 2014 Yorkshire Stage. Passing Ewden Village, between the Broomhead and More Hall reservoirs, you have another steep ascent to Bolsterstone, home to an award-winning male voice choir. You can enjoy a long, occasionally steep, descent past Midhope Reservoir and over Langsett Reservoir, where you join leaf-littered reservoir tracks; there is a hillier road alternative.

The route takes the good-quality, hard-surfaced Trans Pennine Trail along the River Don and around Winscar Reservoir before rejoining bendy, steep roads to reach Holmbridge. There is a long climb up Acres Lane on to a gravel track. You follow the Pennine Cycleway past Meltham and then enjoy the canal path route into Marsden.

◀ HEADING OVER HOUNDKIRK MOOR NEAR SHEFFIELD. © JOHN COEFIELD

Leaving Marsden on the ominously named Mount Road, you have a choice of the busy, fast A62 main road or a stony, grassy and often muddy track across Marsden Moor. You enjoy a long descent into Diggle on the Standedge Trail over the railway tunnel. On disused railway tracks, you follow the Pennine Bridleway through to Bottoms in Mossley. The route here again splits – you can take an urban route through the outskirts of Stalybridge, or the alternative is paved track, stony tracks and reservoir roads. On bumpy, cobbled lanes you reach Tintwistle and join reservoir tracks past Bottoms Reservoir. The route loops past the Roman fort of Melandra Castle then has a short section on the A636 – the narrow, painted cycle lane disappears from the main road at its tightest spot.

The routes reunite briefly at Charlesworth, where you face a long, curving climb on quiet roads. You then either head for New Mills or Hayfield. The New Mills route takes you on disused railway tracks and then an uneven stony track. The route joins the Peak Forest Canal near the Swizzels factory and takes a gravelly path that veers close to the canal edge. The alternative is via the bluebelled Sett Valley Trail into Hayfield and then quiet roads through Chinley and Whalley Bridge. The routes reconnect at Hawk Green.

You follow roads towards Bollington and have another stretch on the curved, busy Buxton New Road before cycling around another reservoir. The trail climbs on wooded lanes through Wincle and Danebridge, again contouring on the border of the Peak District National Park. As you cross Tittesworth Reservoir, you can see the high ridge of the Roaches rising beside you – the gritstone ridge is home to legendary Jenny Greenteeth, who stumbled into Doxey Pool and now lures children into the murky waters.

COUNTRY LANE BETWEEN DANEBRIDGE AND TITTESWORTH RESERVOIR. © CHIZ DAKIN – *GALLERIES.PEAKIMAGES.CO.UK*

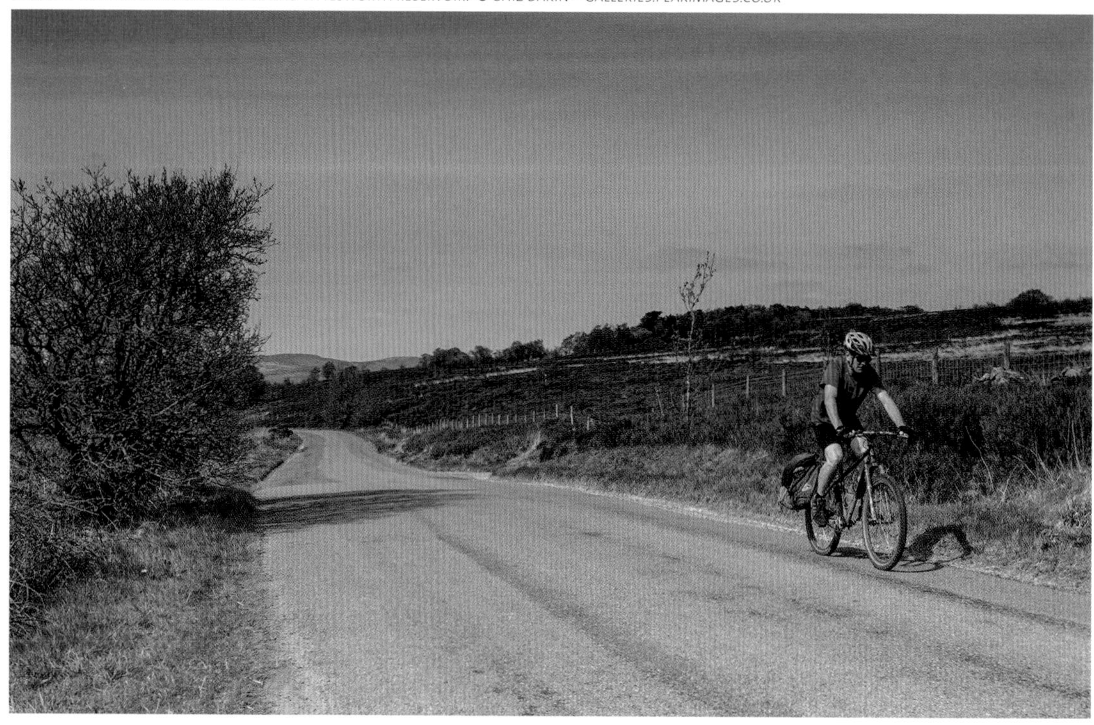

After a long, gentle descent along Blakelow Road towards Waterhouses, you briefly join the lorry-heavy A523. The route takes pleasant lanes through rolling farmland before joining the excellent Tissington Trail on disused railway tracks, on the outskirts of the market town of Ashbourne. You leave the railway at Tissington and climb up the narrow Tophill Lane, to tackle a short stretch of potholed, stony track; there is again an on-road alternative. It is a short road ride back to Matlock's train station.

The Tour is an excellent excuse to get out on your gravel or hybrid bike. Most of the off-road sections are well-surfaced and could be tackled cautiously by a tourer, particularly with appropriate tyres. There are road alternatives for each off-road section, although these are occasionally on busy roads. The Tour is well-served by train stations, and might be attempted on day excursions from Sheffield or Manchester. There are several pubs and cafes en route, although accommodation options are more limited. The Tour often follows NCN and other waymarked trails, but is not waymarked itself.

The Tour de Peak District is a pleasant ride on country lanes and tracks, with fine views across the Peak District. It is a reminder that the moors do not stop at the park's northern edge, and also of the Peak District's urban fringes. The route is rarely flat and never boring, and a good choice for novice bikepackers. Whether you want dramatic gritstone ridges on the horizon, picnics next to sparkling water, mulchy paths through bluebell woods or pub lunches with views of the hills, the tranquil Tour de Peak District will offer something to enchant you.

THE ROACHES, HEN CLOUD AND TITTESWORTH RESERVOIR. © JOHN COEFIELD

20 TOUR DE PEAK DISTRICT: ESSENTIAL INFORMATION

RIDE ESSENTIALS

Start:	**Matlock, Derbyshire, England**
End:	**Matlock, Derbyshire, England**
Distance:	**252km**
Ascent/descent:	**4,270m/4,270m**

HOW TO GET THERE

Matlock has local train services to Derby and Nottingham where connections can be made to mainline services. The closest international airports are Manchester and East Midlands.

TIME TO COMPLETE

Minimum days:	**2 days/21 hours**
Maximum days:	**5 days/29 hours**

PROS

- **Produce** – the Tour passes the Our Cow Molly farm, which produces delicious ice cream and milk, Bradfield Brewery with its Belgian Blue, Bollington's microbrewery with its strong Oat Mill Stout and Holmfirth Vineyard. You should make a short detour to Ashbourne to try their unique gingerbread.

- **Picnics** – there are plenty of spots for an impromptu picnic lunch, but also benches with panoramic views at the top of Greenhouse Lane near Ringinglow, by Bolsterstone's church and in the bluebell wood near the River Sett.

- **Railway** – the Tour not only makes good use of disused railway tracks but also passes by or close to more than a dozen train stations, including Marsden, Chinley, Broadbottom and Grindleford, as well as the heritage railway at Rowsley and Darley Dale.

CONS

- **Hilly** – although there are no monster climbs, the route continually ascends to descend to then ascend again.

- **Roads** – the Tour is often on roads. Some of these roads are main roads, some are busy – particularly in summer – and some have steep ascents or descends with plenty of curves.

- **Sightseeing** – although there are plenty of glorious views and lots of towns and villages, this route does not take you to the Peak District's most famous sites – it doesn't take you to the top of its gritstone edges, to stone circles, to Chatsworth or Haddon Hall, to the Dove Valley or the pudding shop in Bakewell.

VARIATIONS

There are road alternatives for all the off-road sections, although sometimes on busy roads. There is also a link to Grindleford.

GOOD TO KNOW

If you fancy a tougher Peak District challenge, you could take part in the Tour of the Peak Sportive, a 185-kilometre road event that includes a timed climb of Winnats Pass. It follows the route of the classic Tour of the Peak road race, which was held from 1943 to 2005. Mark Lovatt, who was born in Leek on the edge of the Peak, won the race six times in a row (from 1998 to 2003).

FURTHER INFORMATION

Cycling in the Peak District (Cicerone, 2017).

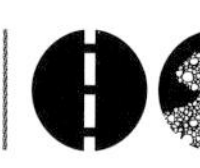

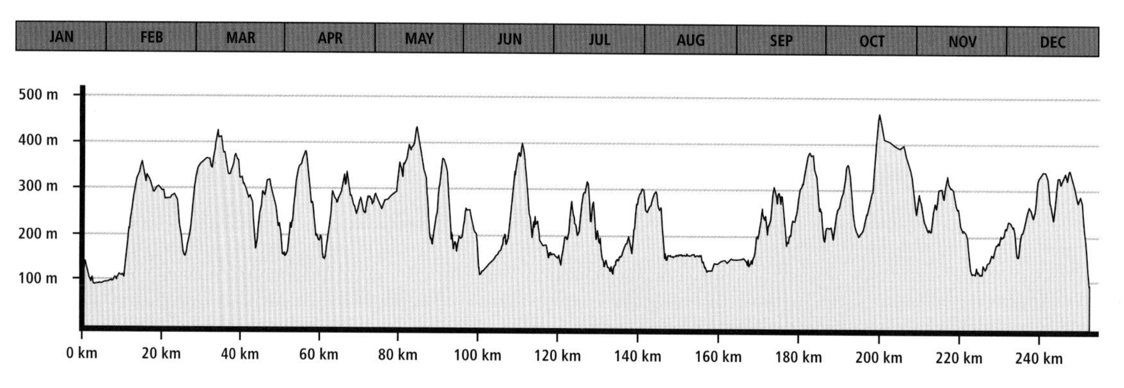

ENGLAND
Huddersfield
Slaithwaite
Linthwaite
Rochdale
M62
A640
Marsden
Meltham
Holmfirth
Diggle
Barnsley
A629
Oldham
A635
Holmbridge
A669
Failsworth
Penistone
M1
Winscar Reservoir
Mossley
Hoyland
Langsett
Midhopestones
A628
Woodhead Reservoir
Langsett Reservoir
Stocksbridge
Manchester
Stalybridge
Tintwistle
Torside Reservoir
A629
Hadfield
Bolsterstone
Hyde
M67
Bleaklow Head
Broomhead Reservoir
Glossop
A6102
M60
High Bradfield
A626
Derwent Reservoir
Stockport
Dungworth
Damflask Reservoir
Marple
A57
Sheffield
New Mills
Hayfield
Kinder Scout
Ladybower Reservoir
Rivelin Dams
A57
Edale
A6
Poynton
Hope
Bamford
Redmires Reservoirs
Castleton
A6187
A625
Hathersage
Peak District National Park
Whaley Bridge
Chapel-en-le-Frith
Dronfield
Derwent
A5004
A623
A625
Holmesfield
Bollington
A6
A621
A61
Macclesfield
Tideswell
Calver
Shining Tor
Buxton
A537
Burbage
Wye
Chesterfield
Langley
A54
A6
Chelmorton
Chatsworth
A619
Bakewell
A632
Beeley
Flash
Monyash
A54
Dane
A515
Rowsley
Wincle
A53
Longnor
Dove
Darley Dale
Clay Cross
Congleton
A523
Manifold
Birchover
Meerbrook
Matlock
S
F
Winster
Biddulph
A615
A5012
Bonsall
A515
Leek
A6
Derwent
N
Onecote
Parwich
B5056
Wirksworth
A53
A523
Carsington Water
Ilam
Thorpe
Ripley
Fenny Bentley
Waterhouses
Belper
0
10 Kilometres
A52
Ashbourne
A517
A52

21

21 TRANS PENNINE TRAIL – 338km

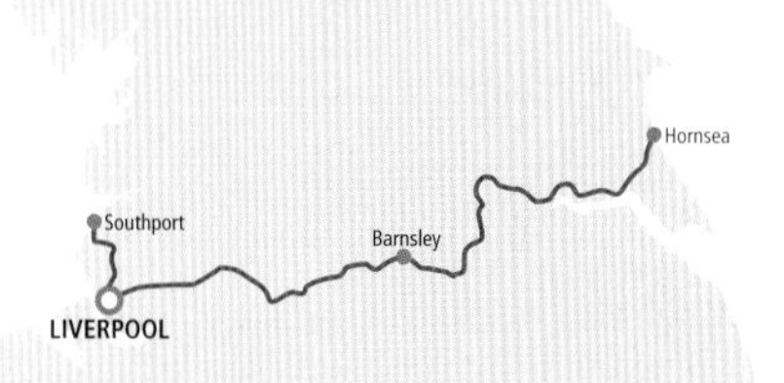

The 338-kilometre Trans Pennine Trail (TPT) is a sea-to-sea route that begins at Southport near Liverpool and finishes at Hornsea near Kingston upon Hull. On often purpose-built cycletracks that take advantage of disused railways, canal towpaths and riverside trails, the TPT is a well-waymarked route and does not feature sustained climbing or technical terrain. It skirts the busiest urban areas, such as Liverpool, Manchester, Doncaster and Hull. You follow the great northern rivers – the Mersey, the Don, the Ouse and the Humber – and climb over the Pennines to explore the edge of the Peak District as you travel from one coast to another.

There is a marker at the Trans Pennine Trail's start by Southport Beach, next to a shoal of metallic fish. You begin your adventure with a fine roll along the Southport seafront, on cycle paths running next to Marine Drive. At Big Ball's Hill you turn inland, following the trackbed of the Cheshire Lines Railway. Near Aintree, you join the grassy towpath along the Leeds and Liverpool Canal; you will have to lug your bike up the stairs at Wally's Steps. You pass the racecourse that is home to the Grand National. Back on the railway tracks you skirt Liverpool, although there is a loop into the city centre.

Near the John Lennon Airport you reach the banks of the Mersey, where you may see grey seals. The route crosses Ditton Brook to climb an impossibly steep ramp, which includes some steps. After the blue Runcorn Bridge you pass Spike Island, host to the Stone Roses's 1990 gig but also once polluted by Widnes's chemical industry. The route takes the wide gravel towpath along St Helen's Canal to reach the outskirts of Warrington. Near the decommissioned power station, which is currently being demolished, you may choose to stop at the Ferry Tavern, a pub that has sat on the island between the canal and the Mersey since 1762. After the wooded Sankey Valley Park, on a short road section you cross the Mersey to reach another towpath along the Manchester Ship Canal.

The route follows the sheltered disused railway track on the old Warrington and Altrincham Junction Railway. A short road section, leading to a waste recycling centre, takes you around Altrincham; this part of the trail also offers several close encounters with sewage works. In the shadow of the M60 Manchester ring motorway you rejoin the Mersey, passing through the nature reserve at Chorlton Water Park.

Near Simon's Bridge, built in 1901 by a legacy from local entrepreneur Henry Simon, you leave the Mersey briefly for a road route through Didsbury but return to the riverbanks to reach Stockport. The Trans Pennine Trail is at its hilliest as it leaves Stockport and heads for the edge of the Peak District. You take muddy trails through the Reddish Vale Country Park, following the River Tame. Near Denton, you face a short on-road stretch including a cut-through on a narrow pathway behind houses, and a short section on a green strip on a busy A road. As the route becomes more challenging you also face more roads, including a ride along the narrow, often busy A560 main road, and a curved road descent into Broadbottom.

◀ BRIDGE OVER THE RIVER MERSEY AND TRANS PENNINE TRAIL, SOUTH MANCHESTER. © SHUTTERSTOCK/IRONBELL

TRANS PENNINE TRAIL BETWEEN PENISTONE AND DUNFORD BRIDGE. © RACHEL DICKINSON – *WWW.INSPIRINGBIKERIDES.CO.UK*

On rolling and sometimes busy main roads, you climb past Glossop, looping past the Melandra Castle Roman fort. Near Woolley Bridge, the Pennine Bridleway offers a brief respite from the roads as you head for Hadfield. You take the broad Longdendale Trail on a long, gentle climb past a series of reservoirs on the northern border of the Peak District. After the reservoirs you face a tricky crossing of the busy A628, a main route between Manchester and Sheffield, and a steep push up a stony track. Your reward is a glorious ridgetop ride on a gravelly, grassy track with panoramic views of Howden Moors. Staying high on the heathered moorland, you have two more crossings of the main road to negotiate before you reach Windle Edge on quiet roads, the Trans Pennine Trail's highest point.

You descend towards Winscar Reservoir, where you join the gravel and tarmac trail along the River Don. The mid-section of the Trans Pennine Trail is a labyrinth, with link routes leading to both Leeds and Sheffield, and despite the excellent waymarking it is easy to find yourself heading in the wrong direction. At the market town of Penistone, you have a choice of trails. You can head north on hilly lanes over Silkstone Common and take advantage of the disused railway tracks of the Dove Valley Trail, passing Worsbrough's historic watermill. A southern alternative also follows railway tracks, past the eighteenth-century Huthwaite Hall towards the busy motorway junction at Tankersley – the TPT passes under the motorway on quiet country lanes. Near Elsecar's industrial Heritage Centre, you join old railway tracks again – although you might choose a short detour to Wentworth Woodhouse, one of the largest country houses in Europe, built on the coal-mining fortunes of the Fitzwilliam family.

The routes reunite just past Wombwell, with more railway trails on the Dearne Way, often by the banks of the Don. Near Conisbrough, with its twelfth-century castle, you cross the Don on the towering, twenty-one-arched viaduct. Through the green fields of Cusworth Hall Park and on leaf-strewn, tree-lined tracks, you head around Doncaster. After gravelly trails and quiet lanes through fields of golden rapeseed, you reach the New Junction Canal and take the towpath. After Sykehouse you take a meandering route on roads and trails through Yorkshire's villages and cross the hectic M62 motorway.

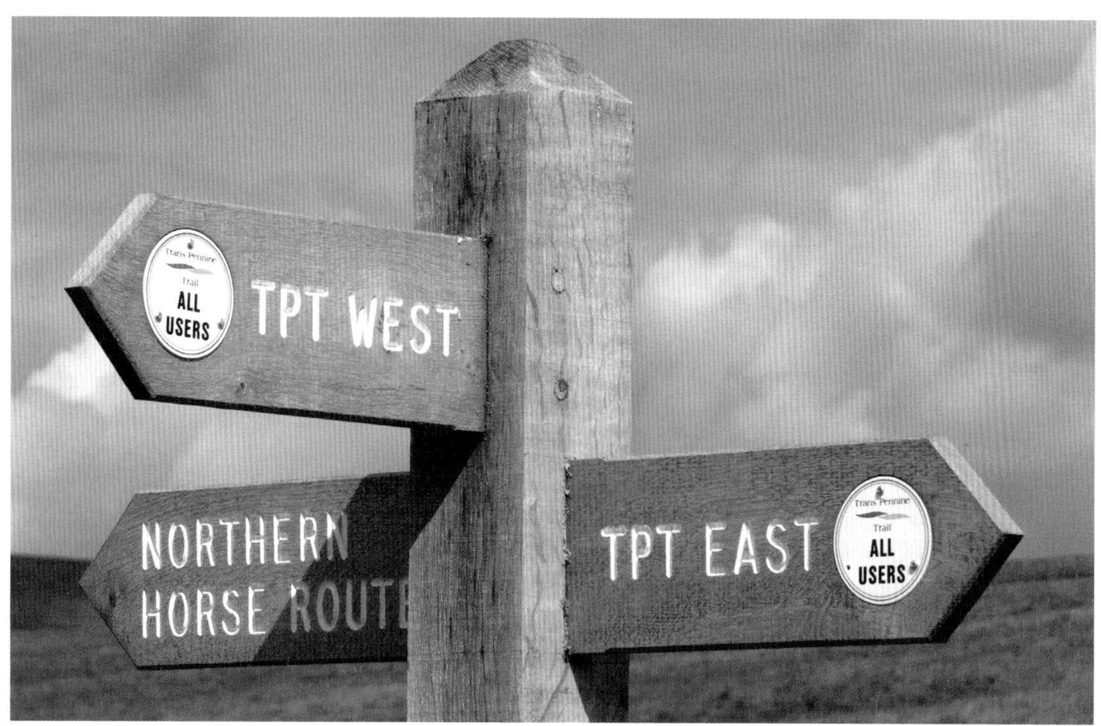

TRANS PENNINE TRAIL WAYMARKER. © RACHEL DICKINSON – *WWW.INSPIRINGBIKERIDES.CO.UK*

After the Viking settlement of Selby there is a spur to York, but the main route continues following the course of the River Ouse. Near North Ferriby, you reach the banks of the Humber estuary. You can see the towering span of the Humber Bridge ahead of you. At Hessle, near the bridge's footprint, you turn away from the water and follow roads into the city of Hull. There is a link to the ferry port where you can board the boat to Rotterdam or Zeebrugge. Otherwise you turn north, on the Hornsea Rail Trail, and finish on the seafront, where you can enjoy an ice cream on the sandy Blue Flag beach.

The Trans Pennine Trail's gravel trails, stone-topped tracks and sometimes muddy sections make it a good route for gravel-bikers. While there is plenty of road, there is lots of off-road track to enjoy, and the route is often sheltered by trees. Good waymarking makes the trail easy to follow, as long as you are not distracted by the many variations. The Trans Pennine Trail is a great way for any cyclist to cross England. On good paths and quiet roads, you are never too far from town but rarely in a busy city centre. You may see grey seals on the mouth of the Mersey or kingfishers on the Ouse, and in 2020 a bearded vulture soared over Howden Moors. If the TPT's watermills, historic houses and dramatic viaducts are not enough for you, you can make detours to the Beatles's hometown of Liverpool, take in the steel city of Sheffield, experience Leeds's vibrant nightlife or learn about York's Roman history on link sections of the trail.

21 TRANS PENNINE TRAIL: ESSENTIAL INFORMATION

RIDE ESSENTIALS

Start:	**Southport, Merseyside, England**
End:	**Hornsea, East Yorkshire, England**
Distance:	**338km**
Ascent/descent:	**1,130m/1,130m**

HOW TO GET THERE

Southport has local Merseyside rail services to Liverpool, where mainline connections can be made. The Trans Pennine Trail passes the international John Lennon Airport between Southport and Liverpool.

Hornsea has no rail services. The closest station is at Arram, on the outskirts of Beverley, but it may be easier to retrace your tracks back to Hull, with its mainline services. The closest international airport is Doncaster Sheffield Airport, and Hull has international ferry services.

TIME TO COMPLETE

Minimum days:	**3 days/24 hours**
Maximum days:	**6 days/33 hours**

PROS

- **Waymarking** – there is clear waymarking along the trail, with fingerposts that indicate towns and distances.

- **Hills** – the trail takes the easiest possible route over the Pennines and across the Peak District. Although there are climbs, very few will force you out of the saddle.

- **Options** – particularly in the mid-sections, there are many route choices, meaning you can decide whether you want to visit the northern cities, prefer road or off-road and want to visit historical landmarks or take a more rural route.

CONS

- **Railways** – the TPT makes extensive use of disused railway tracks – these are often level in gradient and hedged in by trees, with limited views. While many enjoy the easy wheel-turning of good railway cycle paths, you may also find it monotonous.

- **Barriers** – whether it be A-frames, chicanes, gates or steps, you will encounter repeated barriers on the TPT. Some may be difficult or impossible to negotiate on non-standard or heavily laden bikes.

- **Punctures** – particularly on the more urban stretches of the TPT, you may encounter broken glass or metal debris and many cyclists suffer more than one puncture. Carry spare inner tubes or consider tubeless tyres.

VARIATIONS

There are routes that take you through Liverpool, south to Sheffield and Chesterfield and north to Leeds and York.

GOOD TO KNOW

The Trans Pennine Trail owes its creation to meetings organised by Barnsley Council in the late 1980s to investigate the possibility of a long-distance cycle trail that utilised disused railway tracks. Work began in 1989, but it was not officially opened until 2001, after an investment of £30 million and the cooperation of twenty-six local authorities. In 2006, the TPT won the National Lottery's Amazing Space award.

FURTHER INFORMATION

www.transpenninetrail.org.uk; The Ultimate Trans Pennine Trail Guide (Excellent Books, 2017).

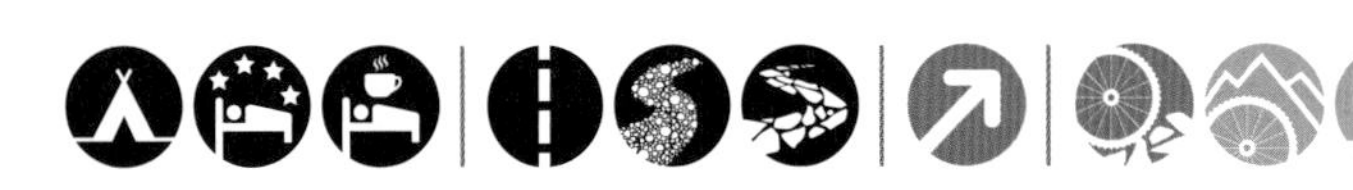

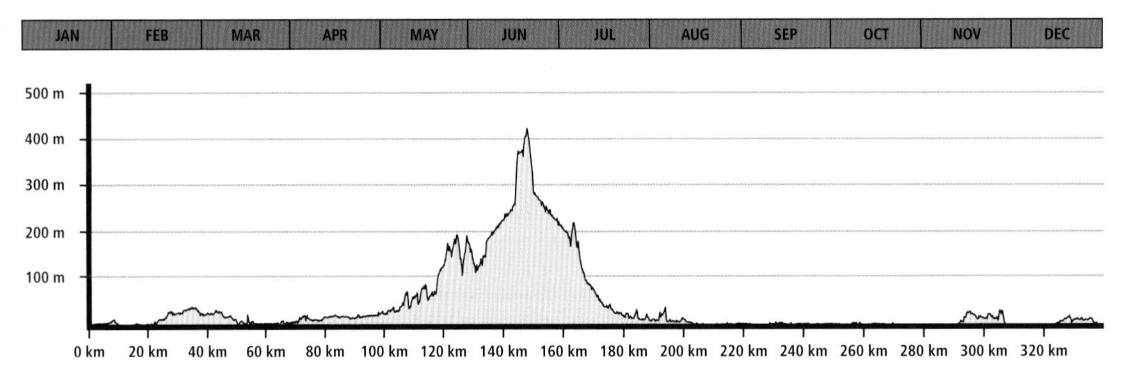

North Sea
Irish Sea
Kendal
Northallerton
Scarborough
Filey
Yorkshire Dales National Park
Ripon
Bridlington
Lancaster
A65
Harrogate
Skipton
M6
York
A1079
A614
Hornsea
A1(M)
Ouse
Blackpool
M55
Kingston upon Hull
Bradford
Leeds
Selby
Cliffe
Burnley
Preston
Blackburn
The Pennines
Howden
M62
South Cave
Hessle
Withernsea
Aire
Humber
Halifax
Snaith
M65
Wakefield
Goole
Blacktoft
A1033
Pontefract
Barton-upon-Humber
Southport
M62
Huddersfield
Rochdale
Bury
A15
Thorpe-in-Balne
Bolton
M1
Barnsley
M66
Scunthorpe
M180
Grimsby
Formby
Wigan
M61
M58
M60
Oldham
Penistone
Doncaster
Manchester
Oxspring
Sprotbrough
Aintree
Wortley
Elsecar
Mexborough
Denton
Woodhead Pass
St Helens
Trafford
M1
M18
A15
M57
Hadfield
Rotherham
Liverpool
Sale
Warrington
Widnes
A57
Sheffield
Stockport
Lymm
Altrincham
Mersey
M53
Hale
Runcorn
Peak District National Park
Retford
M56
Northwich
Worksop
Macclesfield
Buxton
Lincoln
M6
Chesterfield
Chester
A515
N
Mansfield
Crewe
A534
Stoke-on-Trent
Ashbourne
M1
0
20 Kilometres
Nottingham
Derby
Grantham

BENTHAM 3¾
SETTLE 7¼

22

22 WAY OF THE ROSES – 275km

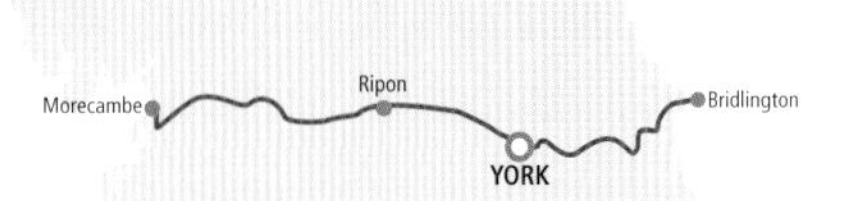

The Way of the Roses is a 275-kilometre cross-country trail that begins in Morecambe on the west coast and traverses Lancashire and Yorkshire, to reach the east coast at the seaside resort of Bridlington. On its way it takes in the historic cities of Lancaster and York, charming Dales villages such as Burnsall and Settle, castles, abbeys and prehistoric stones. The Way passes through the Forest of Bowland Area of Outstanding Natural Beauty, the Yorkshire Dales National Park and the Yorkshire Wolds Area of Outstanding Natural Beauty.

The Way of the Roses starts in the once-thriving seaside resort of Morecambe, on the seafront by the stone jetty. Behind Morecambe's station, you join a cycletrack on a disused railway track. You reach Lancaster and cross the Lune Millennium Bridge, its two steel pylons a reminder of the ships that once crowded the river. The Way skips the centre of Lancaster, preferring to stick to the riverbanks – you will have to detour if you want to visit Lancaster's twelfth-century castle. You enjoy tarmac, riverfront tracks towards Caton, leaving the industrial and housing estates behind you to reach green fields bordered by trees.

Returning to the roads, you cross the River Lune and pass through the Crook o' Lune picnic spot. On narrow, grass-fringed lanes you climb through Halton Park, passing the nineteenth-century country house. The route undulates up and down the sloped riverside, through Gressingham, the village where the eponymous duck was first bred in 1980 (although they are now all bred in East Anglia).

The trail crosses the Lune by the Norman motte-and-bailey Castle Stede. It is an easy, flat route through Hornby and Wray. The Way leaves Lancashire for Yorkshire just south of Low Bentham, where Queen Victoria's bloomers were manufactured. The bumpy Yorkshire Dales rise in front of you, and by Clapham you are on the edge of the national park. You are briefly on cycle paths next to the busy A65 main road near Austwick, but generally on narrow country lanes.

On rolling, stonewalled lanes through green pastures you reach the River Ribble and follow it to the market town of Settle. On High Hill Lane you face a steep climb out of Settle – you will enjoy the long descent into Airton. On the same roads as the Yorkshire Dales Cycleway (see page 147), you pass through the pretty villages of Winterburn, Hetton and Cracoe to reach the popular hikers' and cyclists' destination of Burnsall on the River Wharfe.

After Appletreewick, the village once famed for its annual Onion Fair, you face another stern pull up over Appletreewick Pasture – this section is the highest en route. You can visit the limestone cave system of the Stump Cross Caverns, which were discovered by lead miners in 1860, as you pass them on Greenhow Hill. The descent into Pateley Bridge on an uneven road with bends is dangerous, particularly in wet weather, and should be ridden cautiously.

Pateley Bridge, just outside the national park boundary, is home to the world's oldest sweet shop, which has been selling sweets such as lemon bon-bons, sherbet pips and liquorice since 1827, although the building was originally

◀ THE CROSSROADS IN KEASDEN, WITH THE SUMMIT OF INGLEBOROUGH IN THE DISTANCE. © TOBY CUMMINS

a seventeenth-century apothecary's shop. You ascend to the millstone grit outcrop at Brimham Rocks.

As you descend towards Studley Royal, you pass How Hill Tower – built as chapel in the thirteenth century, it was rebuilt in the eighteenth century as a folly and used as a gaming haunt. The ruins of the twelfth-century Cistercian Fountains Abbey stand at the corner of the Studley Royal Park UNESCO World Heritage Site. After the dissolution of the monasteries, the lands of Fountains Abbey were sold to Sir Richard Gresham and then to Stephen Proctor, who built the grand Jacobean mansion of Fountains Hall. The MP John Aislable, disgraced by the South Sea Bubble, retreated to Studley Royal and devoted his life to landscaping the gardens there. The estate permits cyclists to ride through the deer park on traffic-free trails, offering a pleasant route into the small cathedral city of Ripon.

The route flattens out as you leave the Dales behind you and cross the fertile Vale of York. You are on wider, less rural roads, interspersed with villages. In the shadow of the A1 main road, on the outskirts of Boroughbridge, you can see the Devil's Arrows, three prehistoric menhir stones. Near the village of Great Ouseburn, you pass the grand but now roofless Elizabethan manor of Kirby Hall. Drivers have to pay forty pence to cross the Ure on the Aldwark toll bridge, but cyclists can trundle across the wooden boards for free. On hedgerowed roads through wheat fields, you are nearing the outskirts of York. At the National Trust's Beningbrough Hall you can see the ha-ha, the earthworks wall designed to keep the sheep away from the Georgian mansion's landscaped grounds.

You take traffic-free riverside paths along the Ouse, although you do join the roads to take in York Minster – these city roads will be busy with snap-happy tourists, and you may find yourself in a traffic jam behind horse and carriages. The city of York was founded by the Romans in AD 71, and has been an economic and religious power-house for centuries – most will choose to spend at least an afternoon exploring the city's historic buildings, museums, quirky shops, pubs and restaurants.

ABOVE: ENTERING THE YORKSHIRE DALES ON THE WAY OF THE ROSES. © RACHEL DICKINSON – *WWW.INSPIRINGBIKERIDES.CO.UK*
BELOW: STUDLEY PARK. © RACHEL DICKINSON – *WWW.INSPIRINGBIKERIDES.CO.UK*

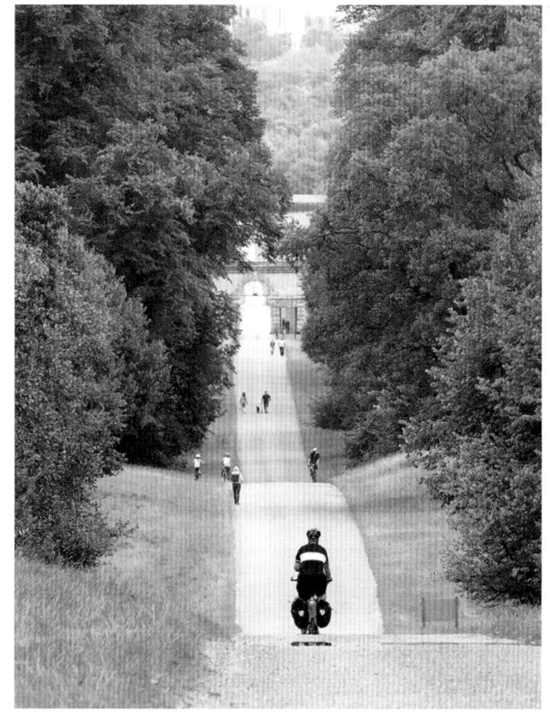

The route takes the green-edged, traffic-free Foss Islands Path to escape the city.

On farm tracks and roadside cycle paths, you reach Stamford Bridge, where King Harold II defeated the Vikings in 1066 just weeks before his own defeat at the hands of William the Conqueror. You reach Pocklington on the edge of the Yorkshire Wolds – there is believed to have been a settlement here from the Bronze Age. You face a rolling ride, on roads so infrequently driven that they are moss-topped, through the farmland, flowered fields, small copses and unspoilt villages of the Yorkshire Wolds.

After the market town of Driffield, 'the capital of the Wolds', there is a brief section of cycle path to give you a break from the main carriageway. In Burton Agnes, you cycle past the large village duck pond and the Elizabethan Burton Agnes Hall to reach the Roman road of Woldgate, which leads you to the outskirts of Bridlington. The Way ends on Bridlington's sunny seafront.

The Way of the Roses can be done at any time of year. It is generally on the road, or roadside cycle paths, but uses some cycle trails. It can be cycled on a tourer, although if you choose a gravel or hybrid bike, you could explore a little more of the Dales. The Way has been waymarked by volunteers, although some markers may be missing or you may have to be eagle-eyed to spot them. It combines national and local cycle trails.

The Way of the Roses is the road route with a little bit of everything: seaside resorts, Dales villages, country houses and York, one of England's most fascinating and historical cities. For every hill that you have to climb there is as much long, flat road, with plenty of opportunity for easy cycling as you enjoy the views.

HEADING TOWARDS CLAPHAM, ENTRANCE TO THE DALES. © *CYCLE.TRAVEL*

22 WAY OF THE ROSES: ESSENTIAL INFORMATION

RIDE ESSENTIALS

Start:	**Morecambe, Lancashire, England**
End:	**Bridlington, East Yorkshire, England**
Distance:	**275km**
Ascent/descent:	**2,240m/2,240m**

HOW TO GET THERE

Morecambe is on the Bentham railway line. It has direct services to Leeds, and connects with the West Coast Main Line at nearby Lancaster. The closest international airport is Manchester.

Bridlington has direct trains to Hull, Doncaster, York and Sheffield. The closest international airports are Leeds Braford and Doncaster Sheffield. Hull has ferry services to Belgium and the Netherlands.

TIME TO COMPLETE

Minimum days:	**2 days/18 hours**
Maximum days:	**4 days/25 hours**

PROS

- **Yorkshire** – this is a route that definitely showcases the best of Yorkshire, from the Dales to the Wolds to the Yorkshire coast. Only thirty kilometres of the route is in Lancashire.

- **Tearooms** – Yorkshire is famous for its tea, and you can sample it at two Bettys Tea Rooms in York. There are also plenty of charming cafes in Burnsall, Settle and Pocklington.

- **Historic homes** – highlights en route include the Elizabethan Burton Agnes Hall, the Georgian Sewerby Hall on the clifftops, the sixteenth-century Fountains Hall at Studley Royal Park and the red-brick Beningbrough Hall, once home to Bomber Command.

CONS

- **Busy roads** – the Way is largely on roads, and most are quiet. Traffic will be heavy as you approach York and Bridlington, and you may encounter increased traffic on scenic roads through the Dales and the Wolds during the summer holidays.

- **Railway crossings** – there are several level crossings, particularly near Lowthorpe, Hetton and Sewerby, which should be negotiated with care, particularly in wet weather.

VARIATIONS

There are no variations, and the route tends to pass through villages and towns.

GOOD TO KNOW

The Way of the Roses is one of six coast-to-coast routes across (Northern) England, based on Sustrans routes – the others are Sea to Sea (C2C), Reivers Cycle Route (which crosses into Scotland occasionally), Hadrian's Cycleway, Trans Pennine Trail and Walney to Wear and Whitby. There is also an off-road mountain bike variation on Wainwright's Coast to Coast, Wheelwright's C2C, devised by Tim Woodcock.

FURTHER INFORMATION

wayoftheroses.info

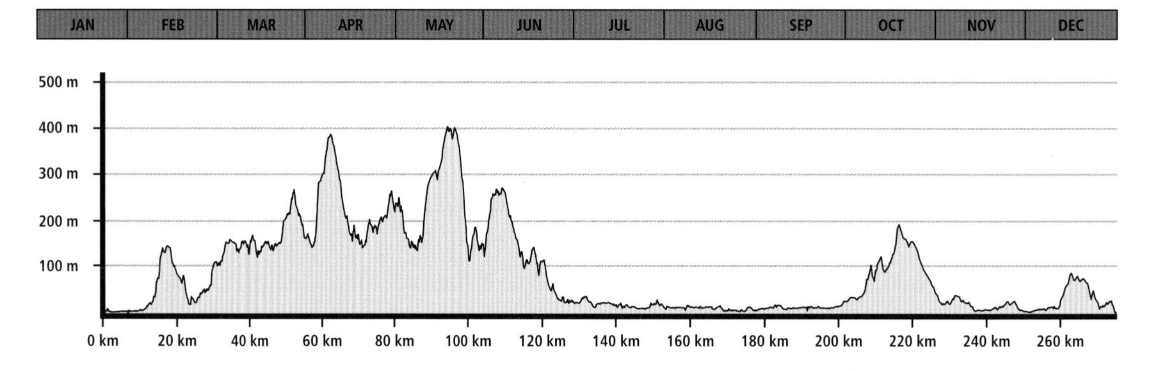

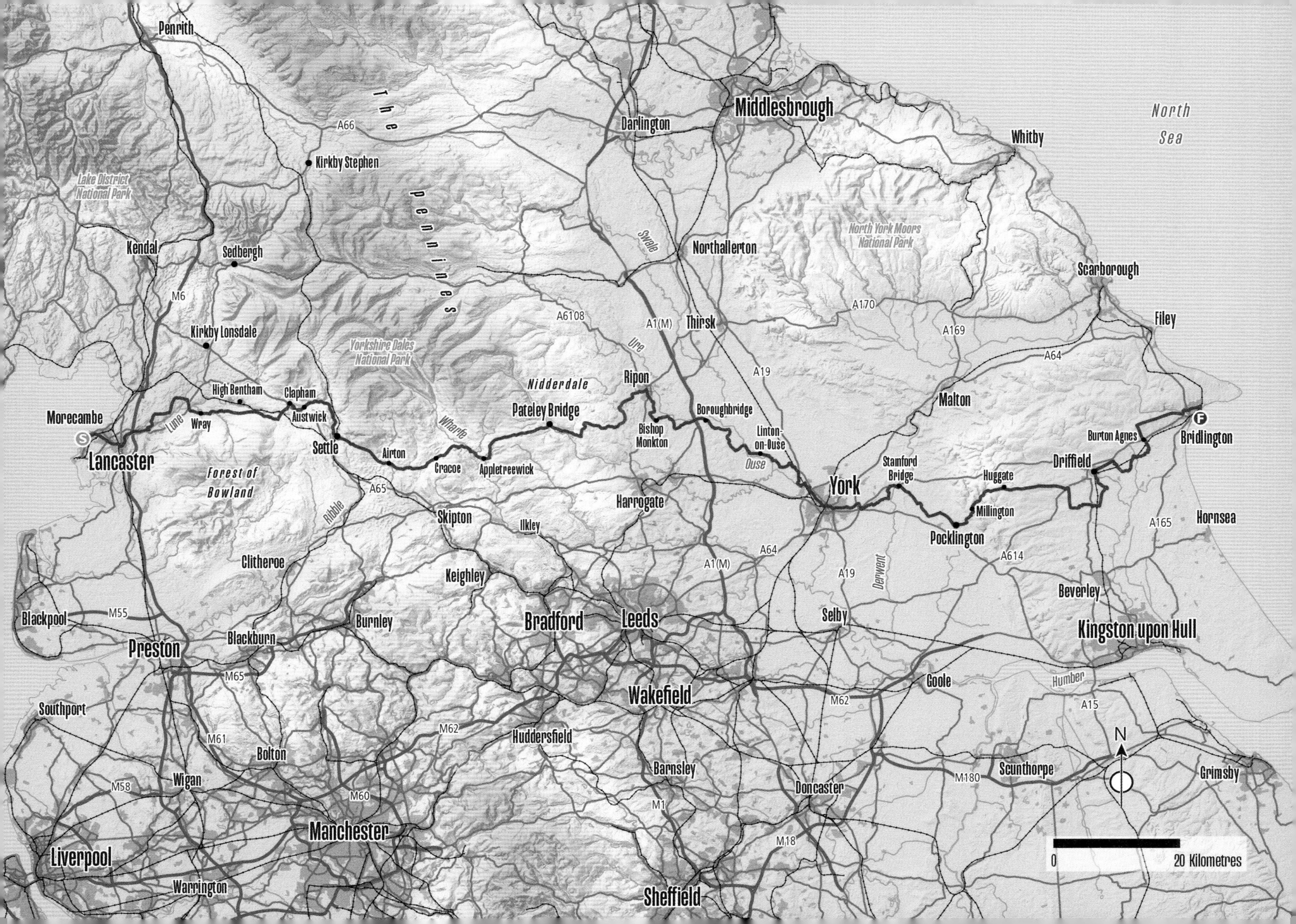
North Sea
The Pennines
Penrith
Middlesbrough
Darlington
Whitby
A66
Kirkby Stephen
Lake District National Park
North York Moors National Park
Kendal
Sedbergh
Northallerton
Swale
Scarborough
M6
A6108
A1(M)
Thirsk
A170
Filey
Kirkby Lonsdale
Yorkshire Dales National Park
Ure
A169
A64
A19
Nidderdale
Ripon
Malton
High Bentham
Clapham
Austwick
Morecambe
Lune
Wray
Pateley Bridge
Boroughbridge
Wharfe
Bishop Monkton
Linton-on-Ouse
Burton Agnes
Bridlington
Settle
Airton
Cracoe
Appletreewick
Ouse
Stamford Bridge
Driffield
Lancaster
Forest of Bowland
York
Huggate
A65
Harrogate
Millington
Hornsea
Ribble
Skipton
Ilkley
Pocklington
A165
A614
A64
Clitheroe
A1(M)
A19
Derwent
Keighley
Beverley
Blackpool
M55
Burnley
Bradford
Leeds
Selby
Kingston upon Hull
Preston
Blackburn
M65
Wakefield
Goole
Humber
Southport
M62
A15
M62
Huddersfield
M61
Bolton
N
Wigan
Barnsley
M180
Scunthorpe
Grimsby
M58
M60
Doncaster
M1
Manchester
M18
Liverpool
0
20 Kilometres
Warrington
Sheffield

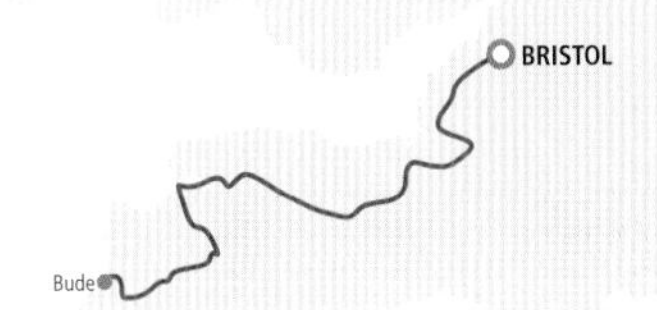

23

23 WEST COUNTRY WAY – 302km

The 302-kilometre West Country Way is an on- and off-road route that wends from Bristol through north Somerset and Devon to the surfer's paradise of Bude on the Cornish coast. The route is part of the longer NCN 3, which links Bristol to Land's End. It follows disused railways, canal paths and quiet country roads, taking advantage of some of the west country's best off-road cycleways. Although it can be cycled in either direction, travelling from Bristol to Bude breaks you in gently with climbs over the Mendips and the biggest hills saved for last. And what better summer's adventure is there than leaving the city streets behind you to head for the coast?

The Way starts on College Green in front of Bristol Cathedral, once St Augustine's Abbey – the green was part of the abbey precincts. Bristol, home to Sustrans, is a bike-friendly city with plenty of cycle routes and facilities – you pass the Mud Dock bike shop and cafe minutes after setting off and the Bristol Cycle Shack is a few metres off-route under the arches near Temple Meads railway station. You could choose instead to start in the Roman city of Bath, a UNESCO World Heritage Site – the Bristol and Bath Railway Path offers a high-quality, traffic-free route between the cities. The West Country Way leaves Bristol on the Avon Cycleway along the river, passing Bristol Temple Meads railway station and following the largely traffic-free Whitchurch Railway Path south.

You are on country roads now, with the occasional neglected shared pathway as you pass the Saxon village of Chew Magna and the large reservoir of Chew Valley Lake. You face your first climb on to the limestone ridge of the Mendips – although the Castle of Comfort pub awaits you at the top, its name reputedly derived from the succour it offered to prisoners sentenced by Hanging Judge Jeffreys on their way to the gallows. The chalk-rich soil of the grassy Mendips are a wildlife-rich habitat, and you can whizz past wildflower meadows buzzing with butterflies.

As you leave the Mendips, you pass Wookey Hole where you can enjoy a round of pirate-themed crazy golf. The limestone caverns are a popular tourist attraction, with their resident witch; the deeper flooded chambers were important in early cave diving explorations. The River Axe, once an important navigation route, springs to life here in these underground caverns.

The route passes the cathedral in the historical city of Wells; the lead roof was melted into bullets during the Monmouth Rebellion, the Duke of Monmouth's failed attempt to dethrone James II in 1685. A well-surfaced track, shaded from the road by trees, leads you out of the city. The trail returns to the roads under the shadow of Glastonbury Tor, which was reputedly visited by Joseph of Arimathea, to reach the religious and sometimes mystical town of Glastonbury.

You are now crossing the fertile Somerset levels, green meadows divided by ditches and drains. The route passes under the M5 motorway to skirt Bridgwater, one of the towns on the spectacular autumn West Country Carnival circuit. You have a pleasant spin on hard-surfaced tracks

◀ THE BRISTOL–BATH RAILWAY PATH FORMS A GREEN CORRIDOR OUT THROUGH THE EAST OF THE CITY OF BRISTOL TOWARDS BATH, FOLLOWING THE TRACK BED OF THE FORMER MIDLAND RAILWAY. © DAVID HARPER – *WESTERNASPECT.COM*

along the waterlily-fringed canal to Taunton. Alternating between quiet roads, good track by the River Tone and more towpaths, you cross the country border into Tiverton.

Back on-road, you climb to the grand Victorian house at Knightshayes, now owned by the National Trust, and have a bumpy ride through country lanes to Bampton and then Dulverton, the gateway to Exmoor. The climbs get serious now as you ascend to the wild, isolated Exmoor National Park. You traverse the park through farmland, wild moor, bracken and heather, and can enjoy views out over the Bristol Channel to the bird-rich Lundy Island. The roads narrow to a grassy, fringed strip of tarmac, barely wide enough for a car, that the moors are in constant danger of reclaiming. There is nothing on these exposed lanes except for scattered farmhouses until you reach the Sportsman's Inn near Exmoor's western edge.

The Way descends from the moors through Bratton Fleming with its little village shop and down to the coast at the historic town of Barnstaple. You now join the tree-shaded Tarka Trail – named for Henry Williamson's famous otter, the trail is one of the longest off-road cycleways in Britain (although you only cycle part of it). This section of the trail consists of tarmacked tracks along a disused railway line. You could take a rest along the way on one of the benches specially crafted by local artists.

You follow the trail through Bideford and Great Torrington, leaving it near Petrockstowe. Your route to the Way's finish at Bude is largely on-road, although a short section through Holsworthy takes advantage again of a disused railway track to divert from the traffic. North Devon offers some final challenges as the route climbs up and down over rolling hills. The route crosses the border into Cornwall just before reaching Bude, and you finally leave the roads behind as you roll into this popular seaside resort on tarmac trails above the Bude Canal. With your journey finished, you can relax on the sandy expanse of Summerleaze Beach and perhaps take a dip in the seaweed-fringed Sea Pool.

ABOVE: THE FORMER MANGOTSFIELD STATION. © DAVID HARPER – *WESTERNASPECT.COM*
BELOW: GLASTONBURY TOR SEEN FROM THE TINY STONE DOWN LANE. © *CYCLE.TRAVEL*

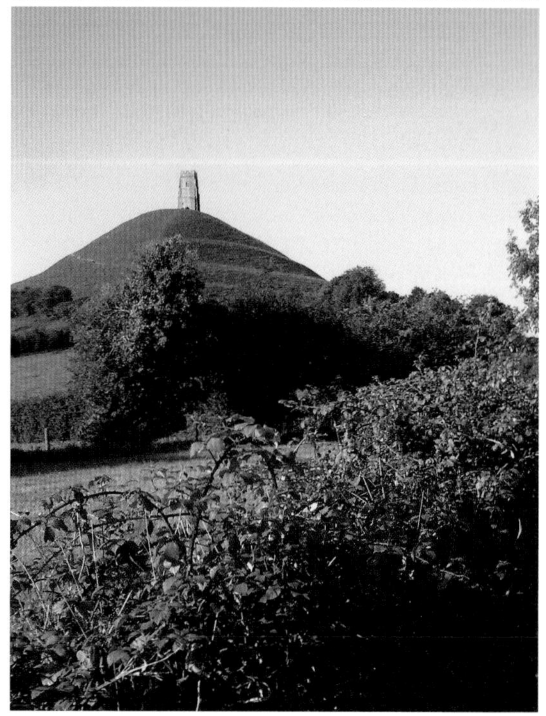

You could extend your adventure by picking up the Cornish Way in Bude and following it down to Land's End, through the foodie fish town of Padstow and across Bodmin Moor; this gives you the opportunity to enjoy the Camel Trail, another great south-west traffic-free cycleway. The West Country Way can be cycled at any time of year, and Devon and Cornwall on the whole enjoy slightly warmer weather than the rest of the UK. The off-road sections are generally well-surfaced and should pose no problem to a tourer. However, a gravel or hybrid would be a good choice and would allow you to discover more of Exmoor by riding some of Devon and Cornwall's bridleways, or to ride south over Dartmoor.

The West Country Way is a great sunny adventure for the new gravel biker in the spring or summer. While the section across Exmoor is isolated and exposed, at other times you are rarely far from a town or village where you can stop for a cream tea. The hills are big enough to warm your legs, but you should not need to get off and push. Bristol is a bike-friendly city and a great place to set out from. With wide skies, wildflowers, high, panoramic moorland views and sea breezes, this is the route that could make you fall in love with cycling holidays.

THE GRAND WESTERN CANAL AND ITS TOWPATH VIEWED FROM EBEAR BRIDGE, NEAR WESTLEIGH. © DEVON COUNTY COUNCIL

23 WEST COUNTRY WAY: ESSENTIAL INFORMATION

RIDE ESSENTIALS

Start: **Bristol, England**
End: **Bude, Cornwall, England**
Distance: **302km**
Ascent/descent: **2,920m/2,930m**

HOW TO GET THERE

Bristol has a mainline railway station with fast connections to London and other cities. It also has an international airport.

Bude does not have a railway station. You will either have to return to Barnstaple, cycle cross-country to Okehampton or continue on to Newquay – these all have regional train services, with connections to the Great Western Main Line. Bude has bus services to Plymouth and Exeter, but bikes will not generally be carried. Bristol and Exeter are the closest international airports, and there are ferry services to France from Plymouth.

TIME TO COMPLETE

Minimum days: **2 days/21 hours**
Maximum days: **5 days/30 hours**

PROS

- **Cheese** – Somerset is famous for its cheddar, but it produces all kinds of quality cheese. You can enjoy cheese aged in the caves at Wookey Hole, Exmoor blue cheese, sweet, nutty Wyfe of Bath cheese and the creamy sheep's cheese Little Ryding.

- **Pubs** – there are plenty of pubs en route where you can enjoy a ploughman's lunch and pint. You'll be glad to see the Castle of Comfort and the Sportsman's Inn after strenuous stretches of the route. You'll have to hop across the river to reach the Cyder Presse at Weare Giffard, where you can sample the local cider, but you pass the fifteenth-century George and Pilgrims, built for Glastonbury's pilgrims.

- **Birds** – you may see buzzards, kestrels and skylarks over Exmoor, and peregrines, fulmars and guillemots close to the coast. Keen birdwatchers should take a boat trip to Lundy Island from Bideford, which has 317 species of birds, most famously puffins.

CONS

- **Grockles** – tourists, or 'grockles', love Devon and Cornwall in the summer – accommodation may be difficult to book, heavy traffic may be encountered and trails may be thronged with walkers.

- **Trains** – the closure of many of the south-west's railway lines has provided cyclists with excellent cycleways but left it difficult to travel the peninsula by train. Buses will not generally transport bicycles.

VARIATIONS

There are no route variations, but you could choose to extend your ride on the Cornish Way, or the Bristol and Bath Railway Path or even to London on the Great Western Way.

GOOD TO KNOW

North Devon is Tarka country, named for Henry Williamson's 1927 *Tarka the Otter*, which describes the life of an otter as it wanders between the rivers Taw and Torridge. You encounter both rivers on the West Country Way and pass close to Tarka's birthplace, near Great Torrington. Williamson's naturalism inspired Roger Deakin, Rachel Carson and Ted Hughes, who became a friend of Williamson's. You cycle past a sculpture of Tarka on the banks of the Torridge, in Bideford.

FURTHER INFORMATION

www.sustrans.org.uk/find-other-routes/west-country-way-bristol-to-bude

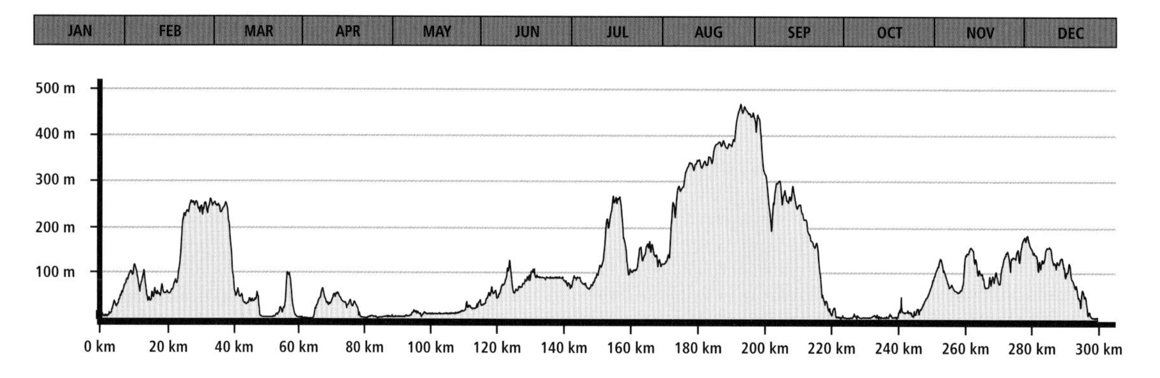

N
0
20 Kilometres
WALES
ENGLAND
Newport
Cardiff
Barry
Bristol
Bath
Bristol
Channel
Lundy
Ilfracombe
Lynton
Minehead
Weston-Super-Mare
Chew Magna
Chew Valley Lake
Charterhouse
Mendip Hills
Priddy
Wookey Hole
Wells
Brue
Cossington
Glastonbury
Bridgwater
Quantock Hills
Exmoor National Park
Braunton
Bratton Fleming
Barnstaple
Bideford Bay
Bideford
Weare Giffard
Great Torrington
Dulverton
Wiveliscombe
Taunton
Langport
South Molton
Taw
Tone
Wellington
Yeovil
Torridge
Chulmleigh
Tiverton
Halberton
Crewkerne
Petrockstowe
Bude
Holsworthy
Cookbury
Sheepwash
Hatherleigh
North Tawton
Cullompton
Crediton
Exe
Honiton
Tamar
Okehampton
Exeter
Bridport
Lyme Regis
Seaton
Dorchester
Launceston
Moretonhampstead
Sidmouth
Bodmin Moor
Dartmoor National Park
Exmouth
Weymouth
Lyme Bay
Tavistock
Princetown
Newton Abbot
Teignmouth
Liskeard
Torquay
Portland Bill
M4
M5
A39
A361
A396
A367
A371
A358
A303
A352
A377
A3124
A373
A30
A35
A382

24 WILD ATLANTIC WAY – 2,765km

The 2,765-kilometre Wild Atlantic Way was launched in 2014 as a tourist driving trail, one of the world's longest coastal routes. But cyclists quickly discovered the joys of exploring Ireland's quiet shores and spectacular scenery, and it has become a popular road route for those who want to discover the quaint villages, historic buildings and dramatic sea views that stretch along Ireland's long, jagged coastline. The route takes you from the wild, isolated Donegal coast, past the rollers of Mayo's surfers' coast, through Yeats country and past limestone karst and high cliffs, as well as looping around Ireland's southern peninsulas that point like fingers across the Atlantic. This route takes you through fishing ports, past prehistoric tombs, stone circles and crumbling castles and leads you to cosy pubs where you spend evenings listening to traditional music and legends told in Gaelic Irish. You'll need a hearty bowl of Irish stew with a generous dollop of colcannon to fortify for you for the next day – the Wild Atlantic Way is a route that revels in Ireland's rugged cliffs rather than a low, sea-level trail.

The Wild Atlantic Way begins in the walled city of Derry or Londonderry, on the border between Northern Ireland and the Republic. There are off-road cycle paths that follow the A2 main road out of the city, but a new greenway route is under construction. You begin with a loop of the Inishowen peninsula, following the shores of Lough Foyle. The white lighthouse at Fanad Head was built in response to the 1811 sinking of *HMS Saldanha*, one of Ireland's worst maritime disasters – the entire 250-strong crew died, the sole survivor being a parrot that was shot weeks later. The route undulates past rocky outcrops and sandy bays to reach Malin Head, mainland Ireland's most northerly point.

Donegal is one of the hillier sections on the route and you can cycle both the Gap of Mamore and the Glengesh pass, which are both long, stiff climbs. The deserted Donegal coast offers stone circles, castles, waterfalls, hills and the opportunity to explore islands. Most will choose to cycle across the bridge to loop around Inch Island. You can also hop on the ferry to enjoy a loop around the quiet island of Arranmore.

The undiscovered cliffs at Slieve League are three times higher than the famous Cliffs of Moher; the road to the viewpoint twists and turns around tight bends as it climbs towards the precipice. You can explore One Man's Pass and the Pilgrim's Path, chiselled into the green mountainside, on foot. At Killybegs, whose fortunes were built on carpet-weaving and fishing, you can see a cluster of replica clochãns, the beehive monk huts. South of the market town of Donegal, you can ride across the strand at Rossnowlagh if the tide permits.

After the seaside resort of Bundoran, with its Fairy Bridges sea arch, the Way barely touches Leitrim. The route heads for Mullaghmore Head, a popular surfing destination. You are now on the Sligo coast, under the shadow of Ben Bulben – this was a shoreline beloved by W.B. Yeats, whose grave is in Drumcliffe churchyard. Near Sligo, you can visit Carrowmore, one of the largest collections of megalithic tombs

◀ LOOKING TOWARDS KILBRICKEN FROM THE R340.
© JONATHAN HOUSEAGO

CYCLING ON THE R340, THE WILD ATLANTIC WAY, NEAR CARNA. © JONATHAN HOUSEAGO

in Ireland, and the tiny Fairy Glen Valley with its stone-stacked Queen Maeve's tomb.

At Céide Fields, a megalithic farming community, you can view the oldest stonewalled fields in the world. Mayo's coastline – with its rugged headlands, sea stacks and island after island – is pirate country, once the domain of the pirate queen Grace O'Malley. If you cross the bridge and loop around Achill Island, you can visit the stronghold tower of O'Malley's Kildavnet Castle; you encounter another of her castles at Rockfleet. The Great Western Greenway, following an old railway line, offers a great off-road route from Achill through to Westport, past Clew Bay, which is reputed to have an island for every day of the year.

After passing below the holy mountain of Croagh Patrick, you climb the Doo Lough pass – hundreds of starving locals were forced to cross this pass in filthy weather, many dying on the journey, in the 1849 Famine Walk. Near Aasleagh, where the pretty River Erriff tumbles into Ireland's only ford at Killary Harbour, you reach County Galway. You face the boggy, mountainous landscape of the Connemara National Park. Past the ruins of the Gothic Clifden Castle, you can enjoy a scenic ride along the exposed Sky Road. If you want to explore the Aran Islands, it may be easier to hire a bike than to persuade the ferry to transport your bicycle. The city of Galway, with its churches, canal and the Claddagh fishing village, is the perfect spot for a rest day.

Near Fanore you encounter the karst landscape of the Burren Park before a spectacular section of the route along the high Cliffs of Moher. You catch the Tarbert ferry to avoid a lengthy detour inland along the Shannon estuary. After Tralee you loop around the Dingle peninsula, long associated with St Brendan – you skirt the mountain named for him. At the tip, looking out towards the Blasket Islands, you may see seals, whales and dolphins. You ride past Ventry Bay, with Mount Eagle as your backdrop, and pass the impossibly long Inch Strand.

The Ring of Kerry picks a hilly route between the MacGilly-cuddy's Reeks to loop the Iveragh peninsula. On old butter roads you reach Caherdaniel, birthplace of Ireland's Liberator Daniel O'Connell, and continue on less-travelled roads to the very tip of the peninsula. The Skellig Islands are now

A BEAUTIFUL MORNING AT GURTEN BAY ON THE WILD ATLANTIC WAY, COUNTY GALWAY. © JONATHAN HOUSEAGO

inhabited by puffins, but Skellig Michael was once home to a sixth-century monastery. Near Kenmare, you can visit the fifteen-stoned Bronze Age circle.

The Beara peninsula is an undiscovered wonder, peppered with Neolithic sites. The fuchsia-fringed roads offer plenty of climbs as they loop the rugged peninsula, past the rainbow-hued villages of Allihies and Eyeries. At the tip of the peninsula, you will probably have to leave your bike behind if you want to take the swaying cable car across the sea to Dursey Island. Across Bantry Bay, you circumnavigate Sheep's Head; there is a signposted cyclist's route around the small, tranquil peninsula. On your next peninsula, you reach Mizen Head, where you can see Fastnet, Ireland's teardrop, so named because it was the last sight seen by emigrants leaving for America. On hilly roads, you turn east towards the colourful harbour town of Kinsale, where the Way ends.

The Wild Atlantic Way is the route that you choose to follow. Even those who drive the route find themselves drawn off-track by the dolmens, castles, cliffs, loughs and deserted beaches; those who cycle have even more reason to pore over maps and pick a route that explores the very best of Ireland's west coast and the quietest roads. The lack of off-road rights of way means that you are usually limited to the roads, although a friendly request will often allow you to explore grassy tracks or stone trails if you are on a gravel or mountain bike. Few attempt the Way, one of the world's longest coastal routes, in a single trip and, particularly on the southern peninsulas, sections of the Way are easily explored as loop routes. The Wild Atlantic Way is too good to rush; it reveals Ireland's culture and history, as well as the conflicts, famine, pilgrimages and prayers, political hope and poets' visions. On a misty day – of which there are plenty – the Wild Atlantic Way will feel an exposed and isolated route, far from anywhere. On the sunny days, when the sea shimmers beneath impossibly high cliffs, the mountains shine green and every corner seems to reveal a crumbling castle besides a sandy bay, you will understand why Ireland's west coast has always attracted artists and adventurers.

24 WILD ATLANTIC WAY: ESSENTIAL INFORMATION

RIDE ESSENTIALS

Start:	**Derry, Londonderry, Northern Ireland**
End:	**Kinsale, Cork, Ireland**
Distance:	**2,765km**
Ascent/descent:	**23,680m/23,700m**

HOW TO GET THERE

Derry Airport offers flights to the UK mainland, but international flights are available from Belfast's airports. Derry's train station has services to Belfast. Belfast and Larne offer ferries to the UK mainland.

Kinsale has no train station – the closest train station is approximately thirty kilometres away at Cork. Cork also has the closest international airport.

TIME TO COMPLETE

Minimum days:	**18 days/173 hours**
Maximum days:	**40 days/238 hours**

PROS

- **Beaches** – among dozens of beautiful, deserted beaches to discover on the Way, you can explore the long sand spit of Inch Strand, Ballydonegan Beach, which was created from the crushed quartz of the copper mines, or the Blue Flag Barley Cove Beach near Mizen Head.

- **Castles** – there are plenty of historic castles to explore on or close to the route, from the sixteenth-century tower house Dunguaire Castle to the thirteenth-century Ashford Castle, remodelled by the Victorians and now a luxury hotel, as well as Baron Headley's nineteenth-century folly Wynn Castle.

- **Culture** – from W.B. Yeats's Sligo, to the poet and harpist Piaras Feiritéar of Killarney, to Peig Sayers, the Blasket Island storyteller, this landscape has inspired generations of poets, storytellers, artists and musicians. It passes through the Irish-speaking Gaeltacht.

CONS

- **Tour buses** – particularly on the Ring of Kerry and near the Cliffs of Moher, you are likely to encounter buses full of sightseers, making difficult manoeuvres on impossibly narrow roads.

- **Driving route** – the Way was conceived as a driving route. This not only means you may encounter traffic, particularly during the summer, but also that there are significant sections where you face a long ride between facilities such as shops, places to stay and pubs.

- **Out and backs** – Ireland's roads often peter out as they reach the coast. If you want to visit all the sea arches, quiet bays and headlands, you may have to retrace your route.

GOOD TO KNOW

Mizen Head to Malin Head is Ireland's End to End. Between 1955 and 2007, the female record was held by Isabel Woods, Ireland's most prolific cycling record breaker. In the 1950s, she set eight road-cycling records, and the End to End is the only record she has lost. She was ahead of the men's record on her Dublin to Derry ride until she encountered roadworks near Omagh. Her End to End record was broken by Rose Leith, who rode a route approximately thirty kilometres shorter thanks to new roads. She cut one hour and nineteen minutes off the record, and was congratulated at the finish line by seventy-eight-year-old Isabel.

FURTHER INFORMATION

www.thewildatlanticway.com

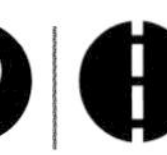

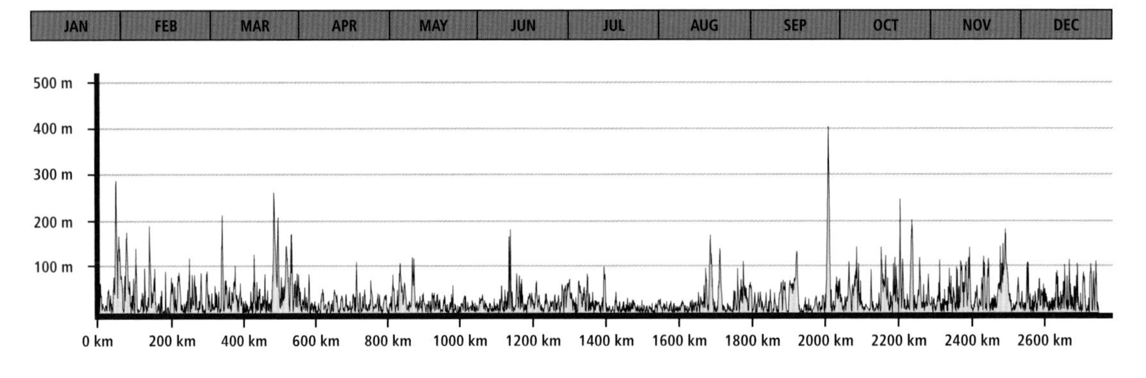

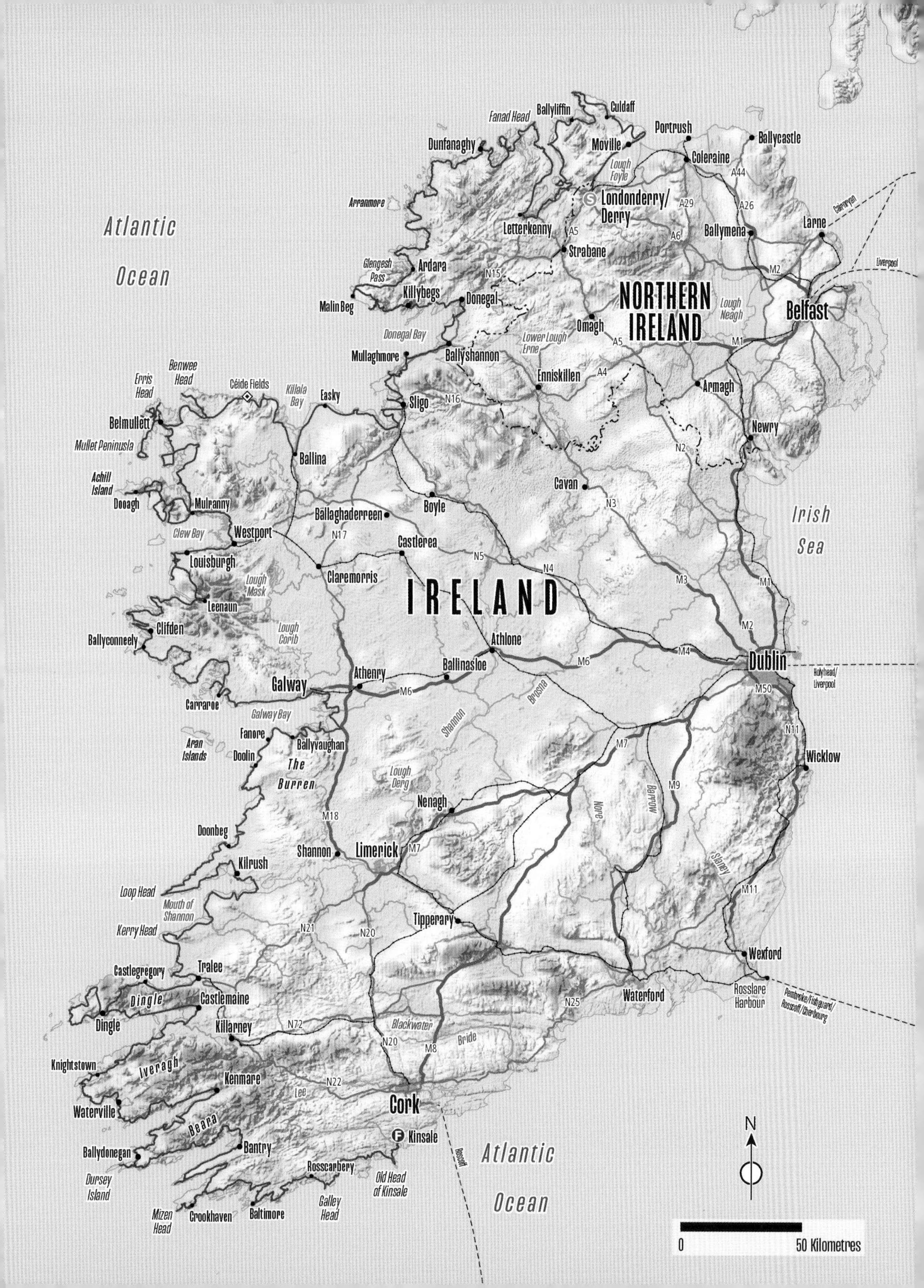

Culdaff
Ballyliffin
Fanad Head
Portrush
Ballycastle
Dunfanaghy
Moville
Coleraine
Lough Foyle
A44
Arranmore
Londonderry/ Derry
A29
A26
Cairnryan
Atlantic
Ocean
Letterkenny
A5
A6
Ballymena
Larne
Strabane
Glengesh Pass
Ardara
N15
M2
Liverpool
Malin Beg
Killybegs
Donegal
NORTHERN IRELAND
Lough Neagh
Belfast
Omagh
Donegal Bay
Lower Lough Erne
A5
M1
Mullaghmore
Ballyshannon
Benwee Head
Erris Head
Céide Fields
Killala Bay
Enniskillen
A4
Armagh
Easky
Sligo
N16
Belmullett
Mullet Peninusla
Newry
Ballina
N2
Achill Island
Cavan
Dooagh
Mulranny
Boyle
Ballaghaderreen
N3
Irish
Sea
Clew Bay
Westport
N17
Castlerea
Louisburgh
N5
N4
Claremorris
Lough Mask
M3
M1
IRELAND
Leenaun
Clifden
Lough Corrib
M2
Ballyconneely
Athlone
M4
Dublin
M6
Holyhead/ Liverpool
Athenry
Ballinasloe
Galway
M6
M50
Carraroe
Galway Bay
Brosna
Shannon
N11
Fanore
Aran Islands
Doolin
Ballyvaughan
M7
The Burren
Wicklow
Lough Derg
Barrow
M9
Nore
Nenagh
M18
Doonbeg
Shannon
Limerick
M7
Slaney
Kilrush
Loop Head
Mouth of Shannon
M11
Tipperary
Kerry Head
N21
N20
Wexford
Castlegregory
Tralee
Rosslare Harbour
Pembroke/Fishguard/ Roscoff/Cherbourg
Dingle
Castlemaine
N25
Waterford
Dingle
Killarney
N72
Blackwater
Bride
N20
M8
Knightstown
Iveragh
Kenmare
N22
Lee
Waterville
Cork
Beara
Kinsale
Roscoff
N
Ballydonegan
Bantry
Atlantic
Rosscarbery
Dursey Island
Old Head of Kinsale
Galley Head
Ocean
Mizen Head
Crookhaven
Baltimore
0
50 Kilometres

Cattle
grid

25

25 YORKSHIRE DALES CYCLEWAY – 213km

The Yorkshire Dales Cycleway is a 213-kilometre loop, entirely on-road, that begins and ends in Skipton. It takes you along the Swale and Wharfe rivers, through Grassington, Hawes, Kettlewell and Malham, and past Barden Tower, Bolton Abbey, Whernside and the dramatic viaducts of the Settle–Carlisle Railway. It is a route to be cycled for the challenging climbs, breathtaking descents and never-ending views.

The Cycleway begins at the top of Skipton's High Street – your ride begins by cycling past the walls of Skipton Castle. You are soon climbing on field-fringed roads with views over Skipton Moor. As you reach Embsay, you may be overtaken by a steam train puffing along the heritage railway line beside you. You face a steep climb up the snaking Barden Road under the shadow of the gritstone Eastby Crag, topping out at the cattle grid near Lower Barden Reservoir. You can freewheel past the fifteenth-century Barden Tower, built as a hunting lodge.

The route contours the hillside above the River Wharfe to reach the pretty Wharfedale village of Burnsall. You climb away from the river, and although you pass the Michelin-starred Angel at Hetton, there are plenty of opportunities to taste Yorkshire's great local produce along the route. The Cycleway rolls through the green, sheep-dotted Dales countryside to reach Airton, where hikers and cyclists can find accommodation at the historic Friends' Meeting House's bunkbarn.

After Kirkby Malham, you face a long climb over Kirkby Brow towards Malham. These roads will not only be traffic heavy, particularly in summer, but are likely to be lined with badly parked cars. The trail passes the entrance to the popular National Trust car park, after which the traffic situation should improve. Malham, with its youth hostel and pubs, is a great place to stop; you can climb the cove to view the limestone pavement and cool off in the wild swimming spot at Janet's Foss.

You face more climbing along the stonewalled Malham Rakes – the limestone pavement is a small detour (less than one kilometre) on foot over Sheriff Hill from the road. On a high, narrow tarmac road, you pass Malham Tarn and can then enjoy an extended descent into Stainforth, where you might want to detour to view the pretty Stainforth Force. The route follows the River Ribble into the market town of Settle. You have to navigate an often-busy crossing of the A65 main road. Heading north, you ride a little above the scenic Settle–Carlisle Railway before climbing towards Clapham. You should enjoy the brief downhill into the village, because you now commence on a seemingly unending climb past Ingleton's waterfalls and still upwards.

The road finally tops out under Whernside, the tallest of the Yorkshire Three Peaks, although you are entering the hilly middle section of the route with plenty of challenging ascents and descents. You are in Cumbria rather than Yorkshire now, and you face a steep descent into Deepdale on narrow, bendy lanes. After the pretty village of Dent, you have a rare flat section beside the River Dee. Another tough climb up through Cowgill and Stone House follows, with great views of the Arten Gill and Dent Head viaducts carrying the railway high above the River Gills.

◀ COVERDALE, YORKSHIRE DALES CYCLEWAY.
© CYCLE ENGLAND

On gentler roads, you face a gradual descent into Yorkshire and the high market town of Hawes, where the white Wensleydale cheese is made. It is easy to keep the wheels turning over on the flattish ride next to the River Ure into Askrigg, the town that the BBC used as vet James Herriot's Darrowby in its 1980s television adaption of ***All Creatures Great and Small***. You encounter a sharp climb on to Askrigg Common, and then a descent down to Swaledale. The B6270 road that follows the River Swale often suffers heavy traffic during the summer. On a narrow bridge, you leave the B6270 to ride a thin strip of tarmac. The Norman church at Grinton, nicknamed 'the Cathedral of the Dales', is home to a colony of pipistrelle bats which the vicar and congregation and have learnt to accommodate, as they are a protected species. The church used to ring an evening curfew bell to guide lost travellers into the village.

ABOVE: MALHAM, YORKSHIRE DALES CYCLEWAY. © CYCLE ENGLAND
BELOW: LOOKING NORTH OVER THE SUMMIT OF NEWBY HEAD TOWARD HAWES AND THE YORKSHIRE DALES. © TOBY CUMMINS

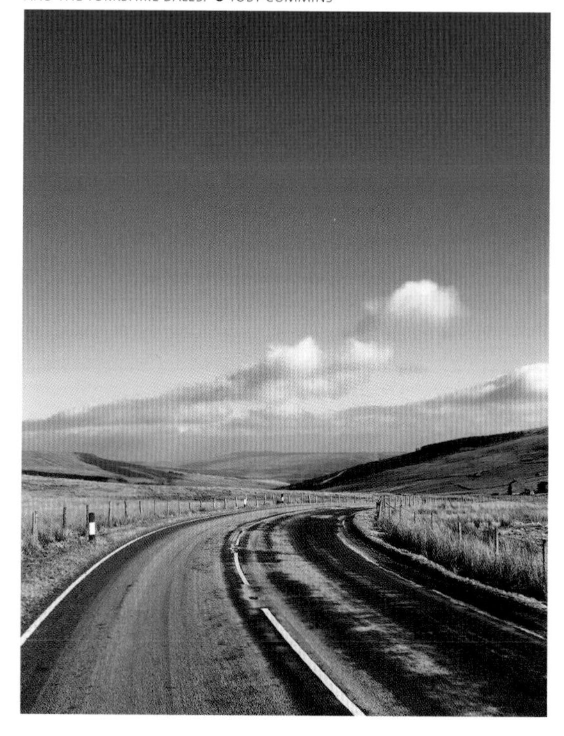

You have another thigh-warming climb up over Grinton Moor, passing Grinton Lodge Youth Hostel. The route descends, often steeply, around Redmire – the army uses Redmire, the terminus of the Wensleydale Railway, to transport armoured vehicles destined for nearby Catterrick, so you may meet tanks on this section. There is a short section on the A684 main road as it passes through Wensley before you embark on your final big and long climb through Coverdale, beginning along Gale Bank. The trail continues ascending through Melmerby and Carlton, with a final sting in the tail – after a steep climb you reach the summit at the waymarker Hunters Stone, which is said to spin around when the Hunter's Hall clock strikes twelve.

Your descent begins gently but rapidly gains momentum, with hairpin bends and gradients of up to twenty-five per cent. Back by the Wharfe, you reach Kettlewell with its teashops and the youth hostel that also serves as village post office and bookshop. You face gentle undulations rather than monster climbs now, as the route nears its end. The Cycleway follows the River Wharfe down to the bustling Grassington; with its teashops, pubs and market square, it is possibly the Dales' most charming village. The trail continues along the Wharfe through Hebden and Appletreewick to Barden. You take a meandering route by the Wharfe, passing the ruins of the twelfth-century

Augustine Bolton Abbey. Leaving the riverbanks, you follow the steam railway back to Embsay, where you retrace your tracks into Skipton.

The Yorkshire Dales Cycleway may be cycled at any time of year, although some roads may be busy in summer and there are high, exposed sections which may be challenging in winter. Although there are some long sections over moorland, there are plenty of towns and villages with shops, pubs and places to stay along the Cycleway. For those who want a longer challenge, there is a 251-kilometre extended route that continues north from Ingleton rather than cutting across the Dales. It skirts the national park, visiting the bookshop town of Sedbergh as well as Tebay, Kirkby Stephen and Reeth before rejoining the shorter Cycleway at Grinton. It offers a chance to enjoy an encounter with the Eden Valley as well as great views of the Howgills and a ride up to England's highest pub, but does not cut through the grassy heart of the Dales. Entirely on-road, with some tricky descents and ascents, this is a great opportunity to get out on your tourer.

For kilometres on the Cycleway, there is not much of anything – be it towns, pubs, stone circles or castles – other than stunning views across heathered moors, gritstone edges, rolling pastures and the bubbling rivers that have carved out the Dales between the hills. You will take country lanes lined by stone walls, under tree arches that are sometimes so narrow that the mossy fells are creeping on to the tarmac. You will discover a landscape shaped by farming and mining that seems little touched by the twenty-first century, and will often find yourself on a high, narrow track that seems to be the only road snaking through the beautiful scenery.

ABOVE BURNSALL IN WHARFEDALE LOOKING UP THE VALLEY. © JOHN KERR/YORKSHIRE VELO TOURS

25 YORKSHIRE DALES CYCLEWAY: ESSENTIAL INFORMATION

RIDE ESSENTIALS

Start:	**Skipton, North Yorkshire, England**
End:	**Skipton, North Yorkshire, England**
Distance:	**213km**
Ascent/descent:	**3,610m/3,610m**

HOW TO GET THERE

Skipton is on the Airedale Railway Line, with direct railway services to Leeds. The closest international airport is Leeds Bradford.

TIME TO COMPLETE

Minimum days: **2 days/15 hours**
Maximum days: **4 days/21 hours**

PROS

- **Hostels** – in addition to YHA hostels at Malham, Grinton, Kettlewell, Hawes and Ingleton, there are plenty of independent hostels and bunkbarns to be discovered in the Yorkshire Dales.

- **Dales** – each Dale has its own unique character, scenery and specialities. The Cycleway takes you through Malhamdale, Deepdale, Wensleydale, Coverdale, Dentdale, Wharfedale and Swaledale.

- **Climbs** – depending on which way you travel the loop, you can tackle some of the Dales' iconic road climbs at Deepdale, Oxnop Scar, Malham Rakes and Park Rash.

CONS

- **Zigzags** – the roads often take a snaking route to climb steep hills. Zigzag sections of road not only make it difficult to see far ahead (and for other road users to see you) but are also challenging on downhill sections.

- **Sheep** – you are sometimes on roads that are just a tarmac strip through boggy moorland, and you should expect to encounter grazing sheep that have wandered on to the lane.

- **Walkers** – the Yorkshire Dales are criss-crossed with hiking routes, and several popular long-distance trails occasionally share the roads. You may encounter trekkers on the Pennine Way near Malham Tarn, A Dales High Way through Deepdale, the Dales Way near Cowgill and A Pennine Journey near Askrigg.

VARIATIONS

There is an extended Cycleway that continues north from Ingleton, through Sedbergh, Tebay, Kirkby Stephen, Tan Hill and Reeth, following the border of the Yorkshire Dales. There are several small detours – to Malham Cove, Ingleton Waterfalls, Janet's Foss, Hardraw Force – that you may want to make on bike or on foot.

GOOD TO KNOW

The Tour de Yorkshire is a road cycling race that was born out of the Tour de France's Yorkshire stages in 2014 (which included routes through the Yorkshire Dales). The Tour de Yorkshire takes place before the May Day Bank Holiday. The Tour usually incorporates sections in the Dales – the 2020 route followed the Yorkshire Dales Cycleway from Gunnerside to Grinton, but the event was cancelled due to coronavirus.

FURTHER INFORMATION

cyclethedales.org.uk/route/yorkshire_dales_cycleway

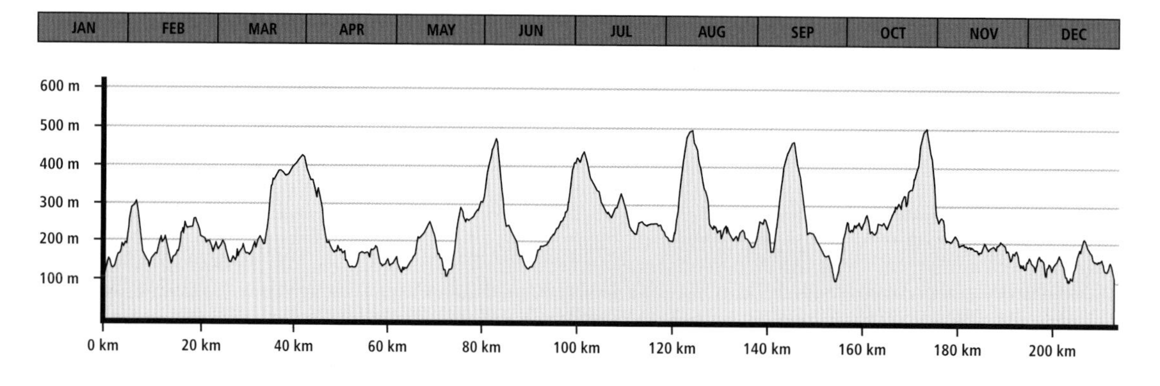

ENGLAND
Appleby-in-Westmorland
B6276
A66
Barnard Castle
M6
Warcop
Brough
Eden
A685
A66
Soulby
Winton
Orton
Kirkby Stephen
Nateby
Arkengarthdale
Newbiggin-on-Lune
Greenholme
Tebay
A685
Yorkshire Dales
B6259
National Park
Howgill Fells
A683
Hugh Seat
Swaledale
Reeth
Gunnerside
Low Row
Grinton
Swale
A685
The Calf
Wild Boar Fell
Great Shunner Fell
Askrigg
Common
Knoutberry Haw
Preston under Scar
Sedbergh
Wensleydale
Askrigg
Redmire
Leyburn
A684
Appersett
Bainbridge
A684
Ure
Wensley
Hawes
B6255
Aysgarth
Middleham
Dentdale
Gawthrop
Dent
Widdale
Melmerby
Lune
Carlton
Deepdale
Dodd Fell Hill
B6160
A683
Coverdale
Whernside
Buckden Pike
Kirkby Lonsdale
Buckden
A65
B6255
Ribble
Starbotton
Wharfedale
Great Whernside
Thornton in Lonsdale
Pen-y-ghent
Ingleborough
Ingleton
A687
Horton in Ribblesdale
Kettlewell
A683
Fountains Fell
Clapham
Malham Tarn
Wharfe
Conistone
A65
Stainforth
Langcliffe
Grassington
Hebden
Settle
Malham
Threshfield
B6265
Kirkby Malham
Cracoe
Burnsall
Appletreewick
Airton
Forest of Bowland AONB
Winterburn
Hetton
Barden Tower
Hellifield
A65
Eastby
Embsay
Bolton Abbey
N
S
F
A59
Skipton
A65
Barnoldswick
Ilkley
0
10 Kilometres

BIG RIDES – AT A GLANCE

	PAGE	COUNTRIES	DISTANCE	ASCENT/DESCENT	MIN/MAX HOURS	MIN/MAX DAYS	TRAIL ICONS	WHEN TO GO											
01 Avenue Verte	3	England, France	394km	2,180m/2,150m	28/38	3/7		J	F	M	A	M	J	J	A	S	O	N	D
02 Ballyshannon to Larne	9	Ireland, Northern Ireland	357km	3,540m/3,560m	23/32	3/5		J	F	M	A	M	J	J	A	S	O	N	D
03 Coast and Castles South	15	England	324km	2,220m/2,130m	21/29	3/5		J	F	M	A	M	J	J	A	S	O	N	D
04 Great North Trail	21	England, Scotland	1,292km	17,400m/17,670m	115/160	12/27		J	F	M	A	M	J	J	A	S	O	N	D
05 Great Western Way	27	England	256km	780m/770m	17/24	2/4		J	F	M	A	M	J	J	A	S	O	N	D
06 Hadrian's Cycleway	33	England	265km	1,510m/1,510m	17/24	2/4		J	F	M	A	M	J	J	A	S	O	N	D
07 Hebridean Way	39	Scotland	323km	2,350m/2,340m	22/28	3/5		J	F	M	A	M	J	J	A	S	O	N	D
08 Highland Trail 550	45	Scotland	884km	13,010m/13,010m	78/108	8/18		J	F	M	A	M	J	J	A	S	O	N	D
09 John Muir Way	51	Scotland	209km	1,630m/1,610m	17/24	2/4		J	F	M	A	M	J	J	A	S	O	N	D
10 King Alfred's Way	57	England	352km	3,510m/3,510m	31/42	3/7		J	F	M	A	M	J	J	A	S	O	N	D
11 Lakeland 200	63	England	206km	6,080m/6,080m	22/30	2/5		J	F	M	A	M	J	J	A	S	O	N	D
12 Land's End to John o' Groats	69	England, Scotland	1,897km	13,720m/13,760m	122/170	12/28		J	F	M	A	M	J	J	A	S	O	N	D
13 Lon Cambria	75	England, Wales	181km	2,080m/2,120m	12/17	2/3		J	F	M	A	M	J	J	A	S	O	N	D
14 North Coast 500	81	Scotland	816km	8,150m/8,150m	52/73	6/12		J	F	M	A	M	J	J	A	S	O	N	D
15 North Norfolk Coast Cycleway	87	England	159km	770m/780m	10/14	1/3		J	F	M	A	M	J	J	A	S	O	N	D
16 Sarn Helen	93	Wales	342km	6,360m/6,320m	28/38	3/6		J	F	M	A	M	J	J	A	S	O	N	D
17 Sea to Sea (C2C)	99	England	219km	3,010m/3,000m	15/21	2/4		J	F	M	A	M	J	J	A	S	O	N	D
18 South Downs Way	105	England	160km	2,820m/2,810m	17/23	2/4		J	F	M	A	M	J	J	A	S	O	N	D
19 Tour de Manche	111	England, France	1,005km	7,360m/7,370m	69/95	10/17		J	F	M	A	M	J	J	A	S	O	N	D
20 Tour de Peak District	117	England	252km	4,270m/4,270m	21/29	2/5		J	F	M	A	M	J	J	A	S	O	N	D
21 Trans Pennine Trail	123	England	338km	1,130m/1,130m	24/33	3/6		J	F	M	A	M	J	J	A	S	O	N	D
22 Way of the Roses	129	England	275km	2,240m/2,240m	18/25	2/4		J	F	M	A	M	J	J	A	S	O	N	D
23 West Country Way	135	England	302km	2,920m/2,930m	21/30	2/5		J	F	M	A	M	J	J	A	S	O	N	D
24 Wild Atlantic Way	141	Northern Ireland, Ireland	2,765km	23,680m/23,700m	173/238	18/40		J	F	M	A	M	J	J	A	S	O	N	D
25 Yorkshire Dales Cycleway	147	England	213km	3,610m/3,610m	15/21	2/4		J	F	M	A	M	J	J	A	S	O	N	D